Joe Gufreda was a loving  businessman and faithful Cath secret that he was afraid to tell

After years of confusion not living his true gender and worked up the courage toward becoming a woman, JJ Marie.

Left-Hander in London: A Field Guide to Transgenders, Lesbians, Gays and Bisexuals—In the Family, On the Job and In the Pew is the candid, funny and sometimes surprising story of that transition. Joe/JJ Marie's sheer ordinariness is what makes this first-hand account so powerful. This could be your neighbor, coworker, cousin, brother or spouse.

Raised in a Sicilian-American household in Cleveland, Joe Gufreda had a "normal" childhood playing sports, scrapping on the playground, serving as an altar boy and, as he grew older, dating girls. But from early on he knew he was different from the other boys: In secret he liked to dress in women's clothes.

Thanks to a lack of information about transgenders in that era, he was confused about what his leanings meant. Was he one of a kind? A transvestite? It wasn't until he discovered a book about transgenders in a college library that he began the journey to change genders.

The title *Left-Hander in London* refers to realizing you are different from most people, but uncertain how to get to that seemingly far-away place where you will be happy. The book traces Gufreda's journey, from sharing his secret with his wife to dressing as a woman at home and a man everywhere else to telling his family, friends and business associates that he was becoming a woman.

Some of their reactions to this earth-shaking news were a pleasant surprise. Others were painful, bigoted and lacking in "Christian" love.

For anyone hiding and suppressing an important secret, *Left-Hander in London* offers a roadmap on how to go public and what reactions to expect. For friends, family and business associates, JJ Marie's first-hand account will give you helpful tips on how to respond to the coming out of a transgender, lesbian, gay or bisexual.

Left-Hander in London is a powerful, amusing and informative book about embracing your true inner self and moving beyond tolerance and acceptance to *enjoying* diversity.

LEFT-HANDER IN LONDON

"A joyful and exhilarating experience. An intimate insight into the joy and pain of a transgender person. Informative but also transformative, Ms Gufreda has a personal and conversational style that make reading of this volume easy and enjoyable. This book will be a great asset... for helping everyone know and understand how we can all live in unity, with diversity— provided love is there as the catalyst."

Friar Justin Belitz, Founding Director of The Franciscan Hermitage, Inc., a spiritual center dedicated to personal growth and development

"In her wonderfully personal way, JJ has done a great job of conveying to the reader her transition process and how it affected her professional life. It's a 'must-read' for everyone in today's ever-changing business world."

Irwin Drucker, Program Director GLBT and International Programs, Supplier Diversity, IBM Global Procurement

"A great, compassionate... textbook for those who feel they are 'out of the mainstream,' and wanting to know how to negotiate the road to freedom."

Johnny Burke, host of Johnny Burke & the Morning Crew on 96 WHNN

Justin,
Thanks for being
there for me!

Left Hander in London

A Field Guide to Transgenders, Lesbians, Gays and Bisexuals
In the Family, On the Job and In the Pew

JJ Marie Gufreda

Enjoy Diversity

JJg

Published by Enjoy Lefty Publishing LLC
http://www.LeftHanderinLondon.com
(317) 885-7811

Requests for information should be addressed to:
jjgufreda@lefthanderinlondon.com

ISBN: 978-0-9846867-0-4

This book is printed on acid free paper.

Printed in the USA

Dedicated to

Our Lady of Lourdes

St. Bernadette

And

My wife, Jo
She knows what they mean when they say
"together through thick and thin."

Acknowledgements

Thanks to everyone that helped and supported me during my writing of *Left-Hander In London (LHIL)*. First, I thank Jo, Joey, Andrea, Matt, Katherin, Kyle and Amanda, Tim, Glor and their families and all my relatives. Your love for me and assistance with the book was invaluable. Special thanks to my editors, Kym Reeves and Steve Hall and my publicists, Mariel Wilding and Leigha Landry. Joey Gufreda helped with technical issues and Andrea Pilz did all the design, artwork and graphics for *LHIL*.

I asked many people to do peer review and help out on the book. I appreciate your time and contributions. If I missed someone, I apologize, but be assured that I appreciate your help. Some of the peer reviewers and people that offered support were Charlie Colosky, Johnny Burke, Dan DeWitt, Geoff Petranek, David Johnson, Michele O'Mara, Vickie Davis, Fredrikka Maxwell, Tony Amaddio, Millie Amaddio, Janet Cross, Michelle Davis, Stephanie Peck, Emily, Sandy and Shannon from IXE, Kristen Smithson, Mary Levell, Jim and Tina Seebeck, Rich and Jan Hammond, Jenny Starnes, Angie Starnes Laninga, Lisa Alberico, Brad Bell, Pete, Kyla and Diane Maddox, Samantha Brown, Jan Kubelsky and Wendy, Benito Cerimele, Tom King, Megan Wallent, Angel Robertsson, Nick Turner, Chloe Prince, Felicia Powers and everyone at the NGLCC, Scott Franklin, Ron Craig, Cynthia Wade, Julie and Randy Dwenger, Natalia Zukerman, Robin Honan, Justin Belitz, Randall Balmer, John Marshall, Indy Rainbow Chamber of Commerce, Irwin Drucker, James Kuester, Joe Maxwell, Rob and Rebecka Kruk, Aurie Chidziva, Tim Ruddell, Terri Friel, Drew Dillon, Mr. and Mrs. Gregg Messel, Lou English, Jeff Ellis, Charlie Peterson, Paige Drymalski, Jeff and Anita Sipes, Jessica Wilch, Vivian Benge, Erin Warnick, Sue Smith, Judy Koch, Bonnie Starnes, Julie and Jo Nemecek, Barb Clayton, Dan Prock, Kathe Perez, Tara Betterman and Melody Layne, Barry King, Terry Hildebrandt, Teddy Gumbleton, Lisa Ryberg, Dr. Christopher Trepel, Jaycee Renee Patterson, Jon Coalson, Annette Gross, Paul Burt, Emily, Andrew, Miranda, Faith, and Sarah Klein, Andrew Tudor, Lizz Schunn, and Barb Milton. I would also like to acknowledge Vincenzo Cancilla Gufreda. He is too little to help with the book, but he brings us joy just by being with us!

Regarding Names of People in the Book

I did not list all the relevant names of many people described in the book. In some cases, if the person had not been very nice or done something that I perceived as wrong or misguided, I didn't see much benefit to listing their name. I am not looking for any paybacks or asking for a fight—just describing things as I perceive them. I write from my perspective. Others may have a different view of what occurred.

I listed some by their names. I am happy to acknowledge the people who helped and supported me when I really needed it. If you are on this list, but not in the book, it is because I didn't write everything down or save each note. I sincerely thank everyone who helped me along the way, even if they are not acknowledged.

If you think you are one of the misguided people I describe or recognize my description of some of the less supportive people, I hope I don't hurt your feelings. May God bless you. Maybe the next person you encounter will feel a little better after being with you than I did.

I use the term "LGBT" to describe sexual attraction and gender non-conforming people. Some folks use other letters as well, such as I (intersex) Q (Queer or Questioning) A (Ally or Androgyne). There are others. For simplicity and since LGBT is most relevant for my story, I'll stick with that. I wish no offense to anyone I left out.

Editor's Note: Tips on Using This Guide

Who Needs Left-Hander in London?

This book was written with the intention of assisting and educating:

- those determining and embarking on their own gender journeys,
- family members and friends who have just received world-rocking news about a loved one's gender identity or sexual orientation,
- people who have encountered a transgender person (or gay or lesbian or bisexual or whatever-designation) and want to know how to react in the best way possible,
- folks who want to understand what someone may be going through as they become their true selves,
- business people who may desire (or are being forced into compliance) to be more inclusive but need a little guidance,
- souls in conflict over their spirituality and organized religion (the Catholic Church in JJ's case) in relation to their sexuality or gender identification,
- clergy and laypeople who want to represent their faith in a more loving and Christ-like manner,
- folks who just enjoy an interesting tale and don't mind learning a little something in the process!

How Do I Best Use Left-Hander in London?

Depending on what you want to get out of this book, here are some tips on finding what you need to know.

The bulk of the chapters are more anecdotal in nature and should give a little more depth and a "human face" via one person's personal journey toward wholeness. It is my hope this will aid in comprehending how someone feels before, during and after they understand themselves and their gender identity -- and have determined they need to make changes in how they express their own true nature.

If you have neither the time nor inclination to hear my personal story, no fear -- I'm not much into guilt, in spite of my strong Catholic roots! Simply turn to the back of the book and check out the Summary, which includes a Chapter Synopsis and Questions Section. The questions should give you food for thought, and the descriptions of each chapter's contents will point you to the section that you feel is relevant to your personal situation or area of interest.

Questions Section

Here you will find some questions you may have for yourself or for someone who is LGBT, as well as some that I have been asked during my transition. As I've told people, you can ask anything you like; I just may not answer everything you want to know!

Resources and Unabashed Hucksterism

I have mentioned several resources that I have found useful during my gender journey, and have included points of contact after the Questions Section. I wish to stress that I am not being compensated in any way for the mention of any particular website, product or program, but simply wish to acknowledge that these techniques or programs worked for my issues, and to suggest they may be helpful to you or your loved ones as well.

Table of Contents

Introduction—A Brief Overview

Left-Hander in London: A Field Guide to Transgenders, Lesbians, Gays and Bisexuals -- In the Family, On the Job and In the Pew will benefit lesbian, gay, bisexual and transgender (LGBT) people who want to "come out" or, in the case of some transgender people, transition. Friends, family and co-workers can also profit because the book can give them a better understanding of people they know that are "different." This is helpful for everyone affected during some of the toughest and loneliest times an LGBT person experiences.

We have all heard of people that have overcome the odds to become successful in many fields. A young person is abandoned by his or her parents, raises siblings without much help from anyone and eventually perseveres through all their challenges and difficulties to become a star athlete. They use their newfound riches to support their family. Another rises from the depths of poverty to a college education and public service as an elected official. It is easy to observe these people, hear their stories and feel admiration and respect for them and their incredible journeys.

LGBT people each have a journey to become the best person they can be and the persons they were meant to be. They must first discover why they feel different from others. For some this happens very early in life. For others, it may take years. Secondly, they have to determine what to do when they realize that they are Lesbian, or Gay, or Bisexual, or Transgender, or however they feel. This *can* be easy, but often leads to pain, broken relationships and broken people. Finally, they live their lives – as they really are or, sadly, hiding their true being. Hopefully, my story will be illustrative of others' experiences.

Does our society view LGBT peoples' journeys with the same understanding and admiration as we do in my example of the star athlete or civic leader who had to overcome so many challenges?

I believe a person can have a satisfying journey despite the inevitable difficulties. Many transgender and "coming out" stories focus on the losses incurred, discrimination faced and problems unsolved. I want to emphasize that people can become their true selves and *not* lose everything and everyone. In fact, the journey can be rewarding and fun, especially if you have a positive attitude, great family, friends and associates, and a good sense of humor.

A note of clarification: Transgender people express their gender differently than most, and some want to change their gender. Gender and sexuality can vary on a continuum and may change over time.

Left-Hander in London is written from my perspective, which is transgender. This is not a scholarly study analyzing the similarities and differences between transgender people and lesbians, gays, and bisexuals. I have gained some relevant insights about others in the LGBT community which might be helpful for people that are uncomfortable around or even discriminatory towards LGBT folks.

When We're Out, We're Definitely Out

Many issues are the same for "LGBs" as for "Ts"—discovering your true self, becoming your true self, determining who to tell and how to tell them, finding how you fit in when you are not "normal," and how to help others deal with the real you.

One of the biggest differences between transgender people and other LGBs is that many transgenders encounter more issues related to telling people or what to do if others discover it on their own. It is harder to hide your gender if you are changing it than to hide your sexuality, as some gays, lesbians and bisexuals do.

In my case, people noticed my hair was getting longer, my ears were pierced, my nails grew longer and my hair magically turned blonde (well, maybe with some help). Hormones and female clothes completed the final demise of the male part of me. After a while, I could not hide my new gender, even if I wanted to (which I didn't). If you are genetically a male and go to the store dressed as a female, people may notice quickly, especially if they knew you previously as a male. Changing gender is not like changing shoes.

Generally, you can't look at LGBs and instantly "tell" they are gay, lesbian or bisexual. They can decide to be "in" the closet or "out." Some hide it better than others. But sexual orientation and gender identification are different; anyone that knew me as Joe knows I have been through some big changes, if they recognize me at all.

Some transgender people go back and forth from one gender to another. In my case, once I started dressing as a female and going out on a regular basis, I realized that my friends and family had to know. I quickly became comfortable going anywhere and doing anything as a female.

It took me many years to discover and understand my true self. I have enjoyed a successful business career, which includes manufacturing industry management and engineering positions, consulting and teaching at a college. I have contributed to three business books and written several magazine articles. My wife and I have been married for over 33 years, and we have three grown children and a grandson.

I always knew, however, that my gender identity did not match that of everyone else I knew.

After a lifetime of hiding and suppressing my real identity, I worked hard to come up with the best transition plan for my family and me. I know of many LGBT people who are hiding or are outcasts. I was determined (and praying) that this would not happen to me. I wanted to keep my relationships with the people most important to me. My journey taught me valuable lessons about myself and my relationships with others. According to some estimates, between 5% and 10% of the US population is LGBT. If there are 30 million LGBT people, you probably know at least a few!

You may be shocked to hear that someone close to you is sharing his or her true gender identity or sexual orientation (or both), especially if it is different than what you previously thought. You may ask, "What can I read to help me process this news about (your relative, colleague or friend)? How do I react to this?"

Left-Hander in London discusses how I told people, and shares many of the loving, questioning and funny reactions I received, as well as those who did not respond positively—or at all.

I can identify and empathize with gays, straights, lesbians, married people, minorities, parents, men and women. I have been a member of many of society's majority groups as well as several minority groups.

Know the old saying about having to walk a mile in someone's shoes before you can understand them? I have done this in a way that most people have not. Walk along with me and hopefully you can get a better appreciation of other people and their journey.

The Church and the Christian Moralists

Left-Hander in London includes a discussion of spirituality and the (Catholic) Church. Many in organized religion shun and reject LGBT people rather than showing the love to be expected from a religious group (or at least that *I* expected). Some religious people attack people that "have the gay" and are afraid of transgender people because they don't understand us or think we are sinning by being who we are.

If you are a Christian, my thoughts on my experience with the Church and some Christians may make you consider unpleasant things about how to properly react to someone whose gender identification is "not normal." Several Catholics who previewed this book told me that they found Chapters 7 and 8 interesting and validating, but painful to read. I only ask that you have an open mind and heart, are considerate of others, and try to gain something from this book that you can use for the good.

Spirituality and Biblical Relevance

In some chapters, I used quotes from the New American Bible, the translation I use. As I was collecting notes, I found many quotes were relevant to the book (and my life) as I read the Bible each day. I soon had a large pile of Bible readings that were appropriate to different parts of what I was planning for *Left-Hander in London*. I decided to include a few quotes that were especially helpful to me.

I have some disagreements with the Church and people I describe as Christian Moralists. In my experience, these people will search the Bible to prove you wrong or find ways to attack you. I am not looking to play the game that one transgender friend called "Dueling Bible Verses." I only want to stimulate your thinking and share how the Bible has been relevant for me, especially when I struggled so much on my gender journey and as I started my transition.

Bottom Line It for Me, Baby: Help for the Reader

People buy books that they would *like* to read every day. But instead of reading the whole thing, they may review the introduction and then simply skim the chapters because:

- They don't have time to read the entire book;
- Something strikes them as uninteresting or boring and their interest grinds to zero;
- They read in a big fat chair or in bed, and even the most exciting book is quickly lost amongst their snores;
- They are easily distracted and something else caught their eye; or
- They don't want to read the *whole* book for *whatever* reason.

If you are one of those people, *I have an extra bonus for you.* At the end of the book is a short summary of the book, along with a description of each chapter. If you want to read the Introduction and/or the Summary, skim *Left-Hander in London* quickly, and then give it away or stick it on your shelf, be my guest! Hopefully you will at least read this Introduction and the Summary and take a look at any particular chapters that interest you. Approach the book however you want. You won't get any guilt from me.

Chapter 1

Left-Hander

I grew up in the '50s and '60s in Cleveland, Ohio. My parents and my entire family were Catholic. I went to Catholic school from grades 1-12 and to a Catholic college for my master's degree. Ridiculously normal, and not exactly the background for swimming against the stream, right?

Experts estimate that only 5-10% of the population is left-handed. When children learned to write when I was a kid, teachers had to decide what to "do" with those students who were left-handed. In many cases the lefties were taught how to hold the pencil and move the paper so the writing would look "correct"—that is, right-handed. In other cases, the teachers or parents taught the students to suppress their stronger left hand and use the right hand. This was one way to help them try to fit in and be the same as others. Some teachers also taught students to be right-handed because it was easier to teach everyone the same way.

There may have also been deeper reasons. Many societies have long considered being left-handed as evil or bad. Lots of terms that refer to left-handed people are not flattering to the lefties! The terms "left-handed" and "sinister" both came from the Latin *sinestra*. Right is often a synonym for correctness while left can mean evil or unlucky. This started in ancient languages, was incorporated into Christianity and continues in many places across the globe. A friend told me that in Arab countries the left hand is reserved for hygiene and therefore viewed as "dirty" and using it is considered a huge insult.

Conformity Required – Right? (See What I Mean?)
Consider a world much more intensely "anti-lefty," where

over time a left-handed person was thought to be less of a person than a right-hander. The stigma and discrimination against left-handed people may have gone on for so long that people forgot that being left-handed was a natural human condition. As a result, the people who were born left-handed were forced to "become" right-handed. They hid and suppressed their natural condition by acting right-handed. They might not even have been aware they were acting anything other than naturally.

They wrote, threw and shot baskets with their right hands. In baseball, even if they wanted, they could not be left-handed because there were no left-handed mitts. Eventually even the term "left-handed" would be so out-of-use that it might be forgotten.

Discovery

Now consider a young boy—let's call him Joey—who was naturally left-handed. His strong hand was his left hand. He kicked better left-footed. He was more coordinated with the left hand and somewhat clumsy with his right. In the environment I described, he did his best to fit in with everyone else. Acting as a right-hander, he considered himself to be a poor athlete and uncoordinated. He felt he was different from other people but didn't know why.

One day, Joey was throwing stones into a pond near his house. He spotted a perfect skipping stone on the ground. For some reason, he picked it up with his left hand and threw it. It went farther than any rock he had ever thrown with his right hand, and skipped six times before it sank into the water—a new personal record.

He looked around to make sure no one saw him do this, and went back to his right-handed game.

He forgot about the incident until another occasion, when he picked up a ball and unconsciously threw it with his left hand.

The same thing happened—he threw it easier, further and better than ever before. He started to get concerned. He knew that people just did not do this. He had never seen anyone throw with that hand. He had previously thought he was a terrible pitcher, but he had a good arm—unfortunately, the *wrong* arm. He felt nervous because he worried about what people would say or do if they found out about his strange trait.

He decided that every once in a while, if it was absolutely safe and no one would see him, he would throw with the wrong hand. He would never let anyone know about it. He constantly looked at the daily newspapers and weekly magazines for information about this strange condition that seemingly only he had.

Every once in a while, he would find something written about someone throwing with the wrong hand, but the person usually did it to be funny and people thought it was hysterical. Joey did not feel that this was amusing at all. He felt normal in this abnormal way, and it caused him anxiety to think about. And he didn't. *Most* of the time.

But every once in a while he would sneak outside after everyone had gone to bed and throw a tennis ball against a wall with the wrong hand. It was great because it was comfortable and so natural. He was terrified that someone would see, but he became good at hiding and suppressing and, as far as he could tell, no one ever found out. He never felt he could or would do anything about this—this was the way his life would be.

One late night, in a dimly lit section of the college library, he was looking around at the old books for anything written about people throwing or writing with the wrong hand.

Not a Lone Weirdo?!?

Amazingly, he stumbled upon a book titled *Left-Handed*. On the cover was a picture of what looked like his strong hand. His hands shaking, he opened the book. The author, long dead, told of something called being "left-handed." The book said a small percentage of the population was this way. It gave some history and talked about the discrimination against left-handed people over the centuries. The book said that there was no known cure for it. If you were left-handed, you just were.

Wow, what now? According to the old book, nothing was wrong with the young man. He was just different from most other people. He decided that he was okay with being left-handed, and he was also thankful since he was a little unique and could see things a bit differently from everyone else. Joey started to wonder what this new information would mean since it explained something important about him and why he didn't quite fit in with the world.

Since he didn't know anyone who was like this, he felt that it was risky for someone to find out his true nature. Joey decided to continue hiding his left-handedness rather than telling anyone what he had discovered.

He did not know what would happen if someone *did* find out, but it seemed too difficult to even contemplate. Fear of the unknown is a powerful force. He pushed the feelings deep down inside, and only allowed them to surface if he thought no one was around, acting like he was right-handed.

Since you've picked up this book, I'm guessing you can already see the parallel, right? The story about Joey is related to me. I am not left-handed, though. I am transgender. The relevance is that most people know someone who is left-handed, but not as many know someone like me who is transgender. I was called Joey when I was young. Later everyone called me Joe, and now my name is JJ Marie Gufreda.

Defining My Left-handedness:

The Human Rights Campaign (HRC) produces a brochure called *Coming out as Transgender*. Their definition of transgender is "an umbrella term that applies to a broad range of people who experience and/or express their gender differently from what most people expect." They also define a transsexual as "a person who—with or without medical treatment—identifies and lives his or her life as a member of the gender opposite the one he or she was assigned at birth."

Given these definitions, both terms apply to me. I prefer and use the term transgender. To me, "transsexual" sounds like it is related to sex; I think "transgender" is the more relevant for me.

The Indiana Transgender Rights Advocacy Alliance (INTRAA) has an information sheet with a diagram of Sex, Sexuality, and Gender, adapted from the <u>Center for Gender Sanity's</u> diagram of sex and gender. It looks like this:

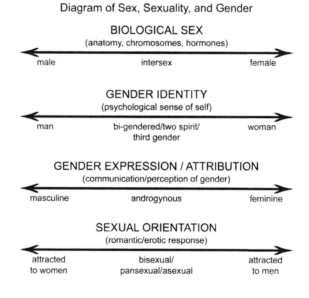

Diagram of Sex, Sexuality, and Gender

BIOLOGICAL SEX
(anatomy, chromosomes, hormones)

male   intersex   female

GENDER IDENTITY
(psychological sense of self)

man   bi-gendered/two spirit/   woman
third gender

GENDER EXPRESSION / ATTRIBUTION
(communication/perception of gender)

masculine   androgynous   feminine

SEXUAL ORIENTATION
(romantic/erotic response)

attracted   bisexual/   attracted
to women   pansexual/asexual   to men

Adapted from INTRAA and Center for Gender Sanity's diagrams

When you attempt to understand someone by using this chart, there is much to consider. As far as I know, I am a male biologically, but I identify and express myself as a woman. I have been married to a woman, Jo, for over 33 years.

Looking at people's positions on this diagram may help you understand another person better. People are not necessarily clearly male and female or gay and straight. Some people's position on the chart can evolve over time.

I have heard of, and read about, some transgender people who always felt that they were the opposite gender. A transgender person who was born male may say something like, "I always thought I was a girl," "I was born in the wrong body," or "When I went to bed, I prayed that I would wake up a girl."

That is not the way it happened with me. I always knew that I was different and somehow things were out of synch. I was always interested in girl things, but I thought that it was better that no one found out. I could never become a girl anyway. It was impossible.

In the story Joey learned to get by as right-handed. I did the same. Even if I did not feel that I was like the other boys, I learned to be a boy. I could get by as a boy. Nothing else seemed possible. You can't dream or wish your way to becoming a girl, can you?

(Later in life I discovered that if you have thousands of dollars and the right physician, you *can* go to bed a boy and wake up a girl!)

Chapter 2

My Personal Odyssey—Uncovering the Real Me

I was born about a month premature in 1954 in Cleveland. Medical issues related to the pregnancy contributed to my premature birth. That was one of the few times in my life that I have been early! I was small and needed to stay an incubator for the first few days. I was the first child for my parents.

We lived in a house in the Collinwood area, a lower- to middle-class Italian neighborhood. It was clean, well kept, and very much a city neighborhood. After a while we moved a few miles away to a similar neighborhood, primarily Slovenian. We lived in an apartment above the store and deli that my mom's parents owned.

My dad was a steelworker and eventually became the union president. My mom stayed at home with my sister and me and, in a few years, my brother ;) she worked different jobs to help the family. Relatives were often around.

One of my early memories was related to gender. In sorting through my recollections, I think this was an actual event mixed up with the memory of a photo we had in the family picture drawer. Memories have run together in my mind after so many years have passed.

I was around four or five. I remember my mom putting me in a dress to see what I would look like. I recall being in the front area of the apartment near the windows looking out on Lakeshore Boulevard, so part of the scene is clear. But I can't remember why Mom did this, where the clothes came from, and whether this was only one time or a repeating occurrence.

I saw the photo a few times in the picture drawer, but later I destroyed it so no one would see the picture of me in a dress. I didn't want anyone to suspect anything about my secret. I would have liked to ask my mom about this before she died, but did not want to open the issue after so many years.

I have curly hair, and it was a big deal with my mom when I got it cut the first time. I think my dad wanted me to look more like a boy and my mom wanted to keep it long and curly. I thought curly hair was always a curse because people considered it feminine. I thought it looked girly on me. I still do, but now I see it as a benefit.

Machismo

Around 1960, we moved to a house in the same neighborhood, about a mile from school. We lived there most of my childhood. I was always one of the "smart" kids in school. Today you might call them geeks! I paid attention and did my work. Only a few of the boys were really worried about school while several girls were in the "smart" crowd.

As school went on, the boys belonged to three groups—the Collegiates, the Racks and the Greasers. I don't remember the difference between the Racks and Greasers, but they used a lot of grease in their hair and wore leather, or at least faux leather, jackets. The Racks and Greasers fought a lot and got into trouble. I was a Collegiate, the group who wore penny loafers and other clothes that we thought college kids did, and avoided getting into trouble.

In the eighth grade, one of the Collegiate kids wanted to hang out with the tough kids. They told him that before he could become part of their gang, he had to beat someone in a fight. I was chosen as the target. He was bigger than me.

I was always timid about fighting, but my dad told me that if I ever got in a fight, I should punch the guy in the nose. He told me that it hurt a lot and usually drew blood, ending things quickly. It turned out that Dad was right.

The guy started pushing me—the preferred way to start a fight in those days. I kept asking him why he wanted to fight. He seemed determined to continue, so after several of his pushes, I punched him directly on the nose. His eyes widened and I could tell that he was surprised. His pride and his nose were hurt. He immediately started bleeding. I gave him a Kleenex and walked away.

The kids laughed and heckled him until he came back and found me for another round. I thought it was all stupid. I asked him if he wanted to do it again, and he meekly said yes. I immediately punched him in the same place, and the blood started again. He stopped and held his nose. That was the end of it.

Some of the girls I liked told me it was cool I won the fight. I was triumphant, but I thought the whole thing made no sense at all. My hand hurt for a week from the punches, probably a lot longer than his nose.

I had some friends at school and mostly hung out with the kids on my block and the next street. I walked to school with Susie, a girl in my grade, and I liked her a lot. At that age guys were not supposed to be friends with girls.

Most of my time with friends consisted of hanging out, throwing a ball against the steps and playing football or baseball on the field down the street. I played Little League baseball and got to be a decent player. My smallish size was countered by my experience, since I played a lot. I never hit with any power, but I was fast and good at placing the ball.

Sounds like a regular childhood, right?

On the Outside, a Regular Boyhood...

During my grade school years, I also became aware that I was interested in girl's clothes.

I got a paper route when I was 12 or so. I woke up at 5 or 5:30 in the morning, and delivered papers in my neighborhood or one nearby. Because no one was around that early in the morning, sometimes I tried on my mother's clothes I found in a basket in the laundry room. The clothes were too big, but if it was available, I tried it on. My sister's stuff was too small.

I used to do odd jobs, and the money was good if I did jobs others did not want to do. A single lady liked to have me work for her. I was cheap labor, and it saved her from the dirty work—outside cleaning, painting and gardening. She commented on how pretty my hair was—that with hair like that, I should have been a girl. I was always excited when she said that, but I tried not to show how it affected me.

When I got the rare chance to be home alone, I went up into the attic by placing a chair under the ceiling cover, moving the cover out of the way, and pulling myself up. After having three kids, Mom had gained weight, but her corsets and dresses from her younger days were smaller sizes.

This effort was a big production. I was always afraid that I would get stranded up there, kill myself on the way up or down, or would not be able to get down and changed back to boy clothes before someone caught me. This never happened, though. Each time was a major accomplishment, and worth every second of the anxiety and all the nicks and bruises.

I looked in the paper, magazines and books for stories about guys who dressed as girls. I cut out pictures of, and articles on, Milton Berle, who often dressed as a woman for comic effect, and Harvard's Hasty Pudding show, where several of the guys dressed up as women. I even memorized a few Ann Landers advice columns—one about a wife whose husband wore her clothes, the other about a girl whose brother would go out dressed as a girl every night for a walk. I remember a *Life* (or maybe it was *Look*) magazine with a feature article about guys who changed their sex from male to female. They looked just like women. I read this several times, but not enough that anyone would notice that I was reading it.

Movies and TV shows also had some cross-dressing. I read with interest about *Triple Echo*, a movie where a soldier hid as a woman on a farm to escape the Army. He eventually liked being a girl and did not want to go back. In the hit film *Some Like It Hot*, stars Tony Curtis and Jack Lemmon were dressed like women for much of the movie. I watched this movie in re-runs on TV.

I always looked for TV talk shows with cross-dressers or guys who dressed as women. I remember one TV show that brought recently married couples to tell a story about their time together to win prizes.

The couple usually came out together, but one show started out with the lady coming out by herself. When the host asked where her husband was, she said that he was getting his dress and makeup on backstage. The host asked why, and she said the producers had asked him to do it. I was all ears and anxiously waited for what was to come.

After the commercial, the husband came out and really looked like a woman. She (the wife) was dressed casually, but he was in a nice dress and makeup.

They told the story of how they came to date. She had been dating a football star, and if the jock found out that she was seeing another guy, that would be the end of that guy. To get around this, her future husband suggested that he would dress as a girl and pretend to be her girlfriend so he could see her without enraging the boyfriend. This went on for months until she finally broke up with the jock. She married the guy who had been her "girlfriend."

The host asked if he had dressed up any more, and the wife said that on their wedding night, he put on her lingerie and wedding dress for fun and that he looked sexy.

This made a big impression on me. The show presented the situation as funny, but this guy clearly liked dressing as a woman

11

and the wife was proud of her girly husband. I was excited by the show but terrified that Mom would realize why I was watching it. I memorized as many details as I could, and then buried the show deep in my mind.

No one knew I thought these things. Except for the occasional article or TV show, I was not aware of any other guy dressing as a girl or changing into a girl. These feelings were so outside what I thought was acceptable that I never considered letting people know about this part of me. It did not seem possible to share this with anyone.

I was good at hiding and suppressing. If the FBI wants to find out how people hide their true identities for years without anyone finding out, I'd be glad to help! It was not easy, but I was good at it. While I was fantasizing about being a girl, I was doing the usual boy stuff. Dad taught us sports, played ball with us and was active with me in the Boy Scouts. I spent my free time with the boys in the neighborhood.

I never told anyone of my interest in feminine things. I felt I was probably the only person like this. I was not macho, but did boy things because that is what I was supposed to do, although I didn't feel comfortable with the way the gender rules were set up.

I had crushes on some girls from school, but was shy around them. The other kids did spin-the-bottle and other kissing games, but I only did that once. I enjoyed it, but I was nervous about the possibility of being "wrong" and being found out.

From the third or fourth grade, I was an altar boy, rising to the position of president of the altar boys in the eighth grade. I thought this made me special, but it really meant that if they needed someone on short notice for 5:30 a.m. Mass, I got the call. I always was religious, attended Mass and felt close to God.

During this time, I experienced my first recognition of anxiety-type issues and symptoms. My mom was a world-class

Italian worrying mother. Like her, I was a worrier—partially because of the stress of concealing my gender issues.

I occasionally felt dizzy, which frightened me. I later learned that these were probably panic attacks. The feelings were terrible. It was many years later that I learned to deal with the anxiety.

My Religious Path

In the summer of 1968 I walked two or three miles to a summer school session to get an early start on my freshman year at an all-boys Catholic high school. On my walk, I met a few girls who would attend the all-girls Catholic school a few miles down the road. I liked one of the girls and eventually asked her out for a football game my freshman year. We only went out once or twice, but I was excited that I had my first date.

As far as I could tell, I was just like everyone else. But I always had lingering thoughts about girls' clothes and girl things. I pushed it down, but it was always under the surface, ready to bob up like a cork. A girly pink cork!

At the 2,200-student high school, I learned a lot about the Catholic faith from the priests and other teachers. They taught us like we were adults with opinions—not kids expected to believe everything we were told. During my sophomore year, I joined a religious group, Sodality. We had prayer meetings and went on some retreats. I was starting to develop my own opinions and think as an adult. The prayer groups got intense, and I felt God's presence. In my mind everything became related to religion; I prayed all the time, all the songs on the radio seemed like they had religious meanings, and I wanted more of a personal experience with God.

A priest at school asked several of us to drive with him to Pennsylvania to speak about our faith to a church group. At the meeting, we prayed together, and they asked me if I wanted the gift of tongues. Not knowing anything about it, I said I guessed it was okay. They laid hands on me, prayed and asked me to pray out loud. I started to pray in tongues. I have been able to do this ever since. Sounds come out of my mouth, and I feel that I am talking directly to God, but I don't understand what I am saying.

On a retreat some years ago, I asked a priest what it meant and why I can do it. He said praying in tongues is a way for your heart to speak to God when you do not know what to say. My gift has been a blessing for me.

I eventually backed off on the religious stuff in high school because it got too intense. I did not lose my faith, but did not think about it as much as I had.

A Normal Good Catholic Boy's Dating Life

My high school years weren't just about learning and developing my relationship with God. We made up for the lack of girls at the all-boys school by meeting the girls after school. I had crushes on, and dated, several girls.

One summer, I dated a beautiful blonde twin. I asked one out but eventually found that I had more in common with her sister. It was mutual. I was always nice to them and appreciated them as individuals. Most of the guys just leered at them because they were so "hot." The girls did not like it when the guys acted like jerks and only liked them because of their looks.

I was always self-conscious about being short. At 5'5", I was one of the 10 shortest students in a class of 500 people. While this was a disadvantage when I was younger, my shortness has become a plus for me now. I can buy women's clothes off the rack and I rarely have problems with pants being too long!

I met my first steady girlfriend when I was a junior in high school. We dated for a few years. She was one or two years younger than me, and very nice. We got along well. My view on sex was a very traditional Catholic one: No sex before marriage, but kissing and petting were okay if you liked each other. I was curious about sex and enjoyed making out with her in the car when I would drop her off at home. It did not go further by mutual agreement.

I ran cross-country during my freshman year and was terrible. I was fast and quick, but not close to the taller runners in long distance races. In addition, running two miles beside Lake Erie in the sleet and snow was not my idea of fun. I gave it up after a year. I never did much with sports in high school.

Outside of school activities, I worked at a pizza shop from age 14 until I was 23. I learned a lot there about taking responsibility, preparing food, dealing with people, gambling, the Mafia, and how the boss hid the gun. I also learned what to do during a bomb threat, how to make weed brownies (a "dope head" worked there part of the time but I didn't eat any), and what happens when a guy gets shot in the parking lot. It was a learning experience, and not only things I wanted to learn!

The boss had a young attractive wife, maybe his second or third marriage. She left her slippers in the pizza shop, and I tried them on when no one was around.

At school, I was involved with student council, religious activities, clubs, dances and doing things with my friends. I had a lot of friends; Don, Dan, Geoff, Ken and John were the closest to me. My friendships with Dan and Geoff became even tighter when they worked at the pizza shop too.

Don once told me that he did not understand why people thought he was gay. I did not know much about gay people, but told him that maybe it was because his hair was light blond. (Obviously, I was not a budding psychologist or scientist!) I always felt that blond hair or curly hair were less masculine than other kinds of hair.

Ironically, he *did* turn out to be gay, as did three others in our group. None of them shared anything about their sexuality in high school. They all dated girls. We only found out later.

I never considered why anyone would be gay. Girls were

attractive to me, and I spent a lot of time thinking about them. I was interested in sex, but I believed in what my parents and the Catholic Church said about no sex before marriage.

But Through and Under It All…

Throughout these seemingly normal years, I continued to have thoughts about dressing in girls' clothes and being feminine, but I did not act on them much. There were limited clothes available and few opportunities for privacy at home.

Once I found an alternative magazine on a magazine rack; it had pictures of what I now know were drag queens. This was exciting to me, but I was afraid to buy it for fear someone would find out.

During a school presentation about sexual deviations, one of the Brothers at school held up a book with a picture of a transvestite. Everyone laughed, but I clandestinely scoured the library to see if I could find the book. I never did.

I knew from my "research" that some guys dressed as girls. Some of them looked good and some looked stupid. I wanted to dress as a girl and be like a girl, but it still seemed outside the realm of reality.

I had tried on some of my mother's things and once congratulated myself that I had worn everything a woman wears—panties, girdle, bra, shoes and a dress. Except for these brief exciting moments, there was no chance to do much more than that. I had never seen anyone in person who did this except for bad costumes at Halloween. Those boys looked like boys in dresses, not girls. If I ever got the chance to dress as a girl, I wanted to look like a real girl. I was terrified that someone would find out about my secret.

I was interested in going away to college, but we never had the money to seriously consider it. I was determined to get a degree. I went to Cleveland State University so I could keep working at the pizza shop and live at home to keep expenses down. My parents were there for me, but I paid for college myself. Ironically, since I had gone to a private Catholic high school, my tuition actually went down when I moved to a state college.

At Cleveland State I tried to make some black friends since I did not know anyone who was black. Cleveland had a lot of racial problems back then, and I found that many of the black people I approached did not like me because I was white. I realized discrimination could go both ways.

My college years consisted of driving downtown in the morning, going to class, studying, occasionally doing things with my friends, and going home to work or do homework. All the wild things that most people did when they went away to college were not available as easily for the students who commuted.

My steady girlfriend and I dated regularly and occasionally drove to Kent State to visit friends. It gave us a chance to be more free and independent—even if just for a weekend. After two or three years of dating, she broke up with me because she found someone she liked better. I never hurt like that before. I only got through the pain because I was coaching Little League baseball. I enjoyed spending time with the kids and teaching them.

Maybe it was coincidence or a subliminal religious thing, but I dated a lot of girls named Mary. Mary and Joseph were in the Holy Family; I thought it might be a sign from God!

It took me six years to get my undergrad degree because I changed my major three times in the same quarter and then took a year off to work in a factory. I was sick of school, not sure of what I wanted to do, and decided to take some time off until I was ready. I always knew I'd eventually graduate.

My Anxiety Shows Itself

In the late '70s I started to get recurring panic attacks. The first one hit me when I was driving around what we call Dead Man's Curve on the Shoreway (our name for the freeway along the lake shore) near downtown Cleveland. I was heading home after a game of flag football on the other side of town.

The panic attack came out of the blue with no warning. It did not last long, but I thought I was dying or going crazy. My head felt like I had been hit by lightning. My heart beat like never before. I thought it would jump out of my chest. I felt nervous and panicked.

After that I continued to get panic attacks off and on, but I never associated this phenomenon with my conflicted feelings about how I felt about feminine things.

Eventually I took a step toward more independence and moved in with my friend Dan from high school and another friend. We all got along well except for the occasional argument about who would clean the kitchen. It generally worked out well for everyone.

One day Dan told me he was gay. To say that I did not react well is an understatement. [Reference Chapter 6 for the whole story on that.] He had dated girls. I did not believe it.

Eventually I got over the shock and accepted it. He was still my friend. I felt bad for him when I realized how hard it was for him all those years when he did not acknowledge his true self. I told him that I did not have much of an opinion about his being gay. He obviously was attracted to guys. I did not feel like it was my place to decide moral issues for other people.

The relationships with my friends stayed the same whether they were gay or straight. I wanted to go with Dan to one of the gay bars he frequented, as I heard that they had shows where the guys dressed up as women. I wanted to see this, but I was working nights and was afraid to suggest it as someone might make the connection that I liked to dress as a woman.

Jo, the One

When I was working and in college, I met Jo, my future wife, at a party for one of my roommates who had just graduated from X-ray school. Jo worked at the hospital in Nuclear Medicine. Jo and I started out as friends but, as our friendship developed, I realized that she was the one for me. Our first date was her coming to my place to watch the Super Bowl—the Vikings against the Raiders. I was never the same after that.

One night she told me about her family and childhood. I locked in emotionally with everything she said and realized that any happiness she had made me happy, and any of her trouble and sadness became mine too. I was ready to marry her. When I proposed, I had to drink some wine before I was brave enough to ask. Fortunately she said yes.

I was happy and emotional during the wedding, but swallowed hard so no one would notice. We had a nice wedding. At the reception, the dancing began as soon as the music started. People were still in the line for food, so the partiers danced around them! The whole day was fun, and we enjoyed every minute of it. They had to kick us out of the hall at midnight. Several of us continued the party by hanging around the parking lot.

Jo and I have been in synch on most things. In marriage, I believe you should make the other person the most important person in your life and realize that you are a couple, where you previously were individuals. Everything is in relation to the other person: Career decisions, where to live, how to spend money, decisions on school.

Jo encouraged me to finish my undergraduate degree and then get my Master's in Business. If she had not supported me on the decision, I never would have gotten my MBA. When I got my degrees, it was truly a team effort.

Small Steps on My Journey

Even with this new life developing, working and going to school, I still had time for dressing in women's clothes.

Jo's things were available and closer to my size. Before we married, I tried on clothes that she left at my place; a skirt and matching top were my favorite. After we got married, I had ample opportunity for "dressing" since I worked the midnight shift and she worked days. I never wore makeup or a wig because these would be hard to hide or change quickly if I had to.

I even wore lace panties to our engagement dinner with our friends in the bridal party. I went to Jo's apartment to shower and change after working during the day. I had forgotten underwear. Jo gave me a black lace pair, the most stretched pair she had. I was distracted, nervous and self-conscious all night knowing that I was wearing panties and wondered if the other people could tell by looking at me. Jo did not know how this affected me. She simply thought it was funny that I was wearing panties.

After we were married for a while, I lost weight because I worked hard on a diet. I was down to nearly 135 pounds and had a hard time finding men's clothes that fit. I bought some dress shirts in the boys department because men's shirts were so big on me.

Money was tight, and I lamented to Jo that men's briefs were expensive. Because I had worn men's bikini-style briefs for years, I suggested women's underwear looked almost the same, but were cheaper. She bought me several women's pairs, and I was in heaven. I also got to wear a pair of her old jeans now a little too big for her. Because they did not have pockets in the back, I was sure people would notice. No one did. The complicated feelings of thrill, shame and rightness were maddening as I went out into the wider world.

Empathy

When Jo got pregnant with our first child, Joey (the name is a tradition in our family), the pregnancy was hard on her. She was healthy, but had constant morning sickness. She ate a lifetime supply of saltine crackers to try to calm her stomach. I was with her every step of the way (as much as a guy could be).

I remember going to a session at the hospital where they teach the couples what to expect during childbirth. I felt bad for Jo and the other ladies; when they had to lie on the floor to do the exercises, it was hard for them to move around because several of them were almost ready to deliver.

After sharing the material and showing the women some exercises, the nurse asked if there were any questions. One skinny guy whose wife was much bigger than him asked how long they could continue having sex before the baby was born. The nurse said that if it was comfortable for both, they could medically have sex all the way up to the birth. The guy got a look on his face like "This is great." His wife's face had the look of death.

I thought that it was uncaring for him to ask that. He seemed so insensitive to how she was feeling. She clearly was uncomfortable. I thought that I must be weird since I was thinking about Jo and the other women having so much trouble moving around, not myself. This guy was thinking about sex right up to delivery!

Jo was in labor for three days with Joey. I guess it was fairly common for a long labor on the first baby, but that is still a long time. I had worked 12 hours on the midnight shift the night before she started into labor, and when I got home at noon, she announced that she was in labor. I jokingly said that this was not a good day for me. But we got ready and headed to the hospital. When the baby finally arrived, we were both exhausted but very happy.

We had started to add to our family and adjusted our lives accordingly. Still, the feminine feelings were always there for me.

A Thrilling Switch, then Nose to the Grindstone

I went out dressed completely as a woman for the first time at Halloween one year. We were discussing costumes; I suggested that I go as Jo and she as me. She "bought" it, and we went out to the party. I already knew her things would fit. I was excited but terrified that Jo or anyone who saw me would instantly know this was something I wanted to do, not just a costume.

For the party I finally got the opportunity to wear everything a regular female would wear. Jo told me to hold still so she could do my makeup. I was so nervous I could barely contain myself. When I came downstairs, I could not believe that I let the babysitter see me as a woman.

The party was a sensory overload—everything from driving in heels to talking to people in a normal conversation when I was dressed as a woman. It was a great, but one-time experience.

Joey was a baby when I worked on my MBA. When not at work, I stayed up all night to study. I got a promotion, and we moved to a small town called Bridgeport in southeastern Ohio, just across the river from Wheeling, West Virginia, three hours southeast of Cleveland and a little over an hour west of Pittsburgh.

The move was stressful. I had never lived away from Cleveland. It was a good career move but a lousy job; the manufacturing plant where I worked was terrible compared to where I had been. The locals did not readily accept anyone who wasn't a native, and we felt like outsiders. I told Jo I needed to survive this job so we could move away. Our other two children, Andrea and Matt, were born there.

I landed a part-time position teaching in the undergraduate and masters programs at Wheeling College so I could stay current on the professional developments in my field, gain some new experience and make a little extra income. I worked hard and enjoyed teaching, even though the money was terrible. Adjunct professors do not make good money. But the experience attracted me to consulting, and that is how we eventually moved away from eastern Ohio to Indianapolis.

My Anxiety Issues Continue…But There Is Help Available

During this time I continued to have panic attacks. I would feel fine for months and then suddenly, they would hit me. After doing some research, our doctor said physical things or issues with your heart could cause feelings of anxiety and that it probably was some minor physical problem rather than mental or psychological problems.

I was relieved the explanation didn't seem as bad as I imagined. Jo eventually found books by Dr. Claire Weekes that explained anxiety and suggested methods to eliminate it or at least reduce the suffering. I was not successful in ridding myself of the problem, but the doctor and then the books helped enormously.

I struggled with anxiety for many years. During therapy when I was sorting out my gender issues, my therapist Michele O'Mara, who can be found via http://omaram.hypermart.net/ thelesbiantherapist/, said that regardless of what I do about the gender issues, I needed to get help for the anxiety problem. She recommended a web site, www.healing-anxiety.com, to finally help me get my anxiety and panic under control. I downloaded the program and it was some of the best money I ever spent. The program explains everything that is happening when you are in the anxiety state. David Johnson, who produced the program, sets you up on the road to recovery.

When I had listened to part of the program, I had a few questions. I sent David an email and later that day, the phone rang. I answered and it was David. I recognized his New Zealand accent from several hours of listening to his program. He introduced himself; shocked and surprised, I said, "Why are you calling me from New Zealand?"

He said, "Well, you had a question didn't you?"

I said yes, and we talked for an hour and a half as he reinforced everything from the program.

I was so impressed that he cared that much about my recovery that he called—and we talked for over 90 minutes! We talked another time later that week to follow up and I was thankful that I had found a source for relief and also made a new friend.

David also has a sense of humor. When my mom died a few years ago, I started to have severe panic attacks. I was taken aback, since I had been doing well and rarely had any symptoms. I sent him an email asking some questions and also informed him about my gender change, which was already well in progress by then.

That night, the phone rang. It was David again. I was feeling a little better that day, but was still rattled that the symptoms had returned.

David said, "How are you?"

I said, "Fine."

He said, "Well, then you don't need to talk to me."

I said, "Hold on, yes I do," and we both laughed.

He told me that my nerves were understandably shocked from the loss of my mom and that I needed to practice what he had taught me more often so I would respond better to stress.

I have been doing much better and will keep working until I am completely recovered. I recommend to anyone who has anxiety, nervousness, panic attacks, phobias, etc. to check out David's site and get his program. Tell him JJ sent you!

The story of my panic attacks might seem a digression from my gender and biographical journey, but hiding and suppressing my gender-related struggles took a big toll on me. The stress contributed to the anxiety and panic attacks.

Fork in the Road – Do I Dare Take the Left?

In 1982, when Jo was nine months pregnant with our second child, Andrea, we were riding in the car at the bottom of the big hill near our house. I said something about women's clothes, and Jo asked why I talked about that so much. Did I want to wear women's clothes?

I saw the opening and took it. I thought that God was affording me an opportunity to get this giant weight off my chest and share this with the person I was closest to. I had never expected to tell anyone about my terrible secret. Given the opportunity, I spilled my guts to her. I was so relieved to tell her.

I shared that I had always been interested in girl clothes and liked to dress as a woman. I hadn't had much opportunity, but took advantage of the times I got to dress. This had been going on for my entire life, but no one knew – but her. I told her that (at that time) I never went out of the house dressed as a female and didn't expect that I ever would. This was true back then, but changed over the years.

She was surprised, but did not react badly to what I said. As long as I did it in private at home, she could live with it.

I eventually recognized that given her condition, this was not the best time to tell her how gender-conflicted I was. Still, I had told the person I loved the most in the world about my secret, and nothing terribly bad happened. Everything went fine with Andrea's delivery, so there was apparently no lasting damage from my poor timing!

I am still sorry for causing Jo stress when she was so close to delivering the baby, but at least my secret was shared. At that time, I thought it was mostly about the clothes. I didn't know much about gender transition.

After the kids were born, Jo asked me if I wanted to dress as a woman for Halloween one year. Like almost all of the guys I worked with in Southeastern Ohio, I had a beard. I wanted to shave it, but was sure that people would figure out the connection between Halloween, dressing as a woman and shaving. I tried on Jo's things with the beard and looked stupid. So I didn't do it.

I was upset that I missed a golden opportunity to dress. After that winter was over, I shaved the beard. Since then, I have had one more short-lived beard. After all the laser and electrology I have undergone in the past few years combined with hormones, I couldn't even grow a beard now if I wanted to.

Jo and I had a great family and worked together to keep everything going well. Jo worked in Nuclear Medicine and took care of most of the responsibilities for the kids and the house. I was in charge of the repairs and helping with the other stuff when there was time. Jo converted to Catholicism in Bridgeport as our family was growing, which made me happy for both Jo and myself. I traveled a lot for work, which was tough on her and the kids. Still, we were in it all together.

Moving -- in Many Ways

I eventually took a job with Ernst & Whinney in consulting. I was excited to be working with a top professional services firm, not as a manufacturing rat in a dying industry. I had broken out of the blue-collar world and was now the professional I always felt myself to be.

When I accepted the post in 1986, the firm gave me three choices for location. We did not know much about Indianapolis, but it got us out of Bridgeport. I moved into an apartment and commuted back and forth on the weekends before Jo and the kids could eventually move to Indianapolis.

Even though I missed my family, I got to dress in the evenings during the week. I brought a box of women's clothes to wear when the shades were down in my nearly empty apartment. I asked Jo to help, and she bought me several female things in Wheeling. I was afraid the cleaning person might look through the boxes and find my clothes, but it felt worth the risk.

We agreed that now that we were in Indianapolis, we would stay at least until the kids got out of school. Jo had to move a lot as a child, and we did not want that for our kids. We discovered that Indy was a great place to raise a family. I worked at Ernst & Whinney (later Ernst & Young) for almost 10 years and then opened my own consulting company, GEI.

When we first moved to Indianapolis, I had limited opportunities to "dress" in our little rental house. A few times when the kids were in bed, I would put on some lingerie and Jo took my picture with a Polaroid camera. She didn't like it, but indulged me—for which I was thankful. I carefully hid everything and eventually burned the pictures so no one would find out.

As the kids grew up, I occasionally wore female items, but it was difficult. There was little privacy. With kids barging in, it is hard to go to the bathroom or change clothes, much less wear women's clothes. I eventually learned through the Internet that loads of men dressed in women's clothes, so I was beginning to realize that I was not the only one. I literally dressed in the walk-in closet with the door locked so no one would accidentally come in on me.

I do not have many regrets from our time together as the kids grew up. Jo and I were focused on each other and the kids. We worked at our careers and went to church, school activities and many of the children's activities and sporting events.

I went through "Christ Renews His Parish," a retreat and renewal program after Jo and I went on a pilgrimage to the shrine in Medjugorje in Bosnia and Herzegovina. I started to read the Bible daily and say the rosary, which I have been doing now for around 15 or 20 years. I needed these spiritual experiences. I also liked to help other people on their faith journeys. I was a leader of our renewal group, and that eventually led to many more retreats and discipleship opportunities.

As the kids graduated from high school in the late 1990's and early 2000's and started to move out of the house, my cross-dressing increased. I asked Jo if she would mind if I dressed totally with clothes, a wig and makeup, which I had previously only dabbled with. She was not excited about it, but said it would be all right.

When the Levy Breaks...

This started the flood of dressing like a woman. Every step I took led to another one:

- I tried more clothes.
- I got wigs.
- We went shopping for more women's clothes.
- I took pictures of myself with the digital camera.
- I shaved my legs one winter, but was terrified that someone would find out.
- I went in our pool at night in a women's bathing suit in the spring and fall. I shaved my legs and body during the winter. I timed it so I got a chance to go in the pool at the beginning and end of each respective season. I had to hide my shaved legs and wear long pants if the weather got warm. One Memorial Day holiday, it was over 90 degrees, but I felt I could not wear shorts, because my hair had not grown back yet. I didn't want anyone to notice.
- I got extremely depressed every spring because I would start to let my hair grow back. I waited longer and longer to stop shaving.
- That led to shaving all the time, since I hated to go back

to having hair in the summer. I finally decided that I did not care what people thought. No one even noticed or, if they did, did not say anything to me.

- I dressed up more often.
- I started to think that I looked a little better, and dressing female became comfortable for me.
- This started to become a regular thing, and I was often dressed at home.
- I started to take on more of a woman's role and do things that guys from my Sicilian background just did not do. I used to cook only for special occasions, but started to do most of the cooking, especially when I was dressed female. I helped with the laundry and the cleaning. I also started baking. It was fun and made me feel more feminine. I previously had been unable to successfully bake anything, but was now a decent cook and baker. In the evenings after work, I became like a traditional housewife. I did almost all the shopping. After all the years of doing it all herself, my wife was happy to get the help.
- I started to dress every opportunity when I was at home, and started to wear nightgowns to bed (with a bra and silicone inserts) every night. I installed better blinds so the neighbors or passers-by could not see in.
- I sat in the dark backyard or made the "mailbox run" late at night when I was dressed as a female. The chances of running into anyone out on the street were remote. Dressing in my female clothes to get the mail and newspaper from the boxes in front of the house felt good, but I always had remorse that I had to hide in the dark.
- I finally got brave enough to go out. One year around my birthday Jo indulged me, and we went to a hotel just far enough away from home. We waited until around 11

p.m., had a short walk around the parking lot and then got in the car to get gas at a brightly-lit gas station. I was so excited, I could barely contain myself.

- On Halloween of 2006, I dressed as a female and gave out candy. It was awesome. Jo had a headache, so I was on my own. Several people saw me as a woman. I discovered if I did not talk in my normal voice, only two of the people who knew me recognized me or realized that I was a guy. No one else did. One of the people was a neighborhood lady who realized that it was me and said that I looked really good. I was energized. When the trick or treating was over, I did not want the night to end. I told Jo that I was going to the grocery store since I had a "legal" excuse (Halloween) to be out dressed as a female. The funny thing was, no one knew, or at least reacted like they knew, that I was a male. I was excited and amazed. I hated to have the night end. I chewed a lot of gum and drank water in the car because of my nervousness; my mouth was dry all night. But I did it. I went out as a woman. The floodgates just broke, and the dam was destroyed so badly that it could not be repaired.

I went to a grocery store that had high school kids working the cash register. They didn't notice anything different about me. In fact, they ignored me and focused on their conversation with each other.

I was so excited that I had to figure out somewhere else to go. By now, it was about 10 p.m. on a weeknight. I decided to go to the liquor store. The reaction was the same: "Hi ma'am, the total is $xx, thanks." I was in heaven. This was before Indiana passed a law that *everyone* has to be carded to make an alcohol purchase, thankfully!

When I came home from the store, I felt like I had started to run on all my cylinders for the first time. I had spent much of my life worrying about what would happen if someone ever "found out" about me or saw me dressed. But I had just talked to several neighbors, given candy to the kids and gone out in public with no negative response at all. No one seemed to notice. They just treated me like any other woman.

I felt a combination of exhilaration and emptiness. The next day I had to go back to normal "guydom." That was distressing and depressing.

I was now *sure* that I was a Left-Hander. I was comfortable with the change to female. The question was, "What do I do now?"

Chapter 3

In London

I envision my left-handed doppelganger, Joey, in this way: Joey heard about a wonderful place called London, across the sea. It had been there for many centuries. The people living there spoke with a bit of an accent so they sounded the same, but different. He read stories about many interesting places to see, food to enjoy, and people to meet in London.

But the most intriguing and exciting aspect of London was that left-handed people lived there. No one seemed to think that anything was abnormal or irregular about this at all. The more he learned about London, the more he dreamed about it, and the more excited he became.

Joey's problem was that he did not know anyone who had ever been there. He had never heard how to get there, and that it must be a fairyland—something out of make-believe. He could only experience London in his imagination. London sounded like where he belonged, but he got more and more depressed and unhappy because there did not seem to be any way to get there.

After many years of dreaming that he would someday both see London and perhaps even *live there*, the feelings became so strong that Joey decided that he could not hold it in any longer. He *had* to find a way to get to London.

As he scoured everything he could find, he discovered people who had not only visited London—they told him that there were regular flights there! It was not easy or cheap, but you could go just about any time you wanted to. He could hardly contain himself and decided that he was going to change many things in his life. Joey discovered that he *could* go to London and desperately wanted to; he just needed to figure out how.

~~Joey~~ *JJ Takes a Trip*

In my case, I knew that a London for transitioned from male to female people existed, but didn't know how to get there from the anxiety-laden world where I was living.

On my somewhat naive journey, it seemed impossible for someone to change from a male to a female. As I met more and more transgender people and learned about the treatments available, a huge weight was lifted from me.

I could get laser and electrolysis to remove hair. Hormones would feminize my body and release my true spirit --I found this out firsthand after I started on the hormone treatments. I could work to feminize my voice. Surgeons had done hundreds of facial feminizing or gender reassignment surgeries and could help me, as long as I had the money! Exactly when I would arrive in "London" was not that important; I just wanted to start the journey as quickly as possible.

Yes, JJ, There Is a London!

The same thing happened with me as the story about little Joey finding a book about being left-handed. While getting my undergraduate degree from Cleveland State University, I also found books about transgender topics in the library. It turned out that there *were* people like me. This was in the late '70s, and several of the books were about cross-dressers or transvestites.

I figured I must be a transvestite. I loved dressing as a girl even though I rarely had the opportunity. I was dating, and was attracted to girls. I was different from a lot of guys in my approach to dating: I was into romance and did not view my girlfriends as being just for sex. I decided that being a transvestite must be the reason things were so different for me.

I was energized and excited to learn more and more about "London." But I still felt strongly that, even though I was figuring things out, I would never let anyone know. I carefully looked at those books when no one else was around. I had to be sure no one would figure it out.

I continued this way for several years. I was interested in girl things, but I suppressed and hid it from everyone. Without realizing it, I was becoming an expert in hiding and suppressing. I ignored the feelings as best as I could.

When I was 23, I married the right person for me—Jo, my soul mate, my best friend. Even with a world of new experiences in front of us, the gender issues did not go away—they just stayed under the surface. In addition to an exciting new life with the one I loved, I now had access to a wardrobe of clothes close to my size! She and I are around the same height, 5'5". I did not get the opportunity to dress often, but I tried her things on if I got a chance. Being like a woman was always in the back of my mind.

After I told Jo about my gender struggles, she was understandably not excited about the news. But she said that if it was important to me, she could live with it, as long as she was not involved (What this meant would eventually become an item for discussion.) and no one found out. I was ecstatic. The secret was out, and besides shocking Jo, nothing bad happened.

I am glad I told Jo and everlastingly grateful that it went well. "Well" is a relative term that varies whether you ask Jo or me what it means. I was jubilant that she knew and that we were still together. She would have preferred that I wasn't like this, but our relationship and our feelings toward each other were still strong.

If I was to get to "London," I would have to figure out how to tell everyone else I knew as well. I pushed this to the recesses of my mind for years because I was afraid of what would happen if people found out. We were so busy raising the kids and making a living that I focused on the family and ignored my gender conflict. As a friend described it, I was wearing my "man mask."

The Mask Begins To Slip

After the kids grew up and moved out, I started to dress completely as a female at home. We had a few "bounce backs" with the kids—the furniture moves back, the dog moves back, the kid moves back, the kid moves out, the furniture and the dog finally moved, etc. Of course we were happy to have the kids around, and I still had opportunities to dress for long periods. Jo and I had the house to ourselves much more than when the kids were younger.

When the kids finally moved out completely, I was dressing one or two days a week. Eventually that became all weekend. This quickly turned into every day after work and every chance I got. I would shave my face with an electric razor when stopped at the traffic lights while driving home from work or as soon as I got home so I would not lose any "girl time."

I would walk in the door and immediately change into my women's clothes. The only time that I wore male clothes outside of work was when Jo and I went somewhere. We went out less and less because once I was dressed female, I did not want to change back to male. I dressed female two-thirds of the day, and for most of the weekend. I would change to male for church on Sunday, but switch back to female as soon as we got home.

I started to collect clothes and shoes, and Jo kindly helped with the shopping. When I wore wigs, I started to feel more female when I dressed. They can be hot and a hassle, but I looked more female. I experimented with makeup and even though I was not that good at it, I was improving. Most of my clothes were dressy outfits. I did not have many casual clothes, jeans, etc. I wanted to look as much like a woman as possible, and dresses and skirts seemed the best way to do that. I was excited to wear the clothes that were, for the most part, not readily available to me for my exterior life.

Jo hung in there, and I got more and more comfortable when

I was dressed female and less comfortable dressed male. One day, Jo said, "It will never be enough for you. The more you do it, the more you want." I thought about it and realized that she was right.

I hated dressing male and acting male when I had to go out or to work. I loved dressing female. I was overdoing it—few genetic girls wear dresses every day. I started to be more of a normal girl. Over time, I changed from dressy clothes to regular female clothes—clothes that most women I knew wore most of the time.

I was feeling trapped, stuck in the house all day. I bought blinds so we could block the windows. I did not want the neighbors to look in the windows and see that I was dressed female. I did not want to shock or surprise anyone. I would peek out when I let the dogs out into the fenced area in the backyard. Sometimes during the summer, I would wait until late at night and go out in the backyard and walk around or sit on the chairs or swing. The backyard is fairly secluded, and while the neighbors might see me if they were out, it was late and dark. I felt safe.

I felt exhilarated and free during these times. I thanked God often that I had the opportunity to be out as a woman. I was beginning to make up for all the years that I could not be a girl and had to try to be a guy. Jo was right. It was not enough. I did not want to just be a woman at home. I wanted to go out. I did not want to change back to being a guy when I had to go out of the house or work. I realized that this was no longer about the clothes. I was not a transvestite. I *needed* to be a woman all of the time.

Next Stop, London (By Way of Music City?)!

In late 2006, a few months after my successful excursion on Halloween, I decided to go out to a "real" place with real people, so I attended a Tennessee Vals Christmas party. The Vals are a Nashville, Tennessee-based social and support group for transgender persons. I had heard of the group, and Nashville was far enough away (a four- or five-hour drive) that I would not chicken out after driving that far and spending the money on a hotel room. There was also a minimal chance that even if people realized I was a guy, they would not know me.

The Vals offered to have someone come to my hotel room to get me if I was too nervous to go to the meeting by myself, and I took them up on the offer. One of the members and the hotel's events manager knocked on my door to be sure I would feel safe on the long journey (to me, anyway) down the hall, onto the elevator and down another hall to the meeting room.

After a few minutes, I relaxed and had a good time meeting the other girls. This was the first time I met a person dressed convincingly as the opposite sex. I listened intently to everyone's stories and experiences. I met several friendly people including Vickie and Fredrikka, with whom I still keep in touch.

When I got to the meeting room, they had a bar and bartender. I was so nervous and exhilarated at the same time; I thought the first thing to do was to get a glass of red wine to help me relax. Vickie came over to get a drink and realized that I was "new." She started to chat and invited me to join her at her table. We all had a great time and everyone was incredibly cordial to me.

After the dinner event was over, they provided a hospitality suite, and we sat around and talked until two or three in the morning. I realized that while I felt right at home, I had a lot to learn.

Roxie, the president of the group, had spent an hour answering my questions on the phone before I committed to attend the meeting. She helped me feel comfortable and at ease. At the hospitality reception after the meeting, she was having a hard time getting the cork out of the wine bottle with the corkscrew and asked, "Is there anyone here not on hormones that can open this?" They all laughed, and I think that I was the only one not on hormones (at that time). Taking female hormones reduces your strength. I "man-handled" it open.

Jo was in Chicago visiting Andrea for the weekend, so I was free until Sunday afternoon. I sadly changed back to my guy clothes on Sunday morning and drove home. I did not want the experience to end, but I was still afraid to drive home as a woman.

I went to a few more events with the Vals, including a few of their regular meetings followed by a trip to a local gay bar that "accepted" transpeople. It was a relaxed environment, and everyone treated us like ladies. We went out to dinner at another gay club one night. I enjoyed my new friends and learning more about them. I initially thought that going to a gay place would make me nervous, but it was fine since everyone was welcoming, gracious and friendly.

I was interested in also going to "regular" places—the types of places I usually go to. I am not a big "bar person" and had not gone to any kind of bars often for several years before I started going out as a woman.

On the Road a Little Closer to Home

I started attending a local Indianapolis gender support group called IXE (Iota Chi Sigma), a gender support group in Indianapolis that holds a monthly social meeting. It was too hard to drive four hours to the Vals meetings every month. The Vals girls also encouraged me to connect with a local group. I appreciated their gentle push. They told me that I was welcome any time, but I needed to find some local Indianapolis-area people to meet so I didn't spend half my weekend driving.

I felt the need to go out more and more. I did not really know where to go where I would feel safe—safe from exposure as transgender, and safe because it's different going out alone as a woman than it was as a guy. I was still self-conscious and nervous that someone might read me as male.

I called a local gay-oriented neighborhood-type bar because I had heard that it was a laid-back place. I asked if a transgender person would feel comfortable there. They said that I would be comfortable and to come by anytime. I went there one evening, and they were friendly and didn't seem to take notice of me at all.

Nonetheless, I felt out of place because I was the only female there and I was alone. I had to start going to regular places, not just places that felt safe. I did not feel right going to bars just to have someplace to go.

Bliss in a Sock Store

Another big breakthrough came when Jo and I took the scenic drive to Nashville, Indiana, which is about 45 minutes south of our house. I had asked her if she would go out with me when I was "dressed." (She had gone with me on a few of the trips to Tennessee, but did not go out with me when I was dressed as a female. She stayed in the hotel. I was nervous going alone, but still was determined to do it.)

She said that she would go out with me to Nashville, Indiana if we went during the day. She is not a late-night person. I had not considered going out in the light of day. I was sure I would be less recognizable in the dark, and I was not confident enough about my appearance to go out during the day.

That was until we drove the winding road to Nashville. Jo and everyone else treated me like there was nothing out of the ordinary and we were two girls out for a fun spring day. I felt so natural and comfortable from the moment we got into the car. I could not believe that I was walking around the shops as a woman and no one seemed to notice. When I went to the ladies room for the first time, Jo said, "Let's go" and held the door for me. The waitress at the restaurant asked us "ladies" what we wanted for lunch. It was such a great day.

The first place we went in Nashville was a socks store; pretty much all they had were socks. We looked around and bought a few pair. I had such an overwhelming feeling of well-being. I don't ever remember feeling quite that way before. It was not happy, like when we got married or when the kids were born. It was more of an "everything is right with the world" feeling.

I thought to myself: I'd bet there never has been a person on earth as happy to be in a socks store as I am right now. I will always remember that experience. I was happening, blooming, becoming.

Helpful Connections on My Journey

- Before I decided to transition and change to a full time woman, I went out as a female several times. One major event was the Be-All seminar (transgender seminar) in Chicago. I was dressed female for the drive there and back and for the entire conference. I did not have any male clothes with me.

  I relaxed and learned from my experiences meeting all of the other people. Most were male to female (M to F). I also made some new friends, including Stephanie, a married electrical engineer from Minneapolis. She told me that her employer was helpful with her transition at work. It sounded like it went smoothly. She also shared about her wife and family.

  The discussion started to give me hope that I might be as fortunate as her if I was brave enough to stop hiding and be myself. I met several people who were married, and I enjoyed learning from their experiences. I especially liked talking with the wives of transgender people so I could learn how to be more empathetic to my wife. I knew that this was all difficult for her. The drive home was enjoyable since I had the opportunity to be a girl in regular situations, not just at transgender meetings.

- I started attending more of the IXE meetings in Indianapolis. I appreciated how they made me feel welcome. Emily and Shannon, the leaders of the group, were empathetic when welcoming new people—especially when I was terrified the first time. I was concerned that someone I knew would see me in the car, I'd get into a wreck (it was raining/sleeting/snowing/icing, you name it, it was coming down that night!) or some other disaster seemingly too terrible to imagine. They had to know I was new because I was wearing a dress and heels. I know now that heels and snow are not that good together!

  I also made several new friends including Sandy and Kristen, who happened to live within 10 minutes of my house. Sandy invited me over for dinner one night, since it would be fun to get together and she knew I was looking for safe places to go dressed. After I started my transition, I went to visit Kristen and her girlfriend, Mary, and I was surprised to learn that they live a five-minute *bike* ride from us. Perhaps trans people were taking over the neighborhood! We have become good friends too.

- The other group that I got acquainted with was the Indiana Transgender Rights Advocacy Alliance (INTRAA). You can see why they use the acronym -- the name is a mouthful. They are the political and advocacy group in Indiana. Affiliated with INTRAA are the Indy Girlz/ Indy Boyz groups. They are support and social groups. I met many nice people and made new friends. Angel, Vivian, Jessica and Erin were especially nice to me. I was struggling with how to keep everything together and wanted to talk to someone. Going back and forth between genders was terrible, and I needed to figure out what to do. They met me at a coffee shop (I don't drink the stuff, but love tea), helped me get comfortable and sort things out. We also went to dinner several times with Angel and Erin and some of the other girls. Jo and our son Joey occasionally attended which made me feel good. Meeting all these trans people was a new experience for them, but I think they felt comfortable. I really appreciate them accompanying me because I was nervous to be out in public. It was a good chance to get out, go to regular places like restaurants and coffee shops, and enjoy my new friends.

I detail these experiences because they are important to me and because I realized that the more I did as a female, the more I wanted to do. Jo was right. Whatever I did was not enough.

Road Work Ahead

I also realized that I would do a lot better as a female if I could work on my body and make adjustments. I shaved my body hair, started to moisturize, practiced with makeup, grew my hair out, started to epilate, etc. I started to consider electrolysis and laser treatments, as well as surgery that could feminize my face and make me look better if the hormones were not enough. Genital reassignment surgery is expensive, so I tabled those thoughts.

I realized that I only needed to look female and not necessarily be gorgeous to be passable, and I had already comfortably been out in public several times. I wanted to go out dressed as a female as much as I could. I already was dressing as a female almost exclusively when at home.

Jo and I started going to a therapist and then several therapists. We went to see Michele O'Mara, who does a lot of gender-related work. We also went to a few Catholic therapists to get the religious view of things.

My business was slow during part of this time, and therapy can be expensive. Jo and I decided to also see the counselors in training at a local college. One of the transgender girls told me that you could get therapy for reasonable prices, since the counselors were grad students under the guidance of a psychologist. They were not gender specialists, but a lot of what we needed was help dealing with marriage and family issues, so it worked out well for us. Michele helped with my general psychological outlook (dealing with anxiety, discovering and confirming my gender identity), and we worked through some of the other issues with the other counselors.

"*I Can't Go Back*"

The real turning point in deciding to transition came when Jo and I went to the Southern Comfort Conference in Atlanta. It is the biggest gender conference in the country. I met many new people, including couples like us who were married and wanted to stay that way. We got to be friends with Julie and Jo Nemecek and later visited them at their home in Michigan. They are nice people, fun to be with, very spiritual and great at sharing and helping others.

The conference offered seminars and workshops, doctors to see and products and books to buy. It was like any other conference, but there were mostly transgender people in one form or another. I say that because there is a lot of variety with transgender people. Some cross-dress and just like the clothes;

some are just into a certain kind of clothes; some only dress once a year when they go to a conference; and some have transitioned and are living a new life as the opposite gender from the way they appeared to be when they were born.

I enjoyed meeting many new people and learned a lot at the different sessions and from listening to everyone. The best times of the week, however, came first with the drive from Indy to Atlanta, which included my first visit to a nail salon and was my first full day dressed and out in public as a woman. Jo and I got our nails done, and I enjoyed how normal it all was. I also liked having good-looking nails!

I also enjoyed the conference's day trip to the Atlanta Aquarium. It is a beautiful facility, and since we are divers, Jo and I like to look at all the fish and other sea critters. After more than 50 dives, my knowledge of sea creatures is this: I look in the books to figure out what they are if I have the time and inclination, or I simply divide the ocean into big guys (sharks and bigger), fish, and critters. It's not scientific, but it works for me! I love the sea creatures, but the most enjoyable part was that we were out, I was a girl, and we had a normal day. Nothing was out of the ordinary. No one treated me any differently than any other woman, and I enjoyed the new me.

We met the Nemeceks for the first time at the aquarium as well. I had corresponded with Julie via email because I saw that she was married and was scheduled to be one of the speakers. I told her I wanted to meet her and Jo (coincidence on the names!), her wife. I was glad to meet another couple similar to us.

Once we got to know each other, we laughed about how boring we are. If you want to know what transgender people and their spouses discuss when they get together, the answer, at least for us, is: the kids, cooking, quilting, and other extremely mundane topics!

Jo did not attend much of the conference. She had a headache, which I am sure was from stress, but we went to the aquarium together and had another normal evening later in the week when we went to Underground Atlanta for dinner. When I say "normal," I mean it's not specifically related to being transgender, just normal stuff like shopping, looking around at the sights and getting something to eat. The normal days with Jo were the most fun for me during the week in Atlanta.

On the drive back, after seven great days of being a female, I started to think about getting home, changing back to male and going to work. I started to get extremely depressed. I felt like something was forcing me down into the seat—like a weight was pushing on me.

I finally looked at Jo and said, "I can't go back." She asked me what I meant. I said, "I can't go back to being a guy. I will for now since we have to figure out what to do, but I can't go back."

That was the final turning point for me. It was the realization that it was not the clothes, not a fad, not a fetish. I had finally figured out the real me, and was ready to go to "London." At the seminar I had met many "Londoners" (I did meet one girl who was a real Londoner from England!), and I wanted to go where they were.

Passport Application

Jo and I met with the therapists, and I drew up many drafts of my transition plan. I was bursting with excitement. I was going to stop hiding, stop suppressing, and become *myself*. Even though I had more questions than answers, when I finally understood that I was transgender and decided that I was going to transition, a great weight was lifted from me.

I had been nervous when I went in public as a female. What if someone who I knew saw me? What if someone figured out that I was (or at least had been) male? All of this fear! David Johnson, in his Freedom from Fear Recovery Program, talks about the "What-If Twins:" "What-If This?" and "What-If

That?" I worked hard to get the What-If Twins out of my life in worrying about anxiety, and I was finally getting them out of my life regarding my true gender identity. I wonder if those Twins figured out that my anxiety and my gender conflict were related before I did? I think they were using the connection to keep me down further – good thing I figured out how to jettison them from my life!

After listening to David's program, I went to the store and bought cheap toy monsters to remind me of the What-If Twins. I found these little guys and emailed their picture to David announcing that I knew what the What-If Twins looked like. Here's the picture:

Taking the Reins

I had admitted and acknowledged to myself that I was transgender. I finally decided that I was going to transition. I was going to put together a plan to tell the people I loved and to tell all the people I knew.

If someone found out, so what! I was going to tell them eventually anyway. Also, if someone saw me and thought that I might be a guy or that I may have formerly been a guy, that did not bother me any more. If they figured out that I was transgender, well, I *was*, so big deal!

I had a long way to go, but I had hit what my niece Angie called "the new normal." I was becoming the real me and I wasn't hiding any more.

Incidentally, after I decided to change to female full time and start hormone replacement treatments, I asked Michele O'Mara, my therapist, when she knew that I was going to transition. She smiled and said, "The first day that you and Jo were here."

I was shocked because at that time, I had no idea where this was going and I was too scared to even think about becoming a full time woman. I asked, "Well, I didn't know! Why didn't you tell me? It would have made this a lot easier!"

She laughed. She told me that I had to figure it out for myself and she didn't want to lead me anywhere—it was all my decision. Live and learn.

Chapter 4

Transition and Circles—Setting Priorities and Boarding the Plane for London

In therapy, we talked at length about the issues related to family that are most important to me. For my transition to go well, the closest family needed to be together as much as possible on the developing plan, and we needed to help and support each other. It was critical to stay together as a family. We have always been close. This was the first priority for me.

Mapping Our Route – Considerations

Here are some issues we needed to address and some thoughts we had when we were deciding what to do:

- Our close relatives would need to know. How and when to do this was an open question, and I was not sure how each would react. I researched this issue as it related to others' experiences. I hoped that after we told the relatives, they would love us the same as they always had, but they might need some time to get used to such a big change. I was confident this was the way it would go for the adults and older kids.

   I was unsure how it would affect the younger kids. I had heard that younger children generally have a fairly easy time getting used to transgender people because they are more prone to accept people as they are. We'd have to see how it worked for us. Many of our nieces and nephews were getting older—high school and college-age—so I guessed that it might not be too difficult for them. I thought they would understand.

I realized that we could risk ending the relationship with someone we love if they couldn't understand or wouldn't accept my family and me. That was a big concern. We decided to do the best we could, be as empathetic as possible and deal with whatever happened.

- I didn't have a handle on issues and possible situations that could occur in the future. Would me wearing a dress/ being female upset or upstage any potential weddings, parties or funerals? What is the effect on potential grandchildren with two grandmas and no grandpa? Do we tell them I used to be male? There are lots of names for female grandparents: Grandma, Nonna, Nanna, etc. We'd figure it out. Again, I decided to do the best we could do, and whatever happened, happened.

- I hoped our closest friends would accept all of us (after all, Jo and the kids would be somewhat guilty by association, so it wasn't just me that was affected) and we would eventually resume the relationship similar to the way it had been.

I have never been that close to that many people outside the family. If it did not work out, and they did not like us any more, then they weren't that great of a friend and I would be okay with a split. Hurt and disappointed, but okay. Jo would be more upset if we lost some of our friends. I would hope for the best and increase the chances of success by trying to communicate well, but I realized that we might encounter problems or friends that dropped off.

- I was not sure at first how to deal with acquaintances and the general public. Some transgender people just leave everything behind, move to another place and start a new life. I had a family and a business, so that seemed to be an unlikely decision for us.

If we stayed where we were and didn't move, we would have a lot of explaining to do with friends, acquaintances and others (church, neighbors, etc) with some percentage of uninformed or bigoted responses possible. I may not care what some of these people think, but I didn't want to pick a fight with anyone and did not want to have to live my life as an advocate or spokeswoman for explaining gender issues. I hoped that it would not be a big issue. If we moved and started out fresh in a new place, many of these issues would not matter, especially since I was getting comfortable being viewed and accepted as a woman.

It may not sound like much to people who are comfortable in their original gender, but "passing" is important to most transgender people. Even if I am totally comfortable with myself as female, I don't want questions about my gender to be the first thoughts someone has when they see me.

Some transgender people have inherent challenges such as being too tall, having hands too big, large Adam's apples and thinning or missing hair for a male to female transition, or being too small or too short for female to male. I am lucky because I am relatively short, my hands are average for a female, I wear size 10 shoes, I don't have a visible Adams apple and I have nice curly hair. I can always be thinner, but that's another issue!
I did not want to live my life hiding my self from others

and not being true to myself because someone might not like me. You only get one shot at life, and I needed to live it for God, myself and my family, not a bunch of other people. I would hate to say that I wanted to live as a female but did not do it because I was afraid of others' reactions. That also seemed impossible to continue to do. I hid for so many years. I couldn't do it any more. I had to transition. Another breakthrough came when I started to feel comfortable in my own skin. I felt female and expected to be treated as such. I think most people pick up on the female vibe.

- I did not have an understanding of the legal and logistical issues if someone dresses female and presents female without actually having surgery. How does it affect passports, driver's licenses, names, credit cards, etc?

As with all other related matters, I decided that we could handle those things as they came up. I eventually got a letter from my therapist that explained that I was transgender just in case, but I never needed it. I changed my name to JJ Marie Gufreda. Needing to change my name on everything that came later in my life has been tedious and a hassle, but not a real problem.

Ready to Roll?

I pondered if I was ready to make the difficult choice for a total transition to female. Could I dress at home as I did for several years, go out more as a female, take vacations or possibly live part-time as a female (e.g. live here as a male in public, but have a second house elsewhere where I lived as a female)? Transition felt right and would avoid the pain of going back and forth.

As I worked through therapy, went out more in public as a female, and moved from having my special times as a female to daily life as a female, I quickly realized that I was ready to transition, and the faster the better. I was not in a hurry for all the physical and permanent changes—hormones, surgeries, name change, etc. I thought that I would get those started when I was ready and it made sense.

My excitement was intensifying day by day to start living full-time as a female and start the process of making all the physical changes. Some people think having genital reassignment surgery (GRS) is the final irreversible step. It may be for some, but for me, when I told everyone I know that I was changing to female, there was no going back.

In 2007, I prepared to roll into transition. I was ready to go. Jo and I had seen gender and relationship therapists—a big help in sorting out what was happening and how to deal with it. I learned about hormones, facial surgery and GRS, and had talked with many transgender people about their experiences. I was finished with laser and had started on electrolysis. All of those changes were starting, although much too slowly for me.

Transition Time

I was most concerned about the people that I was closest to. Jim and Tina were two good friends. I told them about the upcoming changes very early in the process. I was nervous about what to tell people and how to tell them. I hadn't told many people outside of the family. They let me practice "the talk" on them. I did not know how to develop a good way to do it.

"The talk" has changed a lot since that first trial run with my friends. One of the changes was that my speech got shorter. I was so nervous the first time it seemed to take forever. I also found that sending a letter or email gives the person time to process the information before they respond to you.

Jim said something important that stuck with me as things moved along, He said, "We are all going to have to transition with you." I realized that he was right. When people decide to help, support and accompany you on this journey, everyone changes a little.

I developed a few decision rules and a simple model to help me and my family as I started to transition.

Decision Rules for My Transition:

Here are some of the decision rules we came up with:

- Have love and concern for each person that you tell. It will be a surprise, possibly a shock, and it may be something that they never heard about before. Try to have as much empathy as possible.
- Have more information and detail ready, but try not to overwhelm people with too much if they don't want it.
- If someone needs time, that is okay and not unexpected.
- Try to have a sense of humor. You will need it.
- Tell before seeing. As much as you can, try not to surprise anyone and tell them about the changes before they see you dressed as your "new and improved" self. (Okay, it's really the old and normal self, but...)
- Don't apologize. In an early draft of one of "the" letters, I wrote something like, "If you have a problem with this, I understand." My therapist Michele liked most of the letter, but she asked me, "Are you okay if someone has a problem with you because you're changing genders?"

I thought about it and told her that I was not okay with it. These people were my family, friends and work associates. I expected them to accept me as I am.

She suggested that I take that sentence out and not apologize because I didn't really feel that I had anything to apologize about. It was a helpful suggestion, and thinking through the issue helped me develop my thoughts and expectations about others' reactions.

- Do the best you can and whatever happens, happens. You cannot change another person's views or feelings so hope for the best, but try not to be too surprised by anything.

Who to Tell -- And When and How?

I decided that I needed to organize my thoughts about the people in my life. I started to think in terms of circles:

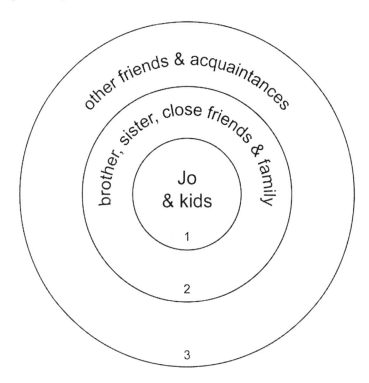

In number 1, the inner circle, the center is my wife Jo. She is the most important person to me, and it was critical to me that I helped her work through many of the issues that she would have and try to help minimize any pain and problems that she might encounter. I can't make her happy—that is up to her—but I can certainly show her my love and help and support her in any way I can.

As much time and effort that I needed to spend helping her with the adjustments was well spent. I could not move further out into the circle until she was ready and committed (as reluctant as she might be) to go with me.

I know several male to female transgender people who had to give up their marriage when they transitioned. Some of them sound relieved that they were "free," and others are upset, disappointed or bitter. In my case, Jo is my soul mate, my best friend, and we could not see either of us going through this or anything else without the other person.

At one point, I asked Jo, "Do you see any possible scenario where we would not go through this together?"

She said, "No."

I replied that we were in it together and would work everything out as we always did. We agreed that we were in it for the long run. That was a good confirmation for both of us. The future was uncertain as it always is, but we would do it together.

The second part of the first circle was our children. I thought it would be hard for them to accept Dad turning into a woman, and I was concerned about how they would handle it, how it would affect their relationships and what we would need to do to keep a good close relationship.

The second circle was my brother and sister, parents and close relatives. Moving out into the last circle was everyone else, in order of how I knew them.

The inner circles included the most important people in my life. I was determined to do the best I could to help them accept me and the changes we all would experience. I also wanted them to understand that I had not deceived them all those years, at least any more than I had been deceiving myself, and explain why I had waited so long to tell them. I tried hard to help them determine how to talk to their friends, gave them educational materials or information that was available and to do anything that I could for the people I love the most. I also invested considerable energy and effort into telling the other people who are close to me.

The planning, soul searching and effort has paid off. I still have close relationships with *all* of my closest loved ones. It has not all been easy for anyone, but it is all worth it. With the people in the inner circles together and ready to move forward, I felt confident that we could handle any issues or problems that might come up as we moved further out in the circles.

Ripples—Moving into the Outer Circles

In the second circle are two bands of people: other relatives and close friends. Jo and I decided that the main rule for this group was "tell before they see." I was concerned about the closest family members—my brother and sister and other relatives. If we were successful keeping these relationships, I was ready for anything that might happen in the outer circles.

As I prepared to transition, I started to deal with a flood of emotions and issues. I was relieved that I was going to stop hiding and was going to let the world see the person that I am. Almost overnight, I went from a lifetime of fear that someone would "find out" to a feeling that everyone will find out sooner or later anyway and, if they do, it is what it is.

The problem quickly shifted from hoping that no one would find out to figuring out how to tell people about how my life would change.

Around mid-2007, I had a life-changing experience that greatly affected my transition, as well as many aspects of my life. I consider this experience a major turning point and freeing moment. I wish I knew the exact time that it happened, because

I would like to celebrate it every year on that date. It was not the kind of thing that happened in a flash. It just happened and, like many things in my life, I figured it out later.

I can describe the event simply: I crossed the "I-don't-give-a-shit line." (Pardon my language, but that is the best way to describe it.) Instead of worrying about everything and everyone, I was determined to do the best I could, and then not worry about it as well as I could.

I previously mentioned the "What-If Twins." These culprits caused me a lot of anxiety earlier because I was always worried about "What if this" and "What if that."

When I first heard of them I realized that the What-If Twins had been hanging around me much of my life: What if I can't get rid of my anxiety? What if someone found out that I wanted to wear women's clothes? What if the neighbors see me dressed? So many interactions with the What-If Twins were paralyzing me and making me anxious.

Jettisoning the Twins

When I finally realized that I *was* transgender and then decided I could not hide and suppress it any more, I felt a release of tension, fear and the dread that this was going to wreck my life. I was transgender; I was changing to a woman, and we would deal with it. If someone was going to find out, instead of trying to hide, I realized that they would eventually find out anyway, so there was nothing to hide.

I laughed to myself when I thought about it. I was going to change to female. Jo and the kids knew, and everyone we knew would soon find out because we would tell them. I had been worried when I went out in public that I might not pass as a female, or someone would figure out that I was male or that I had been male.

I chuckled when I realized that if someone figured it out, then they would realize that I was transgender. Big deal, I *was* transgender. You've heard of "gay-dar?" I am not sure there is a "trans-dar," but if someone figured it out, so what?

As the year progressed I started to change my outlook. I considered my gender journey, all the anxiety and fear from hiding and suppressing and the cost of worrying. I realized I couldn't worry about what people thought or how they reacted. I decided, "I don't give a shit." Do your best, have empathy and hope for the best. I did not have firm expectations of how things would go, but I expected the best.

It was not that I didn't care about other people. I always try to be empathetic. I just decided that I could not make my decisions and live my life to try to make others happy. Each person's happiness is up to them. If someone has a problem with me, or does not like what I am doing, I can only do the best I can and move on from there.

When I analyzed my relationships, I realized that crossing the "I-don'tgive-a-shit line" was a prioritization issue as well. I cared much more about the people in the inner circles. As we moved to the outer circles, if there were losses, then we would deal with them. I was comfortable working with the people closest to me and then developing a plan to deal with everyone else.

Telling Our Children

Jo and I talked about what to tell the kids. There didn't seem to be a great way to tell them what was happening. I just decided that we needed to treat them with as much love and understanding as possible and tell them the truth.

I would try to be ready for any reaction. Based on our relationships and the love we already had, I felt it would go fine—at least as fine as it could go when Dad tells you he is going to become a woman.

In addition to the shock, I guessed they would also think about what it meant to them. What do they call me? What would their friends think? What will their boy- and girlfriends think?

I decided I had to talk to Joey first. I had attended a few transgender meetings at the Life Journey Church, at that time known as Jesus MCC church, on the north side of town. That church was at the end of Joey's street! I knew the chances of us running into each other were slim, but I didn't want him to find out by seeing me as a female, recognizing my car or if, God forbid, helping me if I had an accident or a flat. I wanted to tell him the right way.

We work together, so one day I sat him down in the conference room and told him the whole story. He was shocked and asked some questions, but at the end, he said, "Is this the reason that you are so uptight and crabby all the time?"

I told him that I thought it contributed to a lot of it. It was stressful to hide who I really was.

He said, "Well, if this will make you feel better and more relaxed, then I am okay with it." I am glad we have great kids.

Andrea probably had the hardest time with it. First, I was her dad, and she realized that this relationship would never be exactly the same—not necessarily better or worse, but much different from what she expected.

The other issue was that she lived in Chicago, and as things progressed, I was taking major steps forward while she and her boyfriend Kyle were adjusting to the previous changes. They lived three or four hours north of Indy.

They came home one weekend to visit around Thanksgiving. They already knew that I had been dressing for a long time, but had never seen me. At this point I was dressing part-time, going out occasionally and getting ready for full-time transition.

I told them the first day they were at home before Thanksgiving that I always dressed female at home, but had changed to my old clothes because they were home and had not seen me yet. The next day, however, when they returned from a day visiting friends, I would be dressed normally (for me) and would be female. I told them I wanted them to get used to it and to see me the way I was.

When they arrived home after their visits, we all said hi and no one acknowledged that I looked different. Finally Kyle (thanks!) broke the ice. He looked at my chest, which at that time was enhanced with some padded forms (I was not on hormones yet). He smiled, and paraphrased from a *Seinfeld* episode: "They're real and they're fabulous." We all laughed and we survived the rest of the weekend.

We talked about it afterwards, and the perceptions of the weekend varied for each person.

I was relieved that they knew and had seen me. Nothing apparently terrible happened, and we were together.

They had a tough time adjusting and were relieved to get through it. They were getting used to knowing, even though it was a difficult and slow process, and I was getting used to being myself and not hiding. I give Andrea and Kyle a lot of credit because they tried to deal with the transition even though they were only here intermittently.

Much of the difficulty was that I was progressing so fast at that time. By the next time they were home for another visit I was ready to go full-time, to do anything and everything as a female. They had still not dealt with their own issues: "What does this mean for me?" "How do I tell my friends?" "What if someone sees us in public?" I was going at 65 mph (maybe 100!) and everyone else was 25 to 30, tops. (maybe ten!)

It was strenuous, but we have stuck together even though it's still hard for them. I appreciate Andrea and Kyle getting through it because I know it was, and still is, tough seeing the changes every time they came home.

Our youngest, Matt, is a free spirit. He never cared much for what the teachers thought in school. He dressed differently than the average—sometimes because he was different, and sometimes because he wanted to be different. He had some gay friends and was always welcoming to the people on the fringes and those that had been shunned to some degree by the majority of society.

Nonetheless, I was worried about Matt. Even though he was so accepting of diversity and had always been non-judgmental of everyone, I was concerned how he might accept diversity when it came from someone so close—Dad.

Matt asked some interesting questions. He asked if this was why I had been so uptight. I was a little surprised because he said the same thing that Joey had said. I must have been even more tightly wound than I recognized.

Matt also asked if my dressing at home was why we had bought new blinds for the windows and why we asked them to call before they came over for a visit.

I said that this was correct.

He agreed with Joey's reaction and said that if this would help me be more relaxed and happier, he was okay with it.

After we told the kids, I knew that there was a long way to go, and that everything was not easy or settled, but I was relieved that my biggest concern—how my closest family would do with the news—was going to be difficult, but eventually we would work through everything.

Sibling Surprise: Your Big Brother's a Girl

The other two key people were my sister Glorianne and my brother Tim.

Jo and I talked with my sister when she and her family visited us during the summer before I was ready to transition. I wanted to tell her first, and then she could decide what and how to tell her husband and kids. Their visit to Indy provided the perfect opportunity.

The first thing I realized was that in our family, it was hard to talk privately about something that you did not want everyone to hear about. Jo and I grabbed my sister and took her upstairs to our bedroom, since the sitting room was probably the most private place in the house. We could see everyone outside on the patio and in the pool, so we knew that we would not be disturbed. We were wrong! Her kids called her cell phone two or three times to find out what Mom was doing during the 45 minutes we were talking. We had to rush, but eventually we got it all out.

I went through the entire story and Glor asked several questions: "Were we staying together?" "Was I gay?" "How were the kids doing?"

She was sweet. In addition to being the most shocked that she had ever been in her life, she was so concerned about us. She did not seem to fully comprehend what I was telling her. It was like I was from another planet and had announced that the mother-ship was coming to take us all home.

Like many of the people I know, she did not know much about being transgender. I tried to take my time so she could digest what I was telling her.

After we talked, she did some research and understands much better. She is very supportive. She sent me a birthday card that said, "For my Sister—Sharing a lifetime with you has made me realize I couldn't have a better sister or a better friend." That meant a lot to me. The tears flowed, and that was all right with me.

I was nervous about letting my brother, Tim, know what was happening, but I wanted him to know the real me. When we went to visit in Cleveland, I looked for an opportunity to talk with him where we had some privacy. When we have a family get-together, it is a lot of food, conversation, laughing and chaos. That makes it difficult to talk about something private. Every opportunity I tried I did not get the chance!

Six months passed and I thought surely at Christmastime, I will find a way to tell him. I was ready to go full-time (female) and wanted him to know. No surprises; know before you see! We did not get a private moment again. I was determined, but frustrated.

After the holidays, I called him and apologized that it had to be this way (not in person) but I had something important to share with him and his family that could not wait any longer. I hated to do it on the phone, but it could be a year before we got 10 minutes of private face time.

He was surprised—he wondered how he had not picked up on it before. He was open and accepting, and told me he would tell his wife, Patsy, and their kids—all but the youngest. They wanted to wait for a good time to talk with him—a time that was appropriate given his age, changes at school, and recent loss of relatives. They waited and talked to him within six months.

Patsy and a few of the kids called within a day or two to ask some questions and give me support. I was relieved that we finally got it out to my brother and sister and their families.

My dad passed away a year or so before I made the decision to transition. While I would have liked to share something this important with my parents, I never got the opportunity with my dad. I have no regrets; we had a good relationship, and I can't complain about my upbringing. Compared to some of the soap opera families I have come across, our family was pretty mundane.

Forced Back to Guydom One Last Time

I wanted to tell my mom, but her health was poor. She had multiple medical problems and had progressively worse breathing problems. Tim, Glor, Jo and I talked about it, and while I wanted to tell her, they convinced me that it would not help anything since Mom was failing health-wise. Glor asked me if I was doing it for me or for Mom, and I agreed that it was for me. Nothing good would come from telling someone so sick something as major as that. I would have to suck it up, and hold it in for Mom's sake.

One result of this decision was that I had to change back to male when I visited Mom. I had been living full-time as female for about five months or so, I was on female hormones and testosterone blockers, and I had told many of the people I encounter on a regular basis. I had already transitioned at work. As I got more and more comfortable being a female, and that did not take much time at all, the male part of me was quickly slipping away. I was in "London," and going back where I came from seemed a distant memory.

When I picked a weekend to visit Mom and the family in Cleveland, Jo already had plans to go out of town that weekend. I packed up the dogs and drove by myself. In the weeks before the trip, I was anxious to see Mom and the rest of the family, but I was getting more agitated and upset about having to change to male.

It may seem strange to someone who hasn't been in my shoes, but the more I thought about going back, even for a few days, the more depressed I got. I kept trying to "suck it up," but it was bothering me.

I already had switched over my travel bag for all female travel, and I had to look for some of the few remaining male clothes that I still kept for this type of situation. It took me two days to pack because I couldn't remember what kinds of things I packed when I was male; I had to dig into my memory. It was like that was a faded part of a dream that is mostly gone when you wake up.

I guy-ed up as much as I could, tied my hair in a ponytail and loaded the car. The dogs and I started on the trip and after we were on the road, I realized (as I had done a few times before) that I loaded them in the car without their leashes. I laughed at myself since this was a recurring theme and had to stop on the way to pick up replacements. I stopped at a store and walked to the pet department for a few cheap leashes.

When I started to go out dressed female, I was nervous that someone might "find out" or that I might have someone figure out that I was not born a girl. I only had one negative interaction when I first started dressing; the person said something to someone else. No one has ever said anything to me, if they knew or cared. By this time, I was totally comfortable as a female.

In the store as a male, I felt nervous and self-conscious—even worse than when I first started to dress female. I felt like everyone was looking at me and that they could tell that I was not really a guy. I am sure that no one actually noticed, but I felt out of place.

I felt disoriented and disconnected all weekend. I knew it would be hard, but it was harder than I ever thought it would be. I was happy to see everyone back home in Cleveland, but I was so glad to get home, change back to my clothes and stop pretending to be a guy.

Mom passed away a few months later. We decided I needed to go to the wake and funeral as a guy one more time, since I had not told most of the relatives on that side of the family out of respect to my mom since she didn't know. I wore my regular clothes for the trip, but had to change to guy clothes for the wake and funeral.

I was already in a bad way since I had just lost my mom, and then I was figuring out how to try to be a guy again. I did not know what to do with my hair, which was even longer and dyed dark blonde. I asked my sister what would look the most guy-like and we eventually put gel in it and pulled it back as best we could.

The weekend was rough for me. Mom's passing was tough—we had been close as a family, and now both parents were gone. The mixture of the loss and changing to male were a bad combination for me.

I started to get visited by my old unwanted companions, the anxiety attacks, and the relapse caught me off guard. David Johnson helped me get back in synch with the program to eliminate the anxiety.

I felt stupid wearing a suit and tie at the funeral, but that was the last time I would have to do that. After the funeral I gave away the last male clothes.

Time to Tell

A month or so later, I sent a letter to all the other family members explaining everything that was happening. The brief return to acting male during the funeral was a difficult time. Even with my family and friends there to support, I had a hard time. I don't ever recall feeling so disconnected, fake, and out of harmony with myself—and all while we were working through the loss of my mom. I was sad, hurt and shocked, but I was so glad to eventually get it behind me.

While tough on me and everyone else, the funeral was almost unbearable because it was compounded by my having to change back to a guy for a few days. It confirmed what I already knew— I was not making a mistake in changing gender. I had made the right decision to transition, and I could never go back. I was not denying the past, but having been male was like smoke drifting away after fireworks: There for a time, but only a memory afterwards.

The most important priority in my transition was with my close family. We had gotten through that, and we all remained close. All I needed to do now was to tell everyone else I know!

Chapter 5

More in the Outer Circles

I had some good experiences with my "practice my speech and get input" sessions with some of my close friends. I told them that I wanted to share something that was important to me and previously had been very secret. They knew it must be serious, and I quickly started so as not to worry them. After a while, when I would tell people, I'd often say, "What I am about to tell you is important, but it's not bad. No one is dying or anything like that."

I was a little misleading because the male part of me was dying or already dead. I learned that I would need to understand that almost everyone needed time to mourn the loss of the old person in his or her own way. I tried to be aware of their feelings and adjust what and how I tell people to best fit (as well as I could figure out) their needs. I had help, in that some people told me that they would tell others what was happening and that made it easier for me.

Going out locally was a potential problem. If I saw people I knew, I didn't want to surprise them, but I didn't want to hide, either. This was important to me but also a concern for my children. They needed to tell their friends that their dad had changed. I tried to work through it with them as much as I could.

I only had a few occasions where I ran into people who didn't know about my gender change. I saw one old friend at the store. We hadn't seen each other for three or four years, but we used to get together frequently. He was looking at something in one of the main aisles and had his young son in the shopping cart.

At first, I thought that I'd just walk by. I don't think that most people who knew me when I was a guy recognize me now unless they look closely. I haven't had any facial surgery, but some of the other changes were noticeable. Even though the bone structure is still the same, hormones affect my appearance. I used to have salt-and-pepper short hair and I now have long curly blonde hair. That makes a big difference too.

I walked up to him and said hi. He gave me a "Do I know you?" look. I said, "I used to be Joe Gufreda, but I am transgender and changed to female. My new name is JJ."

I could tell that he was surprised but realized what was going on. We talked about our families for a few minutes, I told him that it was nice to see him after so long, and I went on my way. I have only surprised a few people like that, and in each case, it has gone well—both for me and for the other person—as far as I could tell.

I realized for some people the news would be a shock. First, they did not see something like this happening with me (as I said before, I was a great hider and suppresser). Second, most people don't know much about being transgender, so it takes time for them to process. Some were questioning, but many dealt with it in a matter-of-fact way. They said something like, "Thanks for telling me," and that's all there was to it.

It was important to be ready for the first in-person meeting after I told someone with a letter or on the phone. Many people understandably were nervous to see me because they didn't know what to expect.

Love of JJ at First Sight? Not Necessarily

The process goes something like this:

The person reads the letter or hears the news that I am changing to female. They process it depending on their experience and familiarity with transgender people, as well as their personal comfort level. If the person has questions about their own gender or sexuality, talking with me may scare them. Or they may easily absorb everything I tell them. Once the person processes the information, they get ready for seeing me.

I have an advantage. I can easily be comfortable because I know what the other person is like from our previous relationship, and I know what I am like and how I look. He or she may try to visualize in their mind how I will look and act. They have questions: "What do I call her (I think it is "her," right)?" "Will she make me feel uncomfortable?" "Will she be like the person I used to know?" And finally, "What will JJ look like?"

I think the person develops a mental picture that starts with my old face, the one that they knew. My guess is that they start "Photoshopping" my face in their mind—adding long hair, thinning the eyebrows, adding lipstick and makeup, etc.

The problem is that they are unsure what they are going to experience. Every once in a while, a wild flamboyant drag queen's face will jump into their mental map and cover my face. Then they get nervous until they calm down and realize that I probably won't look like that. When they finally see me, I look different than before, but they know it is me.

"I'm Glad That's Over!"

Judy Koch is a friend who works at one of the parishes where we used to attend Mass. I have known her for several years and enjoy her company. She has an offbeat way of looking at things, so we easily connect. We get together two or three times a year and have lunch, and it's always a good time.

I had told Judy early on about my gender transition, and she had given me good feedback on how to tell other people. Shortly after our meeting, after I went full-time female, I asked Judy if she wanted to go to lunch with Jo and me. She accepted, and we picked her up and went to a nice little restaurant. We chatted and ate our lunches, and things proceeded like any other time we had gotten together. I was more relaxed as a female, true, but otherwise things seemed like they had always been.

After lunch, we were driving her back to church, and she said, "Wow, I am glad that is over."

I was surprised and asked her what she was glad was over.

She said, "Lunch."

I asked why, and she explained that she had been nervous about seeing me since she had no idea how I would act and what I would look like. She didn't know "what it would be like" to spend time with me. She did not want us to feel uncomfortable.

Jo and I smiled. I asked, "Well, how was it?"

Judy grinned and said, "It was just like lunch!" She said she didn't know what she had expected, but she was nervous because she had never had an experience like that.

It was a good learning experience for me, and I try to be cognizant of everyone's feelings and any nervousness they may have the first time we get together. I haven't noticed anything different in the second meetings, but the initial meeting can be a little uncomfortable at first. Judy told me that subsequent lunches were like any other time she got together with any of her other girl friends.

A few people have thanked me for not being "weird." It's funny when they say it, but I think I know what they mean.

Batting Cleanup – Hope We've Told Everyone!

After a while, especially after I sent the Christmas letter to anyone that I hadn't already gotten to, just about everyone who needed to know had been informed.

As I encounter people who knew me when I was male, I'll tell them as best I can. I went to an all-guys high school, and a handful of the friends who have stayed in contact know about the news. If I ever go back for a reunion, I think I'll just show up and see if any of the other people figure it out! They don't look like they did in high school, and neither do I!

By now, I was comfortable in my gender for the first time in my life. Most of the people who were friends, associates or family knew me as JJ. I was feeling content as a "Londoner."

Chapter 6

Reactions: "How ya doin'?"

I have not felt any hesitation or remorse for my decision to transition. Dealing with my immediate family was the most important part of the transition. I would not be ready to move forward until I felt that we could all go through it together. We all were committed to staying together and going on this journey. Their love and support helped me get through the tough periods.

I felt alone some of the time because this can be a lonely road, but I knew that everyone close to me was somewhere on the road with me. I may have been traveling faster (probably a lot faster) than everyone else, but we were all moving forward.

After I shared what was happening with the people in my closest circles, we had to figure out what to tell everyone else and how to tell them. I told some in person, some on the phone, and many by letter or email. This chapter is dedicated to sharing how family and friends reacted to the news of my gender change. Chapter 13 discusses how the people involved with me in business reacted to the transition.

I hope you enjoy reading about how great some people can be and how they show love. Small gestures of love and friendship can make a difference in another person's life. Reading these examples of outreach of love and kindness makes me feel good. Tears always come to my eyes when I read them!

It was a daunting task to tell all our friends, neighbors, acquaintances and relatives. I had to make a list of people I know and decide if I *should* tell them, *how* to tell them, and *when* to tell them.

I worked a lot with Jo, Joey, Andrea and Matt to find good ways to tell people. This was also a subject of many sessions with several therapists. The effort was worth it. I would describe some reactions as touching, curious, funny, hysterical, tearjerkers, empathetic and loving. I will share some of the reactions that did not go so well, but let's start with the positive ones. They energized me and confirmed my faith in humankind.

How I Learned How Not To React

More than 30 years ago, I had unknowingly received a good training session in what to expect when someone is told of a major change. Dan Dewitt and I met in high school, stayed friends in college and became roommates, living with another friend renting the upstairs level of a large double house on the east side of Cleveland.

Dan and I worked together at Guido's pizza after school and saw each other every day when we were roommates. We were close friends. One day, Dan went through a long explanation to tell me that he was gay.

I was shocked. First, this was the mid- to late '70s, and I had lived a sheltered life. I had heard of "being gay," but I didn't know what that meant. I was almost completely ignorant of people being attracted to the same sex, and it did not make sense to me. Dan and I used to double date, and he had been out with several girls. He could not possibly be gay!

Also, I was too ignorant or self absorbed to pick up on any of the many signals that I should have noticed. I did not think that this was possible for a friend of mine; especially someone that I was sure liked girls. It just did not compute.

After the poor guy nervously went through his story, I reacted badly. I acted like a jerk. I probably could use more accurately descriptive words than "jerk," but I am a lady.

I reacted like any good Sicilian—I got mad at Dan. I felt confused, betrayed, hurt—so many emotions at one time. We yelled at each other for a while (I did most of the yelling) and broke off the conversation. We were upset and angry at each other.

When I finally cooled down and started to think, I felt bad. Here was a dear friend and roommate, so nervous to tell me this important thing that he had hidden his entire life. My reaction had hurt him badly. I felt terrible and wanted to make it up to Dan.

The next day, I asked Dan if we could talk about it again. First, I apologized for being a jerk, and explained that I had been so surprised that I did not process the news very well. If he would accept my sincere apology, would he please start over and give me the story again? I also told him that I felt bad for him because he had held it in so long and wished that I could have done something to help in all those years that he struggled.

With that behind us, I was ready to be a good friend again, even though I still had a hard time understanding what he was going through. It would take time, but I was his friend and sincerely wanted to stay that way. His being gay would not change that. We had a good talk and proceeded forward as friends. Things were different, but the same. It was good to know that I was allowed to see how he really was.

We stayed close after we moved; he was in our wedding and we always considered each other good friends. We still are friends, and I enjoy hearing from him.

I learned many lessons that day: Don't jump to conclusions. Listen better. Show a lot of empathy. I felt good that after I took a day to process the news, I finally acted like a friend should act. I think I showed the love and concern I felt for him as a person and a good friend. As I told people in my life about *my* news, I expected a good reaction just as I had (albeit a trifle delayed) given my friend.

Sharing the News Template

This is a version of the letter that I sent most often to people to share the news about my gender change:

Left Hander in London

January 2008

To: My friends and family,

I very much value my family and friends. I really have not had a great number of friends in my life, as I always was guarded with what I would share and how much I would let people know about me. I hope that when people close to me understand me better, they will continue to be close, and hopefully, we can get closer since I will no longer be hiding important parts of myself that I have hidden.

I have had anxiety and panic attacks for the past 30 years. I have not told many people, but I can just say that I hope you never go through this. I have been learning how to deal with the anxiety and fear and recently have been doing better. I begin with the explanation of my fear and anxiety because they are related to the other thing about me that no one (except Jo) knew about me. I am transgendered. I have always known that I was different, but it took me years to understand it, and then it took time to stop hiding and suppressing it.

The explanation of being transgendered that I have used is like being left-handed in a time when no one had been allowed to be left-handed for so long, that there was no term "left-handed" and no consideration that this was possible. Eventually, the left-handed person accidentally found out that they were more effective left-handed, actually significantly better. The more they realized it, the more they understood that they did not fit in. Information about being left-handed was limited, buried in dusty books in the library. But learning this meant that there were others in the same situation. This was similar to my journey of being transgender. I always knew that I was different, but never really understood it until recently.

Jo has known about this aspect of my personality for several years and has worked through the changes as I have learned more about myself. I had been dressing female at home, but when I started to go out and meet people dressed as a female, I really started to understand that perhaps I was not a crossdresser, but really a transsexual. I had real difficulty going back to being male after dressing and the sense of relaxation and well being that I had was impossible to ignore. I finally felt relaxed and that I was at peace with my self. The anxiety and tension were lessening.

I was still terrified that someone, especially our kids, would find out. We decided to tell the kids so they would not find out by accident, and to finally get this secret off my chest. While they were shocked and confused, their acceptance and support was a blessed gift. I could feel layers of fear and anxiety falling off of me.

In the process of telling people, I am ready to transition my gender to match the way I feel. It will not be easy, and there are many barriers to cross. We do not have everything worked out yet, but the road becomes clearer to me every day. Hormones, laser and electrolysis, surgeries and other changes may await me, but I am comfortable with the changes and with dealing with all the decisions and potential issues.

There are many positives too. I have made several new friends and many of my old friends and family have been incredibly loving and supportive. It is all a part of God's plan, and all I can do is try to live in a way that serves him. I have been going out more dressed as my true self, and perhaps the next time you see me, I will look different from the person that you have known for years.

<u>*A few questions and answers*</u>

Why did you wait so long to do this? At first I did not understand how I was different and what to do about it. When I started to understand, I was fearful of how people would react. When I could not hold it in anymore, it had to come out. A state of anxiety and fear is not a way to live your life.

Are you staying married? I have always loved Jo (even before I met her) and always wanted to be with her. We want to stay together and could not take being apart. We have always wanted to be married to each other. We are best friends.

Are you attracted to men? I have always been attracted to women and that has not changed. I have heard it explained that "gender is between your ears, and sex is between your legs." Gender identity is not the same as sexual attraction. Also, I am married and would not want to be with anyone but my wife.

Is this a sin? How is your relationship with God? I have talked with a priest during the past year and we both agree with the way I have always felt, that "you are what you are." God made intersexed people (people that have physical attributes of both genders), he made people with both male and female chromosomes, and he made people whose gender is not even identifiable when they are born. He made me the way that I am. I am not complaining, but dealing with the situation the best way I can. I still feel called to be a disciple to others and have always been an active Catholic. I have gone to Mass as a female and know other Catholics that are transgender.

What causes this? There are many theories, the most popular being related to a hormonal bath at a certain time in the development of the fetus. If this does not happen just right, the body develops one way and the brain another. No one really knows exactly the reasons, but "what it is, is."

Aren't you worried about what people will say or think? I spent so many years in fear and anxiety that I am working hard to drop all of that baggage. Sometime in the past year, I crossed the "I-don't-give-a-shit line," and while I still care for, love and empathize with others, I will not live my life worrying about everything. I try my best, and that is all I can do.

Are there others like you? I don't know anyone nor have ever seen anyone like this. In our culture, many people are becoming more public as more information gets out and there is increasing support—medically, socially and emotionally. There are people at our church that are transgendered, people in all walks of life, and while not a big percentage of the population, there have always been transgendered people. In some cultures, such as in Tahiti, Hawaii and in the Native American cultures in the southwestern United States, crossing genders or having a third gender are a normal part of their society. It is not viewed as unusual in any way. The media is doing a (somewhat) better job in helping with the communication about gender issues and transgendered people. Recent shows on the Discovery channel and Oprah have given a very sensitive and informative look at some of the people and their families.

Who knows about this? Some friends and many close relatives know. We have not told everyone that we would like to know because of timing, logistics and other issues. Also, not everyone needs to know. I am not public at work, and since I have my own business, deciding how to do this is of critical importance. I am not trying to hide any more, but we are careful about whom we tell, and how they find out. Because of this, we ask the people we share this with to hold it in confidence so we can communicate in a reasonable way. We feel that if people try to understand, get the facts, and "work" with us, the chances of keeping and improving relationships is very good. The reception from the people we have talked with has almost universally been very loving and positive.

Thanks for reading and hopefully understanding. Please keep us in your prayers. You are in ours.

Pray for peace

Joe Gufreda (aka JJ Gufreda)

A Most Welcome Loving Response

This is a portion of Dan's response when I sent him the letter:

I haven't had enough time to really digest your letter, as I just read it, so my comments and reactions are purely emotional and visceral but in a good way. From someone who agonized 32 years ago about telling my straight roommates I was gay, I think I can understand, on some level, the burden that has been lifted from your shoulders in your process of acceptance and acknowledgement of who you really are. I am saddened somewhat for the burden you have carried all these years knowing what that was like for the short (by comparison) time I hid my true identity. The important thing is you have come to terms with who you really are.

To me you will always be a good friend, a kind spirit and loving parent and husband. (There will be plenty of time to employ correct terminology once your transition is complete. I will rely on your guidance here.)

Your letter brought tears to my eyes thinking of all you must have gone through over the years and the fears you faced along the way having to consider not only your feelings but also those of your family. You have always been devoted to the safety and security of your children and Jo. I saw that clearly before I left Cleveland and imagine that devotion only grew over the years.

In this 21st Century, for all we have achieved in technology, economics (well, not a great example), science and industry, we still seem to be so antiquated and 20th Century in our ability to accept differences, understand the complexities of the human condition, be inclusive instead of exclusive and show true kindness and compassion to our fellow human beings.

With that said, 2008 probably affords you more history and precedence and hopefully support from the transgender culture in your journey of discovery. I hope and pray that you are able to tap into resources that hopefully will make your transition easier on some or all levels. From your "FAQ" section, it is clear that you have a wealth of information to share and you have done a great deal of comprehensive research regarding this journey.

My hope for you, Jo and the children is that your journey continues on a clear path, filled with love and support from all who surround you.

I feel honored that you shared this treasured information with me. You have my support and prayers for a peaceful journey through this new transition in your life. My love to you and Jo. Let me know if there is anything I can do. I look forward to talking to you both soon.

Dan

I get tears in my eyes every time I read it. What a good friend.

That experience with Dan over 30 years ago was relevant to my current situation. It helped in setting my expectations for anticipating people's reactions. When we would tell someone, I expected a reaction in two distinct parts, especially from people who I was close to, or were "good" friends.

The first part of the reaction should be a pouring out of friendship, concern, love, support, etc. If someone is my friend, I expect him or her to show some love for me for several reasons—hopefully, they were friends and loved me (or at least liked me). They had to feel for their friend who was in such a struggle and held it in for 50 years. They also should show concern for my family and be supportive of us as people during this time of need. I hope I showed that empathy for Dan (after I originally completely missed the opportunity). He certainly showed it to me. No matter what a friend tells you or what they do, hopefully, they can still remain a friend.

I expected the second part of the reaction to be whatever their thoughts were about the content of the news that I was transgender. When I told friends, some people were knowledgeable and understood immediately. Some were completely without a clue about what it means to be transgender. To some people, it was like I was speaking another language! Some had a lot of questions, some needed time to process it, everyone was surprised, and some did research.

I was not surprised by any of these reactions. I guessed that those responses would be all over the map, based on people's knowledge of gender issues, their worldview, their acceptance of new things, their beliefs, and their own gender and sexual identity and comfort with themselves.

Compassion and Empathy Requested, Please

What I wanted and expected was that first part, the empathetic part, should be supportive of me and my family as people. The other part, the content reaction, would vary by person and would be something that we would deal with depending on how each person reacted.

I visualize it this way:

Telling big news
↓
Initial Processing of the news

Empathetic Reaction
(care and concern for me & my family)

Content Reaction
(what they think about transgender people, how shocked they were, how they feel about about me in my transition...)

I expected I would get a good empathetic reaction. Why wouldn't my friends and loved ones show me they care when I share something this important and they know that I need their support? I did not feel that I should be surprised by any response I got from someone's content reaction.

The empathetic reaction of some of my friends helped me, especially during the nervous first months of starting my transition and telling people.

My therapist, Michelle, pointed out that people who are close to you need time to adjust and they will probably mourn the loss of the old person they knew, even though the new person is still right here with them. I observed that with many friends. Their taking time to deal with it still did not change the empathy they had and their outpouring of friendship.

"How ya doin'?"

Rich Hammond, one of the first friends with which I shared the news, was also the first person that I told in a letter, rather than face-to-face. He lives on the other side of town, and I was still nervous to tell friends in person.

I hoped that the letter would explain it in more detail and would also give the recipient time to understand what they were reading. They could process it a little and take some time before they responded if that helped them. I sent the email with the letter attached and waited. I was apprehensive. Rich had been a friend and colleague for many years, and I was sure he and his wife, Jan would be comfortable with the news and we'd remain good friends.

After two nervous days, the phone rang in the evening. I answered, and I heard him say, "How ya doin'?" in his Southside Chicago accent.

I said that I was okay.

Rich said, "No really. How are you doing? I read your letter. Are you okay, is Jo okay, how are the kids? This must be hard for all of you to deal with."

I felt so good that his first response was of care and concern for us. A big worry was partially lifted and I was relieved that I had good friends. Maybe it is more correct to say that they had kept me as a friend.

He told me that he and Jan hardly slept since they read the letter *because they were worried about us!*

He then shared the second part of their reaction, which was confusion and interest to learn more. He asked a lot of questions. I had no problem answering anything they wanted to know and sent them some information so they could learn more.

Rich and Jan's empathetic reaction confirmed my expectation that I should get this reaction from everyone who is really a friend. His "How ya doin'?" helped me get a good start on the transition journey. It was possible! I could do this!

I had sent letters to many of the soccer people—the folks who were involved with the kids' soccer games as they grew up. Several still played in the adult leagues with our kids (now all grown) and socialized outside of the games as well. Watching the outdoor and indoor games was supporting the kids, fun to do and provided good social time.

Oops—Missed One!

The first time I went to a game "dressed," I thought that everyone already knew about my changes. I had told some people in person and sent emails to others. I walked in and a few people said "hi, you look nice," "how are you," etc. I looked at one young woman I know, and her jaw dropped about three feet! She held on to her baby (she was so shocked that I thought she might drop the little guy) and looked at me again.

She said, "You're yanking my chain, right?"

I said, "No."

She asked me several more times and I kept answering that I was not trying to yank anyone's chain.

I finally said, "I am transgender. I tried to send letters explaining it to everyone so they would know about it before they would see me dressed female. I am guessing, from your reaction, that I did not send you a letter yet."

She said, "No, I would have remembered that!"

I apologized for not telling her in advance, but told her that while I tried to get everyone in that first shot, I must have missed her.

She told me she understood.

I sent her the full story later that night in an email. We laughed because the look on her face was priceless. I was sorry to surprise her, but thankful for her nice reaction (after the shock). I was glad that she accepted my apology and we had a pleasant time watching that and other games in subsequent weeks.

We Need To Do Something About Your Hair

One of the funniest reactions was from our niece, Jenny. Jenny has two kids, cuts and styles hair, and lives in Iowa. She would occasionally take a road trip to Indy and visit for a couple of days. Sometimes, she would plan the trip in advance and other times, she would give us a call, tell us she was coming, jump in the truck and be here seven hours later.

During this period I was dressing female all the time at home and was starting to occasionally go out dressed, but few people knew and I was still hiding. I had not told many people. Jo and I planned to tell family as we saw them or when we got the "right" opportunity. I decided that, with Jo's agreement, now was as good a time as any other to tell Jenny, so when she arrived and got settled, I would explain everything.

She was understandably tired from the trip, but listened intently. She only made a few comments as I went along.

When I finished, she looked at me and said, "Uncle Joe, or I guess we have to call you something else now, I have two things to say to you: One: You are not even *close* to the weirdest person in our family, so don't worry about us. Two: we need to do something about your hair."

She also told me that she would inform Jo's side of the family about what was happening. I was able to tell, or rather have Jenny tell, all those relatives at one time—and she would do the work for me! She updated everyone when she returned home. She told them that if anyone had a problem with it, they'd have to deal with her! That was sure easy for me. Thanks again, Jenny.

I think that I have a good sense of humor and it was a big help during these moments. At that time, my hair was getting long enough that I had stopped wearing the clip-on fall that added more length in the back, but I did not style it that much. It was salt and pepper, really more salt than pepper, and I let it go curly. I have naturally curly hair, which is great for being a female.

I asked Jenny what she wanted to do to it, and she said that we'd get into it tomorrow. There was too much to consider that late at night. I was a little shocked that she was so direct, but I was thankful for the styling assistance she gave me the next day.

The next morning, she picked, combed and styled until she was happy with the results. She then announced, "You need to color your hair."

I said, "No way."

In the Hands of the Experts

And like any good stylist, she did not take no for an answer. I coincidentally had an appointment with my regular stylist, Lisa, from the Full Circle salon in downtown Indy. I had seen her several times. Previously, I had been going to a friend's salon for haircuts. I liked it there, but stopped going to them when I started my transition since I had not told them of the change.

I was dressing and going out as a female as much as possible, but I wanted to avoid people I knew that I had not told of the news. Timing was important, and it took a while to let people know. Also, I had to tell groups of people that hung around together. I wanted to share the news firsthand, and not let the rumor mill do the job poorly.

I wanted to find a good stylist in a location where I had less chance to run into people I knew when I was "dressing" part-time. Lisa's shop was downtown, and she was understanding and kind to me when I first started to go to her shop dressed female. She told me that she would open early if I was uncomfortable getting my hair done when other people were around!

I took her up on the offer for a few visits, but soon was comfortable enough to visit any time I need a trim. The first time I visited her, I brought a briefcase with my clip-on hairpieces so she could give her advice on how I looked with them, and she could cut my hair, combine the added piece and show me how to do it myself.

I was pleased later in the year when my hair was long enough to get rid of the falls and just use my natural hair. I learned I can never do it as well as the stylist, but I appreciated the lessons they gave me. My stylists have been friendly, supportive and a big help with my hair.

Jenny went with me to the appointment with Lisa and negotiated with her as to what would be done to me. I did not have much input, except that I was allowed to check with Jo so she would not be surprised. Jo said that she was OK if I colored it, just so it was not blonde. I agreed and waited for their recommendation.

They agreed on the plan and told me that either light brown or blonde was the color I needed.

I replied, "I asked Jo and she was okay with it as long as it is not blonde. You are telling me that blonde is what you recommend? Why?"

Lisa explained that there was so much grey in my hair that if I went back to my original black color, it would look bad. A light color would hide the grey and not look so shocking.

I told Jenny and Lisa that I trusted their judgment and made an appointment for the coloring. We decided on light brown just to be safe, but I have since gone to dark blonde and then to medium blonde! They gave me good advice. I never thought I could ever become a girl, and now I found out that London girls could even be blonde if they wanted!

More Positive, Loving Reactions

The day after I mailed "the letter" to several of our friends, I got a call from a good friend, Pete. We had met him and his wife Diane through activities at church and had known them for several years.

Pete told me that they had received our letter and Diane had insisted that he give me a call to tell us that they supported us and would be there if we needed any help. He was funny, because he said that he didn't think he even needed to call—that we should know that they were behind us all the way and would always be our friends, but since Diane insisted, he dutifully made the call.

I laughed, and thanked him for calling. I appreciated the call and that he didn't think he even needed to call. We enjoy them now even more than before.

No Punch Line

I asked a longtime family friend to come into the office one summer day so we could talk in person. I shared with her about being transgender and that I was going to transition.

When I was almost finished, she looked at me and said, "What's the punch line?"

I was confused by her response and asked what she meant.

She said, "You have a good sense of humor. When are you getting around to the joke?"

I didn't know what to say. I *do* have a sense of humor and like to joke with people, but this time, I was serious. I was wearing shorts that day—we're casual at the office unless we are seeing clients—and said, "Feel my legs. They have no hair on them."

She said, "So? Some guys don't have hair on their legs."

I said I realized that, but I previously had a lot of hair and didn't now.

She looked at Joey and said, "Tell me that he is not serious."

Joey told her that I was very serious.

She looked at me and said, "I am sorry that I did not believe you. I thought you were fooling around. Can you please start over so I can really listen to you this time?"

I went through the talk again. At least I was getting good at it. For almost every person that I told subsequent to that day, I started out by saying, "I have something to tell you, no one is dying and I am not kidding around!"

The Neighbor Version and Their Reactions

I wrote a short version of the letter for the neighbors that we see fairly regularly:

November 2007

To: Our neighbors and friends,

We have been neighbors for a while and I want you to know something about me so you are not curious when you notice the changes that I have been experiencing. I am transgender so you will see me dressing as a female as I transition from male to female. Not much else is different – Jo and I continue to be married, we still take care of the yard and fight with blown fuses on Christmas lights!

We have not shared this with many people and do not plan to make any public announcements to the neighborhood. We just wanted you to know what was happening.

Have a very Merry Christmas and a happy holiday season,

The day after they received the letter, Wendy, the daughter of our next-door neighbor, was outside getting the mail. I had been out dressed (female) in the afternoon and was returning home. She saw me pull in and waved to get my attention. Previous to this moment, I had been successful (as far as I knew) in avoiding having the neighbors see me when I was dressed female. The day after I sent the letter to them, they saw me! She waved for me to come out (into the light of day and in the open!!) so she could say something to me.

"We got your letter yesterday," Wendy said. "Thanks so much for sharing the news with us. You are lovely neighbors and we love and support you however you are."

I thanked her for being a good friend and neighbor, and thanked God that now that they "knew," things would be about the same as they had been. We enjoyed being their neighbors. I would be able to be myself in my own yard. No more midnight mailbox runs or sitting in the yard in the dark!

We talked with the neighbors across the street. Finally, most of the people we talked to on a regular basis were up on the news. No one died from the shock and everything seemed fine.

We did not hear anything for several months from some other neighbors after we sent the letter. I was concerned, and I have a hard time reacting to no response, but I tried to not worry about it. I figured that we'd get a chance to talk when we saw each other when the weather warmed up a little. We didn't see them much in the winter months. Both families stayed inside more during the cold weather, and we rarely did much in the yard when it was below freezing.

We finally received a Happy Easter letter saying they'd been out of town a lot visiting family, so they completely missed sending their Christmas letter. They updated us with their late holiday letter and included photos of the grandkids.

She attached a note that said:

Dear Jo and Joe,

I'm looking forward to seeing all your new outfits Joe.... especially pool-wear!!

I've been gone most of the year, so I've been missing out on lots of things.

Be home on the 18th. We appreciate you as neighbors and friends.

Jo and I were delighted with the nice sentiment and note. Our neighbor has a good sense of humor.

An Outpouring of Support

A friend from church whom we had known for many years wrote,

I want you to know I have the deepest respect and admiration for the two of you and your family.

I love you all. Hang in there, buddy. You are fine Catholics, Christians and friends to me.

Here is a response from our cousin:

JJ,

I must say that I've received many holiday letters over the years outlining the activities of families but none as interesting as yours. As I told my wife, life for "normal" people (whatever that means) is hard enough without having to go through what you have. The decision to tell your family and friends must have been agonizing and I admire you for doing it. From what you wrote you seem to have come to terms with it and are moving forward. We will love and support you any way we can.

The hardest thing for me will probably be not calling you Joey. But perhaps an old dog can learn new tricks.

There are things that everyone thinks they should keep secret and keeping that secret usually works. Until it doesn't. It

sounds like you are lucky to have your wife. In that respect we are both lucky.

Speaking of the "Christmas" letter, one friend wrote:

JJ and Jo, OK—you win for having the most interesting Christmas letter!

I was thankful for such a good friend as Geoff, my high school friend:

Hey JJ...

Well I am so glad that I expressed to you about how I felt about you and our friendship before you sent your e-mail. Nothing has changed and I am beyond happy that you have found acceptance of yourself and peace within your heart and soul. You will always be my friend...a special designation in my life, a special designation that I both honor and value above all else.

Thank you for sharing this most personal of challenges and triumphs with me. We will be both stronger in our friendship and love of one another as you continue your journey...

I received many kind comments from relatives, ranging from unlimited support and a big effort to make me feel comfortable, to honest questioning since they did not know anything about being transgender. Most have at least offered their support and love, and some even told me that they'd like to help me but had no idea of how to do it. This was comforting and made it a special moment when we were finally able to get together in person.

I told my cousin Tony on the phone, and he told his wife Maureen along with my aunt and his sisters. They were so supportive and helped with talking to the other family members about me. By the time we were getting ready to go to Cleveland and see the family, Tony had already told his side of the family, so everyone knew what was happening. All I had to do was show up and answer any questions that they had. My aunt gave me some pretty handkerchiefs and jewelry from some of my aunts that had passed away.

One couple from church wrote me a long letter. They thanked me for sharing my story with them, told me how they had digested the letter, and then showed a lot of support for my struggles and me. They remembered some of the times we had been together and sent their kindness and best wishes.

For whatever problems I have had, and nothing is ever perfect on this earth, these responses shrank many of the problems and caused me to give thanks for the great people with which I have been blessed.

In addition to support and prayers a few funny moments were there too. One friend and I had been close in high school and college, but we rarely see each other since he lives in Michigan and we are in Indiana. His name is Johnny Burke, a well-known radio personality in eastern Michigan. He and his wife Genevieve were accepting—shocked, but understanding and loving, as I would have expected.

Jo and I planned to visit them when we were going to be in Michigan. He told me they were looking forward to seeing us, but how could he introduce me to someone as the best man from their wedding when I look like I do now?

I told him that he should say, "She was the best man at our wedding," and leave it at that.

We both had a good laugh.

I talked with our niece Angie, after her sister Jenny had already filled her in. She had a lot of questions and was thinking about all the upcoming issues for the family and me. She finally said, "It will be hard for everyone to adjust, but when you get to the new normal, things will settle down." I thought that indeed, it would be nice when we got to the new normal.

Another cousin and his wife wrote me a nice letter:

Thank you for your brave and wonderful letter. I cannot imagine how hard your struggle has been. I am so glad you are becoming yourself as God made you.

It is interesting how many people responded that they were happy that I finally figured it out and that I was as God made me. More than a few of my (now) ex-friends disagreed with that!

A couple that we knew from church had moved to another town and we did not see them as much as we used to. They wrote me a nice note that included:

We know that you've had major changes going on in your lives. Thank you for the letter. We also know that your life is based on faith—and that much prayer went into your decision. You will continue to be in our prayers. We look forward to seeing you.

Here is an excerpt from a letter from a friend from church. He was a leader and a Biblical scholar, and we had been in a renewal group together. He is retired and has several medical issues to deal with. I respect him a lot.

Wow, I couldn't begin to express all the emotions that affected me with reading your letter—which I read several times. My initial emotion was that of shock. I harbored an image of you as a virile, self-assured, and leadership {oriented} male so I was quite surprised. An enduring sensation is one of distress and anguish. I couldn't begin to imagine the anxiety and fear you have experienced. By comparison, my cross is merely a toothpick. Finally, I am humbled that you would share your adversity with me and entrust me with your confidence. I will certainly keep you in my prayers and I look forward to seeing you in the near future.

Poetic Positive Reinforcement

I'll end this chapter with a poem that Jenny wrote:

A real friend will love you always
Changes in our lives, should earn their support
Helping you understand and find your way

Change is difficult
No matter how you look at it
Overcoming fear of judgment
Finding the strength to carry you both through

Importance of staying together
Sharing a pace that two can handle
Never leave the other behind
That is the tie that will help you both endure
There will be harder times to come
So always respect your partner
Help each other move forward

That will keep the strength you need
in place, where it always has been
Your family is the most important
When it is strong, and you are standing together
Nothing can break you down...

Chapter 7

In or Out – The Creeping Darkness of Christian Moralism

My brethren have withdrawn from me,
  and my friends are wholly estranged.
My kinsfolk and companions neglect me,
  and my guests have forgotten me.
Even my handmaids treat me as a stranger,
  I am an alien in their sight.
I call my servant, but he gives no answer,
  though in my speech I plead with him.
The young children too, despise me,
  when I appear, they speak against me.
All my intimate friends hold me in horror,
  those whom I loved have turned against
  me.
Job 19:13-17, 19

But I am a worm, hardly human,
  scorned by everyone, despised by the
  people.
All who see me mock me;
  they curl their lips and jeer.
Psalm 22:7-8

As I started to share news about my changes with people close to me and started to transition, I was happy that my family and I had spent so much time and effort working on the decision rules—tell before seeing, spend as much time on the family as needed, show empathy for others' feelings and needs, etc.

I was thankful that it had gone so well with my family and the people most important to me. I was nervous about the possibility of losing important relationships, of hurting or shocking people I love, and for having to make them endure the pain and difficulty to make the journey with me. However, I felt like a better person so even if there were losses it might be a positive for everyone. I could help others who would journey with me if I did a good job in how I told them and how I treated them.

I was concerned that some people might not respond well. In my mind I pictured a cartoon where a character sees something shocking; the character's head explodes and smoke slowly rises out of the neck. Surely that would not happen to the people I told.

I was confident that it would all go well. I was surprised to find out that for some people, I was sorely wrong. Apparently their heads, and our relationships, were about to explode.

Before   After

I needed to tell people the best I could and enjoy the friends who would be my companions on the journey when everyone knew I was now female. If some people decided not to ride with me, then we'd move on and leave them behind. After all, as my friend Jim said, "We all have to transition with you."

Not All Positive Response – Some Negative and Sometimes None

In Chapter Six I shared some examples of how great some people were. My main surprise came from the lack of reaction from many of our friends. Some people who were good friends haven't responded to me; they shy away or look the other way when they see me. Since my transition I haven't seen the children of friends whom I was close to before. These were painful experiences. When it did not go well, it was strikingly different from when it did.

I typically spend most of the time with my family. Jo and I had friends— mostly couples who we had met through the kids' activities, church, our neighborhood. Although I felt uncomfortable being "one of the guys," I did some fun things with male friends. Mostly, Jo, I and the kids did activities together or we socialized with other couples, which was fine with me.

When I told people I was transgender, the reactions basically fell into three categories:

A. Unconditional love and support,
B. Judgment and moral outrage, or
C. They ignored me, did not give me a response or didn't give me much of a response.

The unconditional love and support reaction was great, of course. I anticipated their support and needed friends to count on. I hoped that everyone who I considered a friend would treat me this way. They were my friends; why would I not expect it?

I was risking everything, had a long bumpy road in front of me and needed their friendship and encouragement.

Their kind and considerate remarks made me feel loved and gave me a lot of hope. After their reaction, I would give thanks for such people. My next thought was usually: "They were so nice, and I can't believe I was so nervous about telling them."

I was not totally surprised, but still disappointed by the reactions of judgment/moral outrage and ignoring. I was not naïve enough to think everyone would be accepting. But ending a multi-year relationship (in some cases 25 years or more) in a second when I trusted someone enough to share something this personal and important was hard to take. These were my friends, I thought. Not only were they reacting badly, but some of them were calling me out because they thought that I must be sinning.

Sinner? – The Morality of Being Myself

I am blessed with a good understanding of Catholic guilt. I have told some of my Protestant and Jewish friends that most Catholics are great at guilt. As I understand it, Catholics are second only to the Jews in the guilt department, but we are gaining on them! In a daily prayer book I have used several times, James Metcalf's quote one day said, "Conscience is the walkie-talkie set by which God speaks to us." That sounds about right to me.

If something I am doing is a sin, I just know it. Conscience is not a list of rules to break; it is a guide for being. I have an inherent sense of what is right or wrong for me. I can't speak for other people, but for me, it is almost always clear. I don't always do the right thing, but I usually know what it is.

I can describe it this way: I was discussing one of the many ethical crises in business with Tom King, a client and friend who taught a course in business ethics. I asked him to describe what they talked about in class and how he taught the subject. After he explained the details on the class, I shrugged and said that I had an easier and simpler way (for me) to figure it out. I shared the

JJ Gufreda's Two Rules For Ethical Behavior:

1. If you had a good mom when you were growing up—you knew she watched over you, kept you honest and would punish you if she caught you doing something wrong—then this rule will help you. If you have an ethical or moral decision or have to make a judgment call, use this rule: If you can tell your mom what you are doing, have done or are planning to do, and feel no guilt, no hesitation to tell her, and are sure she won't whack you upside the head or ground you (even though you might be 50 years old or more), then your decision is probably the right one.

    If you think you would be embarrassed to tell her, or if she would probably respond, "What are you thinking?" then you are probably in the wrong. If it is no problem to share, you are probably good! It's not that complicated.

2. If you are doing something you know is wrong, but "they" (someone else besides you) made you do it, refer to rule number 1. For example, if you told your mom, "The boss told me to set up a shell company so investors would think our numbers were still good, even though they are not," or if you say, "I falsified our shipping numbers because the executives force us to have rising sales figures month to month," you better think about what Mom would say. That will help you figure it out.

My mom would have said, "You did what? If they told you to jump off a cliff, would you do it?" Just thinking about this scenario, I would feel stupid to mention it. That would help me think more clearly about not making the wrong ethical choice.

I know that every ethical or moral decision is not that easy, and that is why Tom teaches a class full of exercises and role-playing. But for me, my natural sense of right and wrong is good. (Incidentally, I can be available for seminars to teach the *Two Rules*, but I haven't figured out how to make the class last more than 10 minutes!)

Some "friends" asked me about the morality of being transgender and making the "choice." Did I think that God had a problem with what I was doing?

They did not ask in a way that led me to believe that they were trying to understand; they did it in a way that sounded like "You are doing the wrong thing—just admit it!"

I thought: These are my friends, and they are trying to talk me into admitting that I sinned or am going to sin, even though I honestly did not think what I was doing was a sin. This was not what I expected to hear from my friends.

A few interactions like this led me to another of JJ's rules, and I think this one may be more critical than the *Two Rules*:

JJ Gufreda's Morality Rule:

If you have to look up in the Rule Book (Bible or some other religious book) the scripture or quote that proves that someone else is sinning, you might be doing the wrong thing. Instead, be nice to other people and worry about whether *you* are sinning or doing good.

I read the Bible every day, so I've been through it several times. I haven't found the place (yet) that says that transgender people are sinners! (I usually read it in the morning, and I am not a morning person, so maybe I missed it because I am sleepy and not totally awake!)

Leper or Invisible?

The Leper "shall dwell apart, making his abode outside the camp" – Leviticus 13:46

It was harder to figure out the people who ignored me, or the more than 50 who did not respond at all, than those that were overtly judgmental or hostile. How do you react to no response? What does it mean?

I found out how the lepers felt because when some of my former friends saw me, they ignored me completely. This may have been because I looked so different from when I was male, but I have a hard time believing that I was unrecognizable. This was especially difficult to believe since I had sent them the letter about my gender change. At least with my newly-found pleasant attitude and reduced temper, I usually got a laugh out of being ignored when it happened.

As I said earlier, my oldest son plays soccer. I try to go to the games and watch him when I can. Shortly after I started to transition and was dressing female on a full-time basis, I went into the soccer facility. I walked past a friend of mine. He knew about what I was doing and that I had started the transition to female.

I looked at him so I could say "hi," but he looked past me like he didn't see me. He was looking in my direction, but I could not establish eye contact with him. During the game, he moved around a lot, apparently so he would not sit near me, and every time I looked in his direction, he quickly turned the other way.

I grinned a few times to myself. Even though it was hurtful to be ignored, it was funny to watch his reaction. I started to worry that he might hurt himself because he was jerking his neck so much trying to look the other way! His reaction did not feel at all like he was, or had ever been, a friend. Through his reaction I certainly did not feel the love of Jesus that we Christians are supposed to have! It was weird; to him, I was leprous or invisible.

Amused or Angry? It's Better to Laugh!

The second example was similar, but even funnier. Jo worried that I might say something inappropriate to my former friends who ignored me when I saw them. We hadn't talked or seen each other for several months after I "told them." Jo knew that I felt bad, the situation of losing several friends was hurtful to me, and that I was deeply disappointed with these people. I was okay to move on, but I still felt like I had remained a human person who had feelings. Everyone might not agree that I was still a person with feelings, but I was sure I was right!

I told Jo that I did not know how I would react, and I could not guarantee anything, but I guessed that I would probably say hi, chit-chat if appropriate, and move along. I was not looking for a fight. I lost the desire to talk with the people who I had depended on for support that hadn't been there for me. Still, she was worried.

I finally saw a married couple that I knew was upset about me; we hadn't talked or seen each other for several months. They were about 50 yards away from me in the grocery store parking lot one Sunday. It was a hot day, and I had on a summer skirt and sleeveless top. I was walking to my car and noticed my (former) friends loading their trunk with groceries. I had previously told them about the changes I was going to be making, but they had not seen me dressed female.

I knew that they were not happy with me and that they probably would not ever talk to me again if they could avoid me. Even so, when I noticed them, my first instinct was to wave. When you see someone you know, waving is a natural reaction, right? I waved, and the funniest thing happened.

They both looked at me and immediately stared up in the sky as if a plane was flying too low or a UFO was passing overhead. After a few seconds, they looked the other way, but I could tell that they had their eyes on me; but they would not look directly at me.

I thought, "Don't jump to conclusions. Maybe they didn't see you or recognize you or your car." I knew that was wrong, but I waved again to be sure.

They whipped their heads in the other direction! Their moves were so exaggerated that I started to smile. I got into my car because I didn't want to laugh out loud, but by the time the car started moving, I was laughing so hard I could not stop. My eyes were watering and I laughed all the way home. It was hysterical.

I had thought that I'd feel bad if someone treated me like that, but I reconsidered. If this is the way "friends" act, I don't need friends like that. I chuckled all day and stopped worrying about what I would do if I interacted with the people who were my former friends.

The Head-Scratching Feeling From No Response

The people who didn't respond were difficult to understand. I had a hard time reconciling how a longtime friend would not respond to a personal letter like I had sent; would ignore me; and would stop inviting Jo and I to social activities. (It was okay with me, but it really hurt Jo.) Some argued with me, but many did not respond at all.

I kept thinking, "I just sent you a letter about something critically important to me, and you don't even respond? Even if you had a problem with it, and never wanted to see me again, I think it would be polite to at least send me an email or call and leave a message at my home when you know I am at work! Then you could end the friendship without having to talk with me!"

One friend came to see me at my office after he received the letter. We talked for a while, and he invited Jo and me to go to dinner with him and his wife. He said he'd talk to her and get back to us to set a time. I never heard from him again. I am guessing that his wife decided not to go, but inviting someone to dinner and never talking to them again seems rude to me.

In or Out

I spoke on the phone with Megan Wallent, a transgender woman that I had found when I was searching for professional people who had transitioned at work. I asked if she had lost friends when she told them about her gender change.

In an email she told me an important thing that helped me figure out how to handle any broken or lost relationships. She wrote that she had not lost many friends. When she told them, she did not give them a choice. They could either accept Megan and her spouse, or be out. They could not be in *and* not accepting. For her, it was either in or out; being on the fence was not an option. She was lucky in that most of her friends decided to be "in."

Her experience helped me, and I decided to follow the same path as Megan: When I told our friends, they could either be in or out. They could choose. If they needed time to make the decision, fine, but they had to decide if they were in or out.

If someone rejected me, there was no sense trying to change these people. You can do your best, but people make up their own minds. Those people are "out." You just aren't friends with them any more. The relationship is over. You move on. If someone wants to stay with you, they are "in." There is nothing in the middle. They are out or they are in.

The good news about leaving some of my old friends behind and moving on is that I developed a lot of initiative to meet new people. I like some of the new people I have met. You have to see the good and the bad, and making new friends gives a lot of good!

My Wife and Her Friends

Understandably, Jo struggled with me becoming a woman. It profoundly affected her and raised many questions, which are difficult to deal with. "How could she stay married to another woman?" She is not a lesbian. "How does she deal with her friends, and how do they deal with her?"

She didn't lose friends like I did. I was worried that she might be "guilty by association," but most of her friends either ignored what was happening with me or tried to be supportive of Jo.

By supportive, unfortunately, I mean that some of her friends "helped" by showing pity for Jo. They'd say things like, "I give you a lot of credit. This is a terrible thing that you have to deal with, and I could never be able to do what you did."

When they see our marriage situation as awful, difficult or impossible, I don't understand how that is helpful to her.

To use an example for illustration: Suppose someone's spouse had a severely broken leg and could only get around with difficulty. Their spouse would have to help the person with the broken leg in addition to the normal things he or she had to do.

A friend could say, "I hope your spouse is doing well in dealing with this problem and I feel for you since I know you have extra work to do. Be sure to let me know if there is anything I can do to help out."

They could also say, "Waiting on your spouse all day while he lies around must be terribly difficult and depressing for you. I don't know how you can do it. You are truly a holy person. I only wish that I had the fortitude to deal with such a terrible problem with my spouse."

The responses are similar, but the first one is supportive given a challenging situation. The other is negative toward the spouse and gives pity and not support.

Since my announcement that I am female, we rarely get invited to social events with our old friends. I have (mostly) moved on and I stopped expecting to be invited. They are still friends with Jo, though, and she knows that she is invited when spouses are not there, but not invited (or rarely invited) when it is a couple's event. I don't want to mislead you; we are not hermits and we do things with people, just more with new friends. Some of our friends didn't change the way they treated us at all. If we go out as couples, there are three girls and a guy, where before there were two of each. It changes somewhat when we do things with our gay friends.

The Creeping Darkness of Christian Moralism

I tried to understand how people could reject me after being "friends" for many years. I observed how some people view and try to understand other people. I think that you can look at other people in two ways.

You can say that God created each person as a beloved child and loves each of us unconditionally just the way we are. We can act better or worse, but God always loves us, even if we sin. Christians believe that Jesus came to save us from our sins, so I think we are covered. God loves us.

If you see things this way, you can try to look at other people the same way God does. I try to think that each person has value, each person has good qualities, and I should enjoy each person individually as they are, as much as possible. It is not always easy to do this, but it can be an interesting, satisfying journey if you can see other people as God does.

If you view the world this way, you probably find value and good qualities in people who are different from you, people who disagree with you, and people you don't even know. You generally are tolerant or accepting of minorities and diversity. You may even enjoy meeting people who are different from you to see what you can learn from them.

Alternatively, you can observe, judge and interact with people in a way I call *Christian Moralism*. It is hard for me to define, but I see it as a predominant way for someone to look at the world. It seems to be more prevalent with people who consider themselves traditional or conservative Christians. Their logic goes something like this:

- I try to be a good Christian.
- I want to do God's will.
- I strive to know what God wants so I can do His will.
- When I have discerned what God wants, then I can do His will.
- I am uncomfortable with, or don't like, gays, Muslims, blacks, whites, transgender people, liberals, conservatives, whatever. (You can fill in any person or group with which you may not agree with or like.)
- Since I know and do God's will, these people (or the things they do or "choices" they make) must be bad and against God's will. I know this because I am uncomfortable with them and think they are doing the wrong thing. Or I just don't like them and I am close to God.
- I need to "save" that person (the Bible tells us to "correct," doesn't it?) or possibly, I need to do what I think God would want me to do. I should take some action against them. Perhaps God is too busy, has other worse people or bigger problems to look after and needs my help.
- It is okay and probably good for me if I gossip about, make fun of, reject, ignore, or hurt the people that are

obviously out of God's favor.

If you follow the progression, it makes a sort of sense, but the logic is flawed in several places. I try to act according to my sense of right and wrong and do what I think God wants me to do. But I don't claim to know what God wants, especially regarding other people. It is hard enough figuring out what *I* am supposed to do.

Good vs. Evil – I'm Evil?

I theorize that lots of people view the world in the Christian Moralistic way, and I think the number is growing. As they see it, life is basically a fight between good and evil.

When I came out as transgender and transitioned to female, I found out that some Christian Moralists had me on the side of evil! That was a surprise to me. I always thought I was trying to be on the good side! How would *you* like to wake up one day and learn that in the battle between good and evil, you were evil?

Thanks for Your Support – NOT!

Here are some excerpts from a letter I received from a devout Christian friend. I have not heard from him since he wrote me this letter. My inserted comments are in parentheses.

Joe (he did not call me by my female name. I found that people who don't like that I am transgender go out of their way to call me Joe, my old male name, as many times as possible!),

Glad to hear your family is doing well. Your letter has caught me off guard and has caused me to do some deep thinking. I have been praying a great deal over how I would respond to your letter/if I should respond to your letter.

Joe (see what I mean!), *as a brother in Christ, I feel I am*

obligated to tell you that you are living in sin. (I am not sure that this is the most loving way to start a letter. At least, I would be surprised and scared if Jesus sent me a letter with a first line like that!) *I am not basing this on my personal feeling alone. I am basing this on scripture.*

It says in Deuteronomy 22:5: "A woman must not wear men's clothing, nor a man wear women's clothing for the Lord your God detests anyone who does this." What is detestable to God can in no way be "...a part of God's plan..."

(I had hoped to be a part of God's plan, but now I find that I blew that. I still am going to keep saying my rosaries every day just in case I get in on a loophole! By the way, just to put things in perspective, here are a few other quotes from the same chapter in Deuteronomy: "You shall not sow your vineyard with two different kinds of seed; if you do, its produce shall become forfeit, both the crop you have sown and the yield of the vineyard. You shall not plow with an ox and an ass together. When you build a new house, put a parapet around the roof; otherwise, if someone falls off, you will bring blood-guilt upon your house. You shall not wear cloth of two different kinds of thread, wool and linen woven together."

A few other biblical abominations include "varying weights and measures" (Proverbs 20:10); "a harlot's fee or a dog's price for any kind of votive offering in the House of the Lord, your God" (Deuteronomy 23:19); and "every proud man" (Proverbs 16:5).

My point is that I am not sure we can take everything in the Bible literally. One of the verses in Deuteronomy states, "Of the various creatures that live in the water, whatever has both fins and scales, you may eat, but all those that lack both fins and scales you shall not eat; they are unclean for you." If you ever had a lobster or clam chowder, you might be in trouble!)

Back to my former friend's letter:

God also says in Galatians 6:1 (I thought St. Paul wrote the letter to the Galatians, but what do I know?) *"Brothers, if someone is caught in a sin, you who are spiritual should restore him gently. But watch yourself, or you also may be tempted."*

So, I pray that I am being gentle, and my goal is to restore you. Please don't see me as being a "holier than thou" type of person. I am very much aware that I too am a sinner. I write this letter because I am hopeful that you will be restored and build you up so that if/when I am sinning a brother may come along side me and stand beside me and keep me from falling deeper into whatever sin I am falling in to. (Well, it won't be me. I am not a brother any more!)

Why God allows people to be hermaphrodites, alcoholics, gluttons etc. we don't know. (Wow, I am not in good company. I am not sure hermaphrodites, now called intersexed, and gluttons are in the same category!)

You say that "the anxiety and tension were lessening" after you told your kids about this. But, alcoholics feel anxiety and tension lessening when they have a drink, and one drink is not sin. (Ask a mental health professional if being an alcoholic and transgender are the same!)

God speaks frequently on marriage and the position of the man over the woman. Scholars believe that the verse in Deuteronomy was written to prohibit perversions as transvestitism or homosexuality, and that the God-created differences between

114

man and woman are not to be disregarded. Cross reference verses are Leviticus 18:22: "Do not lie with a man as one lies with a woman; that is detestable." and 20:13: "If a man lies with a man as one lies with a woman, both of them must be put to death."

(First, I was not aware that God actually wrote the book. I thought inspired writers wrote it. If this is God's will, as far as I know, we have gone against the Bible and selectively decided that we won't kill these people, at least in the United States. I wonder why that is! If we are following the Bible, shouldn't we stone the evil-doers and throw the other sinners outside the camp? What they have done is a perversion; "their blood will be on their own heads.")

So even though you say that "gender is between your ears and sex is between your legs" this transgendered desire you have is a very dangerous thing to be trifling with.

God has given sex as a great gift and even though I don't know what you are meaning by "hormones, laser and electrolysis, surgeries and other changes are in progress or may await me," thinking that your transgendered life style is "ok" is not, based on what He says in Deuteronomy.

Also, in I Corinthians 7:3-5, it says "The husband should fulfill his marital duty to his wife, and likewise the wife to her husband. The wife's body does not belong to her alone but also to her husband. In the same way, the husband's body does not belong to him alone but to his wife. Do not deprive each other except by mutual consent and for a time, so that you may devote yourselves to prayer. Then come together again so that Satan will not tempt you because of your lack of self-control."

Like I said, I don't know what you mean by the surgeries comment, but will you be able to do what God says if you continue down this road?

Joe, (again) *also remember that every day is closer to when God is coming back, no one knows when this will happen, which is why we need to live as though He is coming back today.*

Joe, (all right, I won't point them out any more!) *as a brother in Christ I emplor [sic] you to realize that this is most definitely a sin and that you need to repent and ask forgiveness and seek counseling to help you deal with this.*

(The funny thing is that I did seek counseling from five therapists, including two Catholic therapists, and none of them thought I was sinning. I also do not think what I am doing is a sin. If I have a good conscience and do not think I am sinning, does another person have the right to decide for me? God knows what has been happening with me, and I have spoken with Him/Her at length about it.)

A good verse to hold on to is I John 1:9 "If we confess our sins, he is faithful and just and will forgive us our sins and purify us from all unrighteousness." This verse is so comforting.

Joe I have been praying for you frequently since receiving your email, and I continue to pray that you will seek Gods grace and turn from this sin.
If there is anything I can do to help you or your family, please don't hesitate to ask.

Your brother in Christ

To tell you the truth, instead of praying for me, I prefer that other people accept me just as I am. They don't need to look up readings in the Bible (with cross-references) for proof that I am sinning. It would also be nice if they did not stop talking to me after they decide that I am a sinner. I don't need the prayers if that's the way to get them.

More "Support"

Here are excerpts from another letter from some former friends. They attached a document supposedly published by the American Catholic bishops. The document was mostly about homosexuals and how they are "disordered." I did not see how anything in the document related to me, but obviously they had looked it up to help straighten me out. Keep in mind *JJ's Morality Rule!*

Dear Joe (again, they won't call me by my legal and preferred name)*:*

Relying on the grace of Christ, and having had time for prayer and reflection, we must tell you that we are gravely concerned about the course of action you are proposing, and the life which you are more and more living even now.

It is well beyond our competence to address these issues from a therapeutic standpoint, but as friends who share your faith, and understand that love and support for a person can involve challenging them, we felt that we could not remain silent, less [sic] you take that as a sign of our approval. We are not, in your terminology, "okay" with this.

Joe, you are a man of faith, and you should believe and acknowledge that you are made in the image and likeness of God. He willed you to be a man; it was not an accident of chromosomes.

Further, you are an image of Christ through the sacrament of marriage. God has given you the gift of manhood and the gift of sacramental marriage. This is what you should be committing yourself to, not to a disordered inclination to "become a woman."

*That you have these feelings, Joe, is not in dispute. But they are disordered. God did not make you this way, but you have become so through the course of your life due to causes that you yourself do not understand in all likelihood. But even if, for the sake of the argument, one accepts the premise that God made you this way, it does not follow that you should act on these inclinations. God could also, arguably, be said to have made people alcoholics. (*I don't know if all Christian Moralists compare notes on the link of being transgender to being an alcoholic, but they both used that example.) *That doesn't mean He is willing them to be drunks. He has made people with bad eyes; should they not seek help from doctors who can correct their vision problems?*

We pray, Joe, that you and Jo seek help from a good Catholic psychologist. You should avoid therapists and groups that only serve to affirm you in this disorder.

(I shared this comment with two of the therapists that we had been seeing. They were both insulted. Just for the record, we looked for therapists who understood what we were going through and could help us sort it out. I don't know any transgender person who tried to find therapists who agree with them! I think what my former friends were saying is that I should find a therapist who agrees with <u>them</u>.)

You should not suppress these feelings, but deal with them through the light of the Gospel. God will give you the grace to carry this cross.

Our concern extends to Jo, who has suffered greatly through the years, and to your children, who need a father. Your decisions have far-reaching and potentially devastating consequences for all of them. Your business, your friends, every relationship you have will be effected [sic] in untold ways by this, if not destroyed.

You are not alone in this struggle. We are your friends, Joe, and we want what is best for you. (They didn't even talk with me for a few years after the letter!) *Please reconsider your plans, seek help, find good spiritual direction.*

The attached document is from the USCCB [United States Conference of Catholic Bishops]. It was issued in November 2006, and while it primarily deals with homosexuality, it contains much wisdom regarding your situation. Please read it prayerfully. We will help in any way we can, Joe. Our prayers are with you and your family always.

I wrote them a letter telling them that I was disappointed to receive their letter, but was much more disappointed that I did not feel that they showed me any empathy or concern. Instead they pitied my wife and judged me.

When I talked about this situation with my friend, Rich Hammond, Rich gave me this comment:

"Love thy neighbor as thyself. I think the Bible says that. God does not need any help. Rich says that."

I read the Bible every day and I found several passages

regarding judging. Much of the book of Job relays how Job's friends "comfort" him by telling him that all of his problems were caused by him being a sinner. He continually said that he thought this was not the reason, but they kept at it. God was not happy with them, and at the end of the book, would not even accept their prayers unless Job interceded for them.

I don't want to get into dueling bible quotes, but it seems like Jesus, many of the Old Testament writers, and the apostles were against judging, so I thought I'd share a few of the passages.

Who are you to pass judgment on someone else's servant?
Romans 14:4

Then let us no longer judge one another, but rather resolve to never put a stumbling block or hindrance in the way of a brother.
Romans 14:13 (I hope he means sister too!)

Stop judging, that you may not be judged. For as you judge, so will you be judged...
Matthew 7:1, 2

Therefore, you are without excuse, every one of you who passes judgment. For by the standard by which you judge another you condemn yourself, since you, the judge do the very same things.
Romans 2:1

Hear now the rebuke I shall utter and listen to the reproof from my lips. Is it for God that you speak falsehood? Is it for him that you utter deceit? Is it for him that you show partiality? Do you play advocate on behalf of God? Will it be well when he shall search you out? Would you impose on him as one does on men? He will openly rebuke you if even in secret you show partiality.
Job 13:6-9

{Jesus said,} First take the log out of your own eye, and then you will be able to see clearly to take the speck out of your brother's eye."
Luke 6:42

Do not speak evil of one another, brothers. Whoever speaks evil of a brother or judges his brother speaks evil of the law and judges the law. If you judge the law, you are not a doer of the law but a judge. There is one lawgiver and judge who is able to save or to destroy. Who then are you to judge your neighbor?
James 4:11,12

"Judge not…"

Is all this judging Christian behavior? Is that the way people would like to be treated? I scanned a bumper sticker I purchased at a bookstore in Indianapolis:

GOD save us from Your Followers

There is a story in the Old Testament where David was traveling with his officers and a man started cursing him. When an officer tried to silence the man, David stopped him, saying, "Perhaps the Lord will take notice… and give me some blessings to take the place of the curses." I think, in my case, the Lord has favored me because he has given me some nice blessings.

Because of such reactions, I coined the term "The Creeping Darkness of Christian Moralism." In my observation, this kind of thinking and behavior does not lead to good, but tears people down, bruises them and creates division. It grows because people think they are acting for God. I am trying not to judge the people I am calling Christian Moralists, but all of this scares me. I just want the hurting of others to stop.

I realized why these two letters bothered me so much. It wasn't that they disagreed with me or did not accept me. Each person is entitled to his or her own beliefs and opinions. As I mentioned earlier, I noticed there were two parts when a friend responded positively to me:

The first part was care and concern for Jo, my family and me. People would say things like, "I feel bad for you that you had this bottled up for so long." "Is the family okay?" "I couldn't sleep because I was worried about you."

The second part of the reaction was whatever they thought about me being transgender—confusion, understanding, excitement for me, questions, concern, etc.

The support in the first part of the reaction was warm and helped me feel the love and friendship we had.

By contrast, when I got a response from someone that I am calling a Christian Moralist, it was very clear that the friendship, love and empathy were not there. I did not feel that they cared about me at all. They just judged me and wanted to save my soul by telling me I was wrong. If I am right or wrong, ultimately God is the judge, but I expected my friends to care about me. I surely did not feel that love and concern from my Christian Moralist ex-friends.

They cared about me enough to do research to prove that I am sinning, but not enough to show me any love or friendship. They were not there when I needed them. Many did not respond at all. I thought about the bracelets printed with WWJD (What Would Jesus Do?). I have a hard time seeing that He would want us to condemn instead of love. That's just me! I think He actually touched and healed the lepers. I don't think Christ was a Christian Moralist!

Jesus' style of evangelization was just the opposite of what we often do. The earthly way is usually coercion, arguments, threats of eternal damnation, or pounding on the other person until they conform. Jesus invites us to follow Him; He attracts us to Him. He loves and respects each person as one of God's creation, and we have the freedom to choose Him or not, to choose God or not. I think He'd rather we were more His way than our way.

If you are going to judge another person, you better be sure you are right. How should I react to a person if they are judging me? What if they are "helping me" by changing me to the way they think I should be? The judging person obviously believes what he or she is saying and also believes that not only is he or she on God's side (good), but they have an obligation to attempt to change me. There is no way for me to respond. I won't change him or her; he or she won't change me. They are out. I moved on. I hope the Christian Moralists are wrong about God's plan. I was hoping to get to heaven!

Remember that in the 18th and 19th centuries, people who were left-handed had it "beaten out of them."

Discrimination Follows Judgment

It was not a long time ago that overt discrimination against blacks was common in our society. I watched the movie *The Express*, about the football player Ernie Davis. He played at Syracuse University in the late 1950s. It is bizarre to watch because of the way people reacted to him because he was black. It looks unreal now, since many of the current sports heroes are black, but people in the movie discriminated against Davis and treated him badly because of their "religious" beliefs.

At one point in the movie, the football teams were jawing back and forth across the line of scrimmage. The other team's players were saying things like, "I am going to send you back to Africa."

The Syracuse center said, "Let's just play football."

The opposing lineman asked, "You call yourself a white Christian?"

The center laughed and responded, "I'm Jewish!"

Religion can contribute to a lot of hate and lack of love. Racism still happens of course, but with a black president in the White House, it is a little harder for people to practice openly in the current situation! I hope we never get back to those days.

I just think that you should be careful when deciding that other people are sinning. You might be wrong. I have two problems in trying to judge other people (really three, if you include the fact that I am often the one that is being judged):

1. In Christian theology, many people believe that God is the judge and Jesus is the Savior. You go to hell if God judges that you rejected Him or have too many sins, but Jesus died for our sins, so hopefully, that will help save us since everyone is a sinner. The judging part is scary, because if He gives you a thumbs-down (does God have thumbs?), you have to spend eternity in hell. All of it is pretty hard to understand, and we really can't fathom God's disappointment with the things we do or understand God's mercy, love and forgiveness. Jesus saves, so I hope I am included in his saved group!

   If I make myself the judge, that could make me somehow responsible for determining if someone else is a sinner and thus has rejected God, is living in sin and will (may?) go to hell when they die.

   I don't know about you, but I am hoping that I get in (to heaven), and that everyone else gets in too. Even if other people are "bad to the core," I don't want to see them spend eternity in hell. Maybe they have a last minute turn-around, or maybe God was in a merciful mood that day and gave them a pardon, or maybe Jesus does save us from our sins.

Whatever the case, I don't want to be the one to judge— to suggest to God that another person is a sinner. If I am judging, God knows, right? If He is listening to you, will He agree with you and decide to judge that person as a sinner? That is too big of a job for me, and I don't want anyone to go to hell. I hope we all get mercy. Judging other people is too risky for me. Maybe not for Christian Moralists, but it is for me.

2. The second problem with judging is that you may not understand the other person's situation; you might not understand God's will or might get either one wrong. Didn't the Bible say that God's ways are not our ways? His thoughts are not our thoughts? His thoughts are so much above our thoughts that they are as high as the heavens (that's from Isaiah). Isn't a thousand years like a day for God?

    I can try to understand and do what God wants, but I am too small to know God and to understand Him enough to judge someone else. Didn't Jesus constantly surprise the disciples? After three years of being together, Peter messed up so much that Jesus *"turned around and, looking at his disciples, rebuked Peter and said, 'Get behind me, Satan. You are thinking not as God does, but as human beings do.'"—Mark, 8:33.*

If Saint Peter could not get it right after years of living with Jesus, being taught by Jesus, and being selected as the one to lead the Church, I certainly can't claim to know what God wants or how God thinks!

Look at it this way: God created everything and everyone. We are all made out of the same stuff. He made some black, some white, some Asian, some straight, some gay, some transgender, some asexual. Some are Muslims, some are Jews, some are Buddhists, some are Hindus, some don't have an organized religion, some are Christians, etc.

Rather than picking out the people or groups that I think God has judged or will judge negatively, I prefer to accept people as they are and love unconditionally. I am not saying I am good at it, but I am trying.

Diversity: Part of God's Plan?

Maybe God likes the diversity. I read somewhere that 45% of the population in Africa is Muslim. If you believe that being Christian is the best way to go (on the freeway I saw a billboard that said "Jesus is the only way to heaven"), what if it is God's plan to have all these different religions?

I heard the Dali Lama speak at Indiana University, and while I am not Buddhist, he sure sounded like he was connected to God. I have a hard time seeing how God would not want a person like that in heaven just because he is not a Christian.

Regarding being transgender, God knows what I have been doing and the pain I had when I hid and suppressed it. He or She never gave me any guilt about it. He or She knows that I did not feel that I could go on any more if I stayed the way I was.

Many transgender people ponder suicide. I can't believe that God wants us to be that unhappy. I am just not smart or clever enough to think this up myself. If I get to heaven, I may ask God what He/She had in mind in making me this way, but I surely am not complaining about it. I am happy to be me.

Christian Moralists Have Many Concerns – How To

Discuss Differences of Opinion

Transgenders being transgender and gays being gay are not the only issues important to Christian Moralists. Abortion is a favorite and for many, it is the most important issue in the world. I want to share a story about how to disagree with someone on an issue such as abortion without turning it into a hate-fest.

Christian Moralists have some funny ways of looking at abortion. It is disturbingly easy to find news stories describing times when the zeal to stop abortion included bombing the abortion clinic and killing the doctors who perform abortions.

I am against abortion. Abortion is an end to a life, and usually bad for the mother and everyone involved in the decision; it is common for guilt and remorse to show up years after the baby was aborted. However, fighting people that are "pro choice," especially in a hateful way, will not solve the problem. Abortion is a difficult, complicated issue.

In the fall of 2008 I wrote a letter to the Obama campaign telling them I was voting for Senator Obama, but disagreed with him on abortion. Here was their response:

Thank you for contacting Senator Obama to advise him of your opposition to abortion. We appreciate your strong feelings on this difficult matter.

Senator Obama believes that every abortion is a personal tragedy, and he has struggled deeply with this issue. He believes that government must do better at encouraging alternatives to abortion. And he supports proposals to decrease the costs of adoption and make the process easier. He cosponsored the Prevention First Act with pro-life Senator Harry Reid, a bill which seeks to expand access to preventive health care services that help reduce unintended pregnancies, reduce the number of abortions, and improve access to women's health care ...

In the final analysis, however, Senator Obama believes that only a woman, her family, her doctor and her conscience should make the deeply personal decision of whether or not to end a pregnancy. For women who choose it, he will work hard to keep abortion safe, legal and rare—in line with the Supreme Court decision in Roe v. Wade.

This is a controversial issue, and we appreciate your deeply held beliefs ...

Obama for America

I have a hard time arguing with Obama's logic. I don't totally agree with everything he said, but according to their response, he is not pro-abortion, but pro-choice. The woman, not the government, has the right to make the choice. Another way to look at it is that the choice is made by the woman—not the Christian Moralists or the Catholic Church hierarchy who, by the way, are men.

Just because you disagree with someone should not mean that you hate them or treat them with disrespect. I believe that a person is a person when he or she is conceived. Others think it takes a month, three months or whatever. I don't know for sure, and neither do they. I think dialogue and constructive discourse with love in our hearts would be a better way to find solutions to the problems associated with abortion than some of the hate spewed out by Christian Moralists (in my opinion).

Hearing another Viewpoint

I met a nice woman from Planned Parenthood at a conference. I emailed her afterwards and asked her if she would spend some time with me on the phone describing her job and Planned Parenthood. After years of not hearing anything positive about the organization, I asked questions and tried to listen with an open mind. We spent almost an hour and a half on the phone and I enjoyed hearing what she had to say. They do much more than abortions and she shared some perspectives that I had not considered. I appreciated learning more and I really tried not to jump to conclusions or judge. I appreciated her openness, sharing and the time she spent. It was a very good experience for me. I felt that I understood them a little better after our call.

Christian Moralism dominates our political landscape. In the name of religion, we have bitter good-versus-evil battles about gays versus straights, the environment, medical research, war, torture and health care. Problem solving, consensus building and mutual benefit have been replaced by the battle of me versus you.

It is a Creeping Darkness that divides and doesn't solve anything. If we had the opportunity to ask Him, I don't think Jesus would like it.

Incidentally, just because someone is a "Good Christian" or very religious does not necessarily mean they are what I call a Christian Moralist. I just have problems with people who immediately judge me and treat me in a less-than-nice way because they don't like what I am or what I am doing or because they think I am sinning. The biggest sign for me was the presence of or lack of empathy. Whether they understood or "agreed" with me is another issue.

Empathy Makes Good Christians

I received letters from two different friends. Both of them are very religious and both had concerns about my welfare, but both were supportive of me as a person, and I felt their love and genuine concern. Even if they did not understand, they still were with me.

One of the friends wrote that he was sorry to hear of my problem. He had been praying for me and likened my situation to a cross to bear. He recognized that everyone has his or her crosses.

I don't view being transgender as a cross to bear, but he did, especially after reading my letter. Yes, it has been difficult, but I am thankful for each day I have been female. He may not have understood me (I don't either!), but he is still my friend.

Would God Really Make Someone Transgender?

I commented earlier that I have no desire to play Dueling Bible Verses with people who disagree with me or with what they call my "lifestyle" or my "choices." For many transgender people I talk with, the "choice" is some form of transition—either hormone replacement, changing their wardrobe, surgeries/ other treatments or suicide.

They find a way to live as their true gender, or they commit suicide. Not everyone has surgery or lives full-time, but each transgender person has to decide how to deal with it. Suicide is far too common in transgender people. For many trans people, committing or not committing suicide is the "choice"—not being transgender. I am not sure how they define lifestyle, but for me, *being* is not a lifestyle!

For the people who argue that God would never do this—or, as one person kept saying, He would not make us disordered— here are some things to consider:

There has been research about the causes of people being transgender. Some scientists suspect that genetics play a role. Others believe that it is from a hormone rush during the mother's pregnancy, and others theorize that it is from something in our childhood. In most cases, people simply don't know for sure.

For me, I am what I am, and I am happy with the way God made me. I doubt that most left-handed people are clamoring for a scientific explanation for why they are not right-handed. They just are.

In some cases, there are clues as to why a person's gender may be out of sorts from the norm. I made a few transgender friends in Indianapolis when I first started going to gender-related meetings and met other transgender people. One of those friends, Erin, told me about several of the transgender people she had met over the years.

One of Erin's friends is Chloe Prince, who has a condition called Klinefelter's Syndrome. She describes herself as a very special person because she was born a 47 XXY intersexed person, and they are, indeed, rare and unique.

In addition to being a nice person to talk with, I had a lot in common with her. I was especially interested in talking with Chloe because she has similar gender issues to mine, but she also has some physical characteristics from both males and females because of her chromosomal variance. She is an intersexed person. She has chromosomal parts from both genders.

After Chloe told me a brief version of her gender story, I asked her how people reacted to her because of her gender change. I was interested to learn if people reacted differently to her than they did to me. In my case, as far as I know, there wasn't anything physically different with me as from any genetic male (before I started hormone treatments), while in her case she had both male and female chromosomes.

The way Chloe saw it; doctors know some of the reasons that she is the way she is. (In addition to the Klinefelter's syndrome, a bee sting was involved! It is quite a story.) In my case, they don't know the reason for my gender incongruence yet, but eventually someone will get a better understanding than we currently have.

After describing Christian Moralism, I asked if she had encountered people who argued that God would never do this to someone, and that being this way is some form of a sin.

Surprisingly (to me anyway!), she *had* encountered this. I asked if the people involved knew that she had both male and female chromosomes, and that God did in fact make her that way. She said yes, they knew it.

Now, I am not a scientist, and I don't know all the new technological advancements and treatments. But I know that she didn't choose her chromosomes. I think God gives those to you free of charge. There are not many people like Chloe, but there are some others with this condition. It seemed to me that it was part of the variation of God's creation and part of the natural state of being human. It is not good or bad, just unique and different from most people.

How a Christian Moralist can accuse her of making this some kind of choice and arguing that God would never do anything like this is beyond me. It is like saying that God would never make someone left-handed, or taller than 6' or have one eye blue and the other brown. Who is to question God's actions or motives? (I think He or She likes the variety. If you could create billions of people, wouldn't you want a little variety?)

In any case, Chloe is what she is. It was interesting that much of what she described in her story was similar to my gender experience. The only major difference was her physical chromosomal uniqueness and the way that manifested itself for her.

It's probably evident that I have problems dealing with the people I call Christian Moralists. My description of "Creeping Darkness" probably gave it away! As I tried to understand it, I thought that maybe they seem to be so judgmental because they don't feel comfortable with diversity that is outside some range in their perception. If you don't think it is real, it probably isn't real for you.

My feeling is that God made transgender and other LGB people that way. Who knows what His or Her reasons are or how God decided these things? Instead of questioning God's motives or deciding what He or She will or won't do, maybe it's better to appreciate the differences in people. There can't be too many kinds of flowers to enjoy. Maybe we should look at people the same way!

Whatever the reasons that someone is transgender, it appears to me that they really *are* trans. No one would go through breast reduction and genital surgery for the F to M's nor hundreds of hours of laser and electrology and genital surgery for the M to F's if they didn't really feel that they are the other gender. It's expensive to throw out almost all of your clothes and buy an entirely new wardrobe and risk your business and career. I'm just not smart enough to figure that out if I really wasn't transgender.

"You Have to Understand…"

Let me finish by sharing a story about a gender meeting I attended. There were male-to-females, female-to-males and people in the middle, as well as some of their family and friends. Each person introduced him- or herself (and this included the people who didn't identify as a him or a her!).

One formerly female person said that he had told his family about his gender journey and upcoming chest reduction surgery and they reacted badly. He painfully described in detail how they rejected him. After a few minutes, he realized that he was criticizing his family in front of all these people, so he stopped and said, "Well, you have to understand: My family is very religious." Everyone in the room groaned and offered their condolences!

Shouldn't the response have been the exact opposite? If someone's family were very religious, I would hope they would love and support their children, especially when they have been struggling with their gender throughout their lives.

A mother of one of the transgender people was sitting next

to me and she was incredulous that someone had rejected their own flesh and blood.

Hopefully, as people understand gender and sexuality issues better and love each other more, in the future, perhaps the reactions will be better.

Every friend declares his friendship,
but there are friends who are friends in
name only.
Is it now a sorrow unto death
when your bosom companion becomes
your enemy?
"Alas, my companion! Why were you
created
to blanket the earth with deceit?"
A false friend will share your joys,
but in time of trouble he stands far off.
A true friend will fight with you against
the foe,
against your enemies he will be your
shieldbearer.
Forget not your comrade during the battle,
and neglect him not when you distribute
your spoils
Sirach 37:1-6

Chapter 8

Bad News and Good News—The Church and Spirituality

Lord, avenging God, avenging God, shine forth!
Rise up, judge of the earth;
give the proud what they deserve.
How long, Lord, shall the wicked,
how long shall the wicked glory?
How long will they mouth haughty speeches.
go on boasting, all these evildoers?
They crush your people, Lord,
torment your very own.
They kill the widow and alien;
the fatherless they murder.
They say, "The Lord does not see;
the God of Jacob takes no notice,"
Understand, you stupid people!
You fools, when will you be wise?
Does the one who shaped the ear not hear?
The one who formed the eye not see?
Does the one who guides nations not rebuke?
The one who teaches humans not have knowledge?
The Lord does know human plans;
they are only puffs of air.
Happy those whom you guide, Lord,
whom you teach by your instruction.
You give them rest from evil days,
while a pit is being dug for the wicked.
You, Lord will not forsake your people,
nor abandon your very own.
Judgment shall again be just,

and all the upright of heart will follow it.
Who will rise up for me against the wicked?
Who will stand up for me against evildoers?
If the Lord were not my help,
I would long have been silent in the grave.
When I say, "My foot is slipping,"
your love, Lord, holds me up.
When cares increase within me,
your comfort gives me joy.
Can unjust judges be your allies,
those who create burdens in the name of the law,
Those who conspire against the just
and condemn the innocent to death?
No, the Lord is my secure height,
my God, the rock where I find refuge.
Who will turn back their evil upon them
and destroy them for their wickedness.
Surely the Lord our God will destroy them!
Psalm 94

I love the Psalms. I can always find something in them to help and comfort me. I read them every day. I read this one shortly after I had some issues, actually several issues with the Catholic Church, and it really hit home. I don't want the Lord to destroy the Church, or anyone else like it says at the end of the Psalm, but much of the rest of the Psalm rang true for me.

Sports

I would like to start this chapter with a story not about me, but about someone else. I have gradually been losing interest in pro sports. When I was a kid, I had been a dedicated baseball fan (I rooted for the Cleveland Indians, so you had to be dedicated). But when they had the big strike in the early '80s, I thought they were being greedy. I thought, "If they are willing to go on strike and ignore the fans, then I don't need to be a fan any more."

It was tough to ignore baseball during the first year, but after a few years I couldn't even name some of the teams, much less the players. I felt bad that I didn't watch the games when the Cleveland Indians (from my hometown) were in the playoffs. Most of my family members were big fans, and I hoped the Indians would win, but I just couldn't watch it.

A few years after the strike, the steroid issues became public, and the entire thing turned me off even more. A strike also killed my interest in hockey. I have had some interest in other sports, but much of American sports seems to be based on how to glorify yourself—egotistical basketball superstars, arrogant athletes dancing in the end zone. ESPN shows the dances and celebrations several times in slow motion after the game. After I started on female hormones, all that macho crap was lost on me.

At this point in my life, I watch the Indianapolis Colts and soccer and I watch boxing. We'll see if I keep interest in pro football after the lockout of 2011.

Interestingly enough, I love boxing. I know it is violent, and people get hurt, but it is a fascinating spectator sport. First, it is one versus the other. Coaches help, fans cheer, but at the end, the skill, smarts and will of one boxer wins out over the other one. Do you like the underdog to win? Boxing is great for that. There are fights where one boxer who was losing the entire match makes a late knockout, and wins in the last minute (or seconds—I have seen it).

One other reason to watch boxing is that the athletes have skills and talent to do things that you can't do. I don't think most people can hit the heavy bag for three minutes, much less get hit while you are punching. Most boxers are incredible athletes.

It may not make much sense, especially since my identity is feminine, but I like boxing anyway.

Parallels—Experiences with the Church

With that as a long introduction, I was watching the HBO series *24/7*, which chronicles boxers, their teams, families, training camp and preparation for the big fight. It is great advertisement for the fight, and it is interesting to see the inside story and get a sense of the boxers and trainers and how they do their jobs. Again, these are incredible athletes with unreal will and work ethic.

I watched the program about the Manny Pacquiao/Ricky Hatton fight preparations. Manny is a religious person, as noted on the program. They interviewed his trainer, Freddie Roach, about religion, and he said that while it was great for Manny, he was not a religious person. When asked why, this is what he said:

"I was born and brought up Catholic, but I'm not a religious person because the last time I went to church, I had a fight with the nun. She pulled me by my hair and threw me down and kicked me. I said: 'Wow. If you weren't a nun, I'd kick your (expletive deleted).' So I went home and told my mom, 'I'm not going back,' so that was my last day of church."

I use that story as an example of what happened to me and many others. I use a capital C when describing the Roman Catholic Church because it is a formal organization and I view it as having the most direct link to Jesus. Obviously, others may have different opinions, but that explains *my* logic!

Many Catholics start out religious or at least in the Church, and then something happens and they are rejected, treated badly, bruised or they get disgusted and leave. Roach sounded like he was telling the truth. Even if it is half true, it is not a good situation, especially his treatment from a "professional" in the church. I doubt that there is much chance that he will ever return to church.

I was what they call a "cradle Catholic." This means that I was a Catholic from birth. My parents were Catholic as were all my relatives. In our family, everyone was Catholic. Jo told me that one of the reasons she wanted to marry me many years ago was that I was a religious person and she thought that was important. She converted to Catholicism and we raised our children Catholic.

I was an altar boy (girls weren't allowed to serve back then, so good thing I got the opportunity while I was still a boy), and was president of the altar servers when I was in the eighth grade. I loved to serve at the Mass; it made me feel close to God. If I remember correctly from 40-something years ago, they had 6:30, 7:15 and 8:00 a.m. Masses *during the week.* They had four servers for each Mass.

I went to Catholic grade school, high school and graduate school. When we got married and started a family, I volunteered to play piano for a "folk" choir at the Catholic Church in Bridgeport, Ohio. I played several years after that when we moved to Indiana. I was on the first "Christ Renews His Parish" renewal group at our church in Greenwood, Indiana, and eventually did "outreaches." These were retreats to help other parishes get started in the process. I worked some high school retreats as well.

Personally, I started saying the rosary every day, hand-making rosaries to give away and reading the Bible and several readings that I picked out that meant a lot to me, every day. The day does not start out well for me if I don't start with the rosary and my readings.

After 15 or so years of making rosaries every day, I stopped making rosaries because almost everyone stopped asking me for them.

I am not touting myself as a good or righteous person, but my relationship with God and the Church was important to me.

Sharing, Seeking Support within the Church

One of the first people outside of the family that I told about my gender issues was the pastor of our neighborhood church. There are several Catholic churches in the area. When we moved 15 minutes across town 15 years or so ago, we did not change parishes. We were comfortable where we had been, and didn't see any reason to change.

I knew the pastor at the other church that is closest to our house, and I used to go to the sacrament of Reconciliation (some people call it Confession) with him and kept in touch. One day, during the sacrament, I told him that I had something important to tell him. I was going to tell him about being transgender during reconciliation since I knew he had taken a vow of silence and couldn't share this secret with anyone. I told him that I didn't think it was a sin, but wanted to be sure my secret stayed a secret until I was ready for people to find out.

He was a little nervous about what I was going to tell him, and was surprised when I told him I was transgender. He agreed that it probably was not a sin and seemed supportive.

When I started to dress female full-time, Jo was hesitant to go to Mass at our old church. We knew a lot of people there, and it was inevitable that many would not know what was happening when they saw me as a female. I was ready to go, but Jo wanted to go somewhere else, at least until we sorted out what and how to tell everyone. I told her that was fine and we went to several different parishes until we decided to go most of the time to the parish that was only five minutes away from our house.

We signed up to be members of the parish and started to go to Mass every weekend. I never got a second look (that I noticed) and since we didn't know many people there, it was not big deal. We were comfortable, the pastor knew what had happened with me, and everything seemed fine.

An announcement in the Sunday bulletin asked for Eucharistic Ministers—lay people who help the priest give out Communion.

I had been a Eucharistic Minister for several years when I was not playing piano, and Jo and I often brought Communion to the sick. It was a great pleasure, since we believe that the Host (the bread that is consecrated for Communion) is actually the body of Jesus Christ. I loved to give out Communion, had taken Communion to my parents when they were sick, and loved seeing the people's faces as they partook of the sacrament. I understood how God loves each person as I watched their faces as they received the Host.

I sent an email to the pastor volunteering to serve again as I had done for many years. I've copied the email chain for you, and you can read the emails that went back and forth between the pastor and me. I removed some names and personal information, because I am not attacking, calling out, or blaming anyone specific, but I want you to get a sense of what happened. It is important to me, because when I got the last email from him, I consider that as the last day I was a member of the Catholic Church.

My initial email to the pastor:

Dear Father,

I was a Eucharistic Minister for several years at {our old church}. When I came out as transgender, Monsignor suggested that I not do that any more since I might be distracting to people. I was thinking of volunteering at {your parish} and attending the training on December 7 since I am a practicing Catholic in communion with the church and received the sacrament of Confirmation (as noted in the bulletin).

Do you see any problem if I start to become active again? I have not done anything for the Church since I left the Archdiocesan Christ Renews group early this year. I feel like I am attending Church, but not in the Church.

His response:

Dear JJ,

I spoke with {the vicar judicial} about this request because I needed to discuss this further before making a decision. While I am sensitive to your situation I must agree with {your old pastor} that it would be too big of a distraction for you to be a minister of Communion at {my parish}.

I was shocked. I was trying to serve the Church in the exact way I had done before, and I was being rejected. I understood that I might be distracting at my old parish because I knew so many people, but at the new parish, I hardly knew anyone. I dress conservatively, just like most women my age, and while I am not a beauty queen, I rarely had anyone pay more attention to me than they would to anyone else.

I Googled the person at the Archdiocese that he referred to and found that he has been active in cases of alleged sexual abuse by members of the Church. He is the canon lawyer, somewhat like a corporate attorney for the Archdiocese of Indianapolis. I thought, "Why would he need to contact someone like that? Was this a legal issue for the Church? Were they considering me as a potential abuser?" I had a lot of questions and wanted answers.

Here is my email asking questions about his response:

Dear Father,

I have been active in the Church for 45 years. I was a server, musician, volunteer, Eucharistic Minister, retreat leader, etc. It now appears that those days are over.

The question for me is what do I do about my role in the Church? I go to Church, but I am not in the Church. My involvement is conditional—I can do this, but not that. At what point does it end for me?

Someone might be distracted, so I can't serve as a Eucharistic Minister. If someone is distracted or uncomfortable with me in their pew, should I be excluded from sitting in that pew? If someone is distracted or uncomfortable that I attend Mass at their Church, should I be excluded? Should I be excluded from teaching Sunday school? Should I be excluded from selling sandwiches at the {church} festival?

When I started my transition, I was determined not to follow the path of most of the transgender people I know, which was to eventually leave their church and attend someplace that is more "accepting." I have the "problem" that I do feel that it is a sin to not attend Mass and I believe in the sacraments. I believe in the real presence of Jesus in the Eucharist. The question for me is what I do with my spiritual life when my Church excludes me, or at least my involvement is conditional. I have to discern what to do.

The questions for the Church are: who do they exclude and from what do they exclude them? For a Eucharistic Minister consider these people:

A transgender person. That person is a distraction and should not be a Eucharistic Minister.

A large black man. Would he be a distraction (at a mostly white parish)?

A person with a facial deformity. Would they be a distraction?

A person that looks gay. Would they be a distraction?

A person that is grossly overweight. Would they be a distraction?

A Hispanic person with a heavy accent. Would they be a distraction?

Should a Catholic pray a rosary that I made? If a transgender person made it, would it be less of a religious object than if it was made in a factory?

My wife, someone that is married to a transgender person and thus could be considered to be in a same sex marriage. Would she be a distraction?

A person with a deformed arm (like the one that Jesus healed). Would they be a distraction?

The second part of the question is from what does the Church exclude people? Just a ministerial role? What about witnessing at a retreat? Working on fund raising? Teaching catechumens? Reading at Mass?

I find it interesting that during my transition, the only exclusions, rejections, or people ignoring me have come from the Church and the people that I refer to as "the Christians"— some of the people that are active in the Church. Everyone else that I deal with treats me with support, empathy and concern and acceptance.

Thanks for your help when I started my transition. I have some thinking and praying to do before I decide what I need to do. I recommend that the Church do the same.

JJ

His response:

Dear JJ,

I am sorry for the hurt you are experiencing.

Wow, that was less than satisfying and yes, that was his entire response! I did not get any answers and was getting the feeling that I was becoming a problem that should go away.

Here's my return email:

Dear Father,

I did some online research as I had never heard of {the Vicar Judicial}. I found that he is a canon lawyer and the Vicar Judicial of the Archdiocesan Metropolitan Tribunal. Much of the information about him that I could find is related to his work heading the task force of the Canon Law Society of America in their development of a paper on "Norms on clerical sexual abuse of minors."

Why did you have to consult a lawyer to see if I could be a Eucharistic Minister after I had previously been a Eucharistic Minister for several years? What is the basis of the Church's discrimination against me? Am I suspected of some kind of abuse or does the Church feel that I am a risk to be an abuser? Does the Church feel at risk because I have been attending Mass and been a member? Do I have a potential legal problem with the Catholic Church?

His response:

As I said before, I am sorry for the anger you are feeling.

It was clear that I was not going to get any answers to my questions. I was frustrated. One of the most important things in my life had been the Church, and I was being excluded, or at least conditionally excluded and I could not get an answer to my questions.

My next email:

I have never heard of someone being rejected by the Catholic Church. I thought that this was the universal Church instituted by Jesus Christ, the Son of God. I would appreciate the courtesy of your or the Church lawyer answering my questions.

Many priests begin Mass by welcoming everyone and thanking the visitors for attending Mass. All are welcome. I would suggest that you and the other priests choose your words more carefully. Everyone is not welcome in the Catholic Church.

JJ Gufreda

I thought that I would surely get some kind of response—guilt is usually a motivator for Catholics. I was wrong.

His response:

JJ,

If you have questions of a legal nature with the Archdiocese of Indianapolis they can be directed to {the Vicar General}. He is the Vicar General of the Archdiocese. His contact information is below: (He listed a P.O. Box address.)

Everyone is welcome in the Catholic Church. Welcoming someone is not the same as agreeing with the choices they are making. Assisting at Mass is a privilege and not a right. Those who assist are called to draw attention to God's word and His sacraments and not themselves. I am no longer going to have any further discussions with you due to your level of hostility. I believe that I have been kind and cordial with you during this time in your life. It is apparent that this has meant nothing to you. I regret that fact.

I had to respond again, but it was clear that I was out and that was the end of a 50-plus relationship between me and the Church—the Church that I thought would be the way to salvation.

My response:

Dear Father,

I apologize if I sounded hostile. I feel that I am being rejected by my Church and I have been an active and practicing Catholic for all my life. This is a very big shock to me. I also did not realize that you did not agree with my choices. They really were not choices. They are necessities.

You were the first person outside the family to share my news. I do appreciate your support and friendship over the past years, especially in the past two years when I really needed it. It has meant a lot to me. I am sorry if I hurt your feelings. I did not want to be nasty. I really don't know how to react as the most important thing in my life was being Catholic, and that basic reality has changed.

I would have appreciated it if you had been able to give me some answers to my questions as I am seriously considering leaving the Church, something that I never thought was in the realm of possibility. The response you and Monsignor gave me was inconsistent with my expectations of the Church. I have always served. I am not trying to draw attention to myself.

I will respect your decision to not have any further discussions with me.

I wish you the best and ask God to bless you.

What now? I was rejected by the Church and had nowhere to turn. I could not get answers from the pastor, and I could not understand what really happened. He had been nothing but supportive for a few years and never gave me any indication that he had any problem with my "choices." I thought it was clear to him, that what I did was not make choices; I was just dealing with the way God made me. I was angry, hurt and felt empty, since the Catholic Church was gone for me. I wrote the Vicar General as he suggested.

He never responded.

We immediately stopped going to that parish since it seemed stupid to go where the priest would never talk to me again. We went to a few different parishes, and I felt more and more distant from the Church.

I forwarded the email chain to a priest I knew who lives outside the U.S. I thought that maybe I was missing something or had misread the situation. I didn't see how this was possible, but I thought that it was worth an email to get another view on the situation.

My email to my priest friend (who I had previously told about my gender situation):

Dear Father,

Please read the emails below from the bottom up. (They had been in chronological order starting at the bottom.)

There is no room in the Church for me anymore. Where do I go when the Church rejects me? ...

Here is his response:

Dear JJ,

You e-mail moved me deeply. Also made me angry about the attitude of so many who are supposed to represent the Shepherd, whose job is to heal the sick, bind up the wounded, strengthen the weak, seek out the lost and bring back the strayed (Ez 34:4). Unhappily the good news is only to be found in pockets.

There is a great confusion with regard to human sexuality within religion in general and within our community in particular. Not that I have the ultimate words of wisdom and insight either. But confusion cannot mean hurting people of good faith.

Your rejecting comes from officials who should be doing better. You are in the difficult position of a prophet in many ways. That pain which the Church causes also invites you deeper and more directly into God. And that in turn is a ministry to the very Church which is hurting you so much at the moment.

What the Church has not yet learned on her journey is that teaching deepens, and that means stepping away from simplistic categories of the past into the complexity of people's experience in the present, to support their search for integrity in front of God, which is what the moral teaching is about, not a series of unalterable rules. They have to guide differently over different terrains of experience and the struggle for integrity.

Anyway please remain assured of my prayers and support.

Yes, particularly {your pastor's} need remains.

In Christ,

Wow, maybe there was some hope, even though I had no idea what I would do next. I appreciated his kindness.

Here is the final email on the subject to my foreign priest friend:

Dear Father,

Thanks for the very kind and Christian response. Misunderstanding or trying to not understand is difficult to take. It seems like they are trying to protect themselves from me. I have never heard of a transgender person being involved with any kind of abuse (I certainly have not). This is not really relevant for transsexuals compared to the rest of the population—male to female people in transition or post-surgery have no testosterone and have lots of estrogen. Hardly the formula for being a sexual predator.

It was interesting that after I sent you the email, I had another round or two of emails with the priest. I asked again for answers to my questions and he said that since I was so hostile, he would not discuss it with me any more. He suggested that I contact the Vicar General, which I did with a letter. I will see what his response is, but I don't expect much.

Also, one thing I recently realized is that the only people that have ignored or judged or treated me badly were Catholics (plus two Protestants). Not in every case, but in general, the most vigorous Catholics were the least helpful and supportive and definitely were not friends to me when I needed them. Everyone else has been great to me.

A disappointing (as if it were not disappointing enough) turn of events was when I called a lady from the snapnetwork.org (support for abuse victims). I wanted to talk to them because there is some similarity between my situation and theirs. As I have written you before, the sexual abuses are terrible and I still can't understand how this happens. I told her that my situation was similar since I knew that they could not get answers from the Church when they had questions and I wanted to know how they approached it.

She told me that the abuse still continues (and in her opinion is worse than ever) and that the cover-ups are more elaborate. People change (religious) orders, move from one diocese to another and change names to avoid exposure. She said that the victims that have tried to reconcile with the Church have been hurt more and worse and did not get any answers or satisfaction.

It was a very disturbing call. I checked out their site, and there are links to daily news reports in secular papers that corroborate her story. I do not have much confidence to talk with anyone or for anything to change.

This is my plan (which can change of course, but I think this works for me):
* I will talk with the Vicar General if he meets with me, but I expect he won't or that he will not be helpful if he takes the time. (As I stated, he did not respond at all.)

* I am now an "attending Catholic." Unfortunately, my wife Jo is having a hard time going, but I hope she comes back. I am still Catholic, but do not participate and I am not a member of the community. I am just there. I can't give up the sacraments and I still love the Mass and believe in the real presence of Jesus, despite the qualities or lack thereof of the priest that did the consecration. I have not decided on what to do about Reconciliation. I never had a problem with it and think it is a blessed sacrament, but I have real reservations now.

* I am done with ministry and any involvement. We'll see what happens. If the Lord calls, I'll try to react.

* I am not complaining or trying to change the Church. From what I have seen, that is impossible.

* I am not giving money to the Church except for special cases and of course to you and your Church if you need it (and I have money). I can't justify funding it while the abuses and cover-ups continue and when they can't even give me the courtesy of an explanation for effectively rejecting me from the Church.

I don't mean to sound hostile or overly dramatic, but the Church was the number one priority in my life and it is hard to re-calibrate my life.

I do appreciate your perspectives and support.

On a positive note—have a blessed Immaculate Conception feast day and a great Advent and Christmas season.

JJ Gufreda

What I've Lost

In a Lenten prayer book the writer reflected on being a Eucharistic Minister. He or she said that "it should be required" because of your intimate interaction with each recipient; you can observe them as they receive the Host or Wine—the body and blood of Jesus, the Savior. I always felt that giving Communion was a way to understand how God could love everyone individually.

Each person comes to the front of the church for Communion, and you can look at each person's face as they receive. Some are reverent, some in a hurry, some in awe. Some are quiet or reflective, some are struggling to get communion when they are trying to keep multiple kids under control. I often used to get tears in my eyes thinking of the awesome love that God has for each of his created people.

Those days appear to be over for me. As my former pastor said, serving is a privilege not granted to me.

I was numb, hurt, angry and deeply disappointed. I cannot speculate on the reasons they decided to exclude me or why they would not answer my questions. I was not ready to give up on the Church, but did not feel like I was a part of it any more, or if I was still a part of the Church, I was definitely a second class member or worse.

Other Sources for Solace

I joined a Dignity group in Indianapolis. DignityUSA (http://www.dignityusa.org/) is an organization with this vision statement:

DignityUSA envisions and works for a time when Gay, Lesbian, Bisexual and Transgender Catholics are affirmed and experience dignity through the integration of their spirituality with their sexuality, and as beloved persons of God participate fully in all aspects of life within the Church and Society.

I met with the group and became friends with some members. There were gays, lesbians and family members. As far as I knew, I was the only transgender person in our local group. There is a national group as well. Two things struck me about the group: everyone seemed to be spiritual, friendly and accepting of everyone, and most of them had been wounded because of their gender or sexual orientation.

I was getting depressed about the Church. I was becoming a magnet for the rejected, disaffected, the bruised and the outcasts. I felt bad that so many people had been excluded. The Church has hurt so many people! To me, it was stupid that we even need a group like Dignity. Everyone should be welcome.

I think that is the way Jesus did it. None of the disciples set up side groups to try to get close to God because Jesus rejected them, right?

I went to one of the Masses of the Dignity group. I was in tears during the entire Mass because I thought this would be the last time I would ever go to a Catholic Church. I was personally hurt, and it didn't matter because I didn't feel they wanted me in the Church anyway. I did not identify with what the Church was doing and how they acted. The Dignity people welcomed me, but the Church as a whole had rejected me.

I was disgusted about the abuse and the lack of concern and love for the victims, and now I was finding all these people (including others, like divorced people, who were not gay) who had also been hurt in some way by the Church.

I thought that before I gave up, I should at least talk to the priest that said Mass. I had never met him before, and I grabbed him after Mass because I needed a few minutes of his time. I quickly explained how I felt and told him that unless he had some other suggestion, that was my last day as a Catholic.

He tried to get me to stay in the Church. His name is Father Justin Belitz and he is a Franciscan Friar. He said that it looked to him like I was a devout Catholic and I shouldn't change that because of something the Church did. He had Mass every Sunday at the Hermitage Retreat and Life Center that he runs. He suggested that the Hermitage was an option, or I should just go wherever I like—don't fight the organization.

He pulled me back in when I had both feet out, a big wind pushing me from behind—and I was standing in slippery oil!

Everyone has been nice in the small group that meets at the retreat house for Mass on Sunday. They asked if anyone could play an instrument, and I volunteered to play piano when they need me. I was a music minister again but I hope that news does not get turned in to the "authorities!" Shhh—don't tell.

Some Good News

Fortunately, I found out about a few people inside the Catholic Church who actively minister to all LGBT people.

One person who especially focuses on transgender people is a Catholic nun, who I cannot acknowledge by name in order for her to be able to continue her ministry. She began her ministry to trans people in 1999. She also ministers to local people where she has lived and trans people like me that are spread across the country. She has a serious medical condition that now limits her active ministry. She won't be able to be as physically present to transgender people but will still work with us via email.

Sister offered counseling and retreats for LGBT people and tries to educate Church leaders and others about transgender people. She has tried to dispel misconceptions and help the priests and religious people understand us better. Because she has had to fly under the radar to a great extent, she hasn't reached nearly as many people as she would have liked, but has managed to open lots of people's hearts and minds.

From her experience, she says few Catholic transsexuals are able to stay in the Church because they clearly feel rejected. She has tried in many ways to raise awareness for us to the hierarchy of the Church. In my opinion, nothing will change at that level anytime soon.

I give her and the others who minister to LGBT people a lot of credit. It's a monumental uphill battle. I think that the Church hierarchy is actually happy with this situation because it is easier if the transgender people just go away. After being rocked by (and losing money from) so many internally generated scandals, why would they risk anyone complaining because they don't want to sit next to a transgender or gay person at Mass? Plus the Pope apparently thinks that the very survival of mankind is at stake because of us!

Sister is unique, however, in that she has helped so many transgender people in various ways on their spiritual journeys. Many of the trans people that I know are spiritual. From my experience, they are introspective and searching for meaning in their lives. They are trying to figure out their true gender and reconciling why they aren't like everyone else. A connection with the Infinite and Almighty is critical to sorting things out.

More Problems

The problems with the Church that I shared earlier in this chapter are not the only problems I have had with the Church. I am concerned about some of the things the Church says about gays and transgender people.

For example, the Pope gave a talk attacking the "Blurring of Gender." According to the BBC, "Pope Benedict XVI has said that saving humanity from homosexual or transsexual behaviour (sic) is just as important as saving the rainforest from destruction."

As I understood the on-line article, and it was hard for me to follow the Pope's logic, he was saying that if we embrace "gender theory" and blur the distinction between male and female, it could lead to the "self destruction" of the human race.

Let me try to understand this. If everyone is gay or transsexual, then there would be no more reproduction and thus the human race would disappear. I guess that is true.

The problem with the argument, from my perspective, is that there have always been gender-variant people. What God had in mind is beyond my understanding, but the creator made them. Other people, such as the intersexed, literally have—were born with— a blurred gender in their body and in fact have parts of both genders at once. As far as I know, God created them too.

I am not too worried about the lack of reproduction because of the existence of the gender-variant people because most of the population is not that way. Also, many gay, lesbian, bisexual and transgender people have children! I don't think the gays, lesbians or transsexuals have been successful at converting anyone—or have been trying.

The Pope's statement seemed stupid, greatly misled and hateful to me, the other gender-variant people and the gays and lesbians. Are those people supposed to feel welcome in the Church? I hope Jesus did not have that in mind.

Just for the record, I personally fathered three wonderful children before I started to transition. The destruction of the human race has been averted for at least another generation even though I am transgender.

Also, the Church keeps reiterating that homosexuality is not sinful, but homosexual acts are. On behalf of all the homosexuals I know, thanks a lot. How does that make sense? God made them with an attraction to the same sex, but they can't act on it. Irrational? Probably. Excluding and rejecting? Definitely.

A few other examples: The Vatican opposed the decriminalization of homosexuality by the United Nations. In some countries, it is legal to jail or in some cases execute people for being homosexual. The Church apparently objected to protecting gay people from violent threats and, in some cases, death. Christian Moralism has usurped Christian love. Pro-life apparently does not apply to gay people. Or maybe it only applies to them before they are born!

The Bishop in Washington, D.C. stated that if the city council passes a same sex marriage law, the Catholic charities won't provide services to the neediest people. They won't abide by the city's ruling that they must allow same sex marriages in their employees. I heard that he was promoted to a big job in the Vatican shortly after this issue played out!

Hurting the poor and needy to prove a point against gays and lesbians seems pretty nasty to me. By the way, I know some gay people in Washington who were married in another jurisdiction where it is legal. They seem to be in love and similar to heterosexual couples I know.

The Pope came out with a declaration that condom use increases HIV/AIDS. I have a hard time understanding that logic as well. As I understand it, the culture in several African countries is such that discussing sex is taboo. Since you don't talk about it, it is difficult to preach about sex or stop the spread of AIDS, which is a big problem. Christian Moralism wins out over the potential survival of millions of people.

My suggestion (not that anyone is listening to me) is to reasonably and intelligently work to understand the reasons for the spread of the disease and use the best solutions that are available. That doesn't have to ignore the morality of the issue.

Self-Serving Sub-Secretum Edict

The issue of the Church's stand on the morality of transgender people was important for me to learn, especially since I was rejected at the local level. Someone sent me an article reporting that in 2000, the Vatican sent a confidential (*sub-secretum* or under secrecy) document that concluded that sex change procedures do not change a person's gender in the eyes of the Church.

The article stated, "The key point is that the (transsexual) surgical operation is so superficial and external that it does not change the personality. If the person was male, he remains male. If she was female, she remains female."

As I read, I had the feeling the people who wrote the article did not really know much about transgender people or, at least, what they wrote was not relevant for me or any of the other trans people I know. The surgery is not superficial to any transgender person I have ever met, and while it does not change the personality, it gets the body to match the personality and the spirit. I was getting more confused as I read on.

Now maybe I am cynical, and maybe I am jaded because of the other problems I have had with the Church, but as I worked through the article, I started to think that perhaps the article wasn't so much about ministering to transsexuals, but about the Church.

You see, if you were born male and nothing can change that fact as the Church has ruled, then you can't have male priests changing to female because they are transgender and thus, there can't be female priests. If a priest has a sex change to female, the Church says the person is still male, even though they look like and feel like they are female. Also, if a female decided to change her gender (of course "decided" is not the right word, but you know what I mean) and became male, she, or now he, could not become a priest because only men can be priests and no matter what she did, she (now he) would still be female.

Self serving? Perhaps. Was the conclusion that we can't have women priests, or something else about transsexuals? You decide.

I certainly don't feel like the official Church is excited about having me around. And by the way, I haven't had any surgery, and they didn't even mention that situation in the document.

Or maybe they did. I did not read the document because it is secret and in Latin (I only took one year of Latin in school), and I am not a bishop, who were the only ones, as far as I know, who were allowed to read it! I am just going by an article that someone sent me and what I could find on the Internet.

They Can't Take My Spirituality Away From Me

Earlier I mentioned I discovered I have the gift of praying in tongues. I am glad that the Divine presence has not rescinded my gift, now that I am having so much trouble with the Church. Hopefully God has not taken away my rights and privileges like the Church.

I continue to lose interest in the Catholic Church. I am constantly bombarded with negative Christian people or actions or pronouncements from the Church that seem to make no sense, or are at least incongruous with what I thought was the right way to live and treat other people.

After what I describe as "Leaking out the Door," for several years, I finally stopped going to church altogether. It is too painful. Being affiliated with the church conjures up so many negative feelings I decided it is better to go it alone. I certainly am okay with God and he or she seems to be okay with me. I miss the Mass and miss the community, but I can't remain a part of an organization where so many, especially in the hierarchy, are hurting sexually abused people, divorced people, women and LGBT people. The Catholic Church is fighting to break up my marriage – and they married us in the first place!

I read an article in a respected publication about the Pope trying to recruit the more conservative members of the Anglican Union into the Catholic Church—with special privileges not available to regular Catholics. They can keep their traditions and if the priests are married, as many are in the Anglican and Episcopal churches, they can stay married.

The only catch is that the people who come into the Roman church have to be against women and gay priests and against welcoming gays into the church. Gays seem to be more accepted in the Anglican Church. Those are the issues that caused the controversy, and the Pope is attempting to unify the Christians that have been separated for 500 or so years—as long as they are against women priests and gays. I was incredulous.

When the news hit the networks, Stephen Colbert did a funny story on Comedy Central's *The Colbert Report*. He had an Episcopal priest, Randall Balmer of Barnard College, Columbia University, as a guest and asked him if he was coming over to the winning side. (Colbert says he is Catholic.)

Reverend Balmer said that he did not believe in unifying against another group and thought that Jesus welcomed everyone.

Everything he said made sense. I've been doing some research on the Episcopal Church. Maybe that will be a better fit for me. Maybe it's appropriate that I get some of my religious revelations from Comedy Central! I have to laugh, or I'd cry.

I don't need to go somewhere where they accept me. After everything that has happened, I try not to care if anyone accepts me, especially if they are overtly and outwardly pious. Rather, I will feel comfortable where I am in synch with the people and organized church. If I find what they do inconsistent with the Gospel as I understand it, then I need to change to be like them or they need to change, neither of which seems likely. Or I need to find something better and just disconnect and find my own way like I have recently.

I wish there was a way to help all these bruised people I meet. I used to offer people who were searching or hurting something in the Church, but the Church or its people hurt many of the people I meet these days. How do I help them now?

I am waiting for God to tell me what He or She wants me to do. I know from the past that I am not a good listener, so He/She may have to tell me more than once! I'll keep the faith, partake of the sacraments if I ever go to church, but I am no longer drawn to the Church. I just need to build on the good, because I've met so many great people since this all started, and ignore the bad, as much as I can. I have met so many disaffected and bruised people. Perhaps I can help them through this book...

Conclusions

I have had the good fortune and been blessed to meet some good and holy people. Many of them have been good church-going people or have been in the clergy.

When I meet these people, I almost instantly feel good about being in their presence. They exude a joy and feeling of being connected with the Divine. I feel better about myself just for having been with that person, but always feel compelled to do better. It is like a feeling of "They have something that I want (a great spirituality and relationship with God) and I'd like to be more like that."

I think that is the way Jesus operates. He draws you to Him. He does not make arguments, condemn all the sinners, and exclude the people that are different. He draws us in.

I would feel better if we had more of the God-magnetized people in the Church instead of the excluders, rejecters and moralists.

When Religion Becomes Evil

When Religion Becomes Evil is a book written by Charles Kimball. He looks at several religions and examines when the sincere attempt to lead people to God becomes a bad thing instead of good. It is an interesting read and he has a good perspective on how things can turn the wrong way.

Kimball lists Five Warning Signs for why people do bad things—sometimes unspeakably evil things—in the name of religion:

1. Absolute Truth Claims: There is one truth and we know what it is.
2. Blind Obedience: Only the leadership has intellectual freedom.
3. Establishing the "Ideal Time:" There is a future time when wrongs will be righted – and we (in our particular religion) know what God will do at this time.
4. The End Justifies Any Means (there may be a lot of this in Christian Moralism!)
5. Declaring Holy War (Is religious terrorism much different from the Pope attacking LGBT people?)

I think it is easy for religious institutions, in their zeal for God and sometimes for power, to cross the line from good to evil. I think that my Church, or at least the one that I used to be a part of, is near or perhaps already over the line. Maybe some dialogue and understanding will help bring them back.

I see the Catholic Church splitting in two. The institutional church is becoming more closed, more conservative and several bishops have stated that a smaller church with better people is desirable. This is how they explain that closing churches is a good thing.

The other church is still connected, but quickly moving in another direction. These are the people that appreciate the sacraments, history, many teachings and tradition of the Church, but feel compelled to think for themselves, be led by God and to be suspicious of the bishops (all men by the way) or the Vatican making decisions for them. I like to think of this growing group as *Diaspora Catholics*.

We'll see where it all goes.

While thinking along these lines, here are some relevant readings that mean a lot to me:

Love your enemies and pray for those who persecute you.
Matthew 5:44

Woe to the shepherds who mislead and scatter the flock of my pasture, says the Lord. Therefore, thus says the Lord, the God of Israel, against the shepherds who shepherd my people: You have scattered my sheep and driven them away. You have not cared for them, but I will take care to punish your evil deeds. I myself will gather the remnant of my flock from all the lands to which I have driven them and bring them back to their meadow; there they shall increase and multiply. I will appoint shepherds for them who will shepherd them so that they need no longer fear and tremble; and none shall be missing, says the Lord.
Jeremiah 22:1-4

<u>*Parable of the Shepherds.*</u>
Thus the word of the Lord came to me. Son of man, prophesy against the shepherds of Israel, in these words prophesy to them {to the shep-herds}: Thus says the Lord God: Woe to the shepherds of Israel who have been pasturing themselves! Should not shepherds, rather, pasture sheep? You have fed off their milk, worn their wool, and slaughtered the fatlings, but the sheep you have not pastured. You did not strengthen the weak nor heal the sick nor bind up the injured. You did not bring back the strayed nor seek the lost, but you lorded it over them harshly and brutally. So they were scattered for lack of a shepherd and became food for the wild beasts.

For thus says the Lord God: I myself will look after and tend my

sheep. The lost I will seek out, the strayed I will bring back, the injured I will bind up, the sick I will heal...
Ezekiel 34: 1-5,11

Chapter 9

Junk that JJ Learned

When I was planning for the book and sorting out how to organize my thoughts, the process started to fall into place. I am what I describe as a "pile-izer." I like to sort through ideas and paper and put them in piles—in my mind, on a table, desk credenza or on the floor (or a combination of all of these).

When I formulated my plan, I started a pile on my credenza. The world has a long way to go understanding and accepting LGBT people, and I thought maybe my book could help open the doors and make others' journey a little easier. As I had a relevant thought or brainstorm, I wrote it down and stuck it on the pile. I collected letters, articles, emails and notes and stacked them on top.

When the pile got about a foot high, I knew it was time to get serious and sort the materials into chapter piles and start writing. I kept a file for thoughts, experiences and ideas that did not fit in any of the chapters but were interesting to share or had been good experience for me. I labeled it "junk" and eventually realized that all of this "stuff" should be collected into a separate chapter about some of the random things I learned. I hope you learn something from my experiences or they get you thinking or at least have fun reading. My journey has included many amusing experiences! Here we go:

Hormones

There is a ton of information available about hormones—in my case, testosterone blockers and estrogen. Transgender people seeking hormones should do some research on their own so they know what they are getting themselves into. Then they should follow their doctor's suggestions and the Standards of Care agreed to by the medical community for the care and treatment of transgender people. From what I know of the standards, they make sense to me.

One of the guidelines is that you need a letter from a licensed mental health professional verifying that you are in fact transgender before the medical doctor will prescribe hormones for you. It does not mean that there is anything "wrong" with you, but it is a requirement that a professional verifies what you already know.

When I am making permanent changes to my body, I appreciate having a professional helping me and giving me advice. I also found that the work on my own and sessions with therapists were helpful in sorting everything out, improving my chances for a smooth transition in the development and sorting out a way to deal with all the relationship issues.

I talked with several transgender people who were excited about changing their hormones through hormone replacement therapy. I was looking forward to it, but was not what I would call excited. I was so happy that I finally figured out what was happening with me and that I decided to live as female—just be myself. I was comfortable with each step along the way. I thought that hormones and anything that came after that would be a bonus.

Unexpectedly, I started to feel more exuberant enthusiasm when I scheduled my appointment with the hormone doctor. That is not the doctor's official title, of course, but that is the term I used. Our family doctor had checked me out and he gave me the okay, so I was ready.

I was feeling thankful and relieved when I picked up the first prescription. I was going to be a good girl—see the doctor, follow the regimen, etc. I had talked to a few girls who had self-medicated for one reason or another. Messing with and adjusting my hormones is not something that I felt comfortable doing without the guidance and monitoring of a professional who knows what to do.

I slowly (very slowly) started to feel and see the changes I had read and heard about—skin gets softer, breasts develop, body hair gets thinner, head hair gets thicker, etc. These changes were all great, and I would check every morning to see if I could discern any new developments.

My friend Julie Nemecek described how hormones gave her a feeling of well-being. After two or three months, I started to feel this. Perhaps the best way to describe it is to say that I finally felt like everything was in balance, all the gears worked and all the chemicals were finally just right. It was a great feeling.

I've described the change like this:

Inside of me, somewhere deep inside, is a lot of me—the feelings, personality traits and inner self that make me the person who I am. I knew much about my good and bad traits but discovered, after changing hormones more good stuff inside that rarely came out before. It was like a thick layer of "black sticky goo" holding the hidden good in there and not letting it out. A graphic might describe it better:

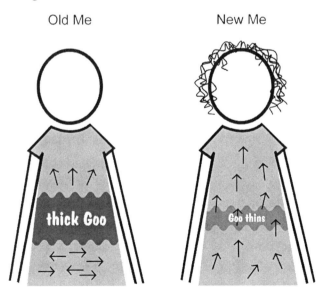

In the "Old Me" graphic, there are two layers of "me" material. The layer on top is all the stuff that people observe when they see me: I have a good sense of humor (maybe "weird" is more accurate), I care about other people, I love my family, I'm polite, impatient, have a bad temper, tell too many stories, etc.

I did not perceive the bottom layer much because it was covered with this thick goo made up of the leftover emotions trying to live the male role, society's expectations, fear, anxiety and testosterone. Actually, it was mostly made up of testosterone.

As I started to change, with the testosterone levels declining and the estrogen rising, the layer of goo became thinner and thinner. After a while, every once in a while a bubble of "New Me"—some feeling, trait or idea—would bubble up and pop out. It was like a surprise as I felt new things first slowly, then more often. I thought, "All of this was inside me, but didn't (or rarely) came out."

What was the New Me going to be? I liked the developing New Me a lot better than the Old Me. A few examples:

Crying

Many people describe how their crying/tearing pattern changes after starting hormone replacement treatment. I expected it and felt ready for it. Becoming more emotional and showing it was fine with me. I was ready for more crying whenever it came, if it came.

I can verify that increased crying is true for me, but the first time it manifested with me was a surprise. Our youngest son Matt and his girlfriend, Amanda, decided to move to Oregon. The oldest children, Joey and Andrea, had both moved out of town for college, but it wasn't too traumatic for me (as it was for Jo) since they moved to Cincinnati and Chicago. Those are two and three and a half hour trips from Indy, respectively. (Well, it should be three and a half hours to Chicago, but with traffic, you never know.) Anyway, Joey and Andrea were within driving distance, so while they were gone, it was not too far to visit with a fairly easy trip.

A trip from Indianapolis to Oregon is a lot different. I knew it would be a while until we would see each other. We went to dinner at Shanghai Lil's restaurant on the north side of town. The family of Joey's fiancée Katherin owns it, and we all love it there. We had a pleasant farewell dinner, and then Jo stayed at Joey's house with Matt and Amanda so she could help them drive the rental truck on the long trip to Oregon starting the next day.

I made the 45-minute trip home to the south side of town, and the tears started as soon as I got in the car. They lasted for almost 45 minutes! I was ready for crying, but 45 minutes at a time? That was tough. I was exhausted and drained when I got home. Crying now comes more often, but I have no guilt or hesitancy to show my feelings like I did when I was a guy.

My Voice

I have done many things to make my appearance match what is inside. Hormones, surgery, hairstyle, makeup and assorted treatments all can help in different ways. One of the most difficult problems to overcome has been my voice. It is unsettling when someone sees a female, but that woman sounds like a man.

I have been using a program I ordered from Kathe Perez at http://www.exceptionalvoice.com/voicefeminization.html. It takes work, but slowly I am getting closer to the voice that I am comfortable with.

Temper and Humor

I am half Sicilian and half Italian. For those of you who think that being Sicilian and Italian are the same thing, let me describe it in the words of my father (the Sicilian). He told me, "There are two kinds of people in this world—Sicilians and people who wish they were Sicilians!" Whether you agree with this is up to you, but that is the way Sicilians see it.

A part of being Sicilian is the Sicilian bad temper. I definitely had this temper, and it was a strong emotion. I didn't get violent, but I got mad. I could literally feel the rage inside of me. Sometimes it got so bad that only downing a shot or two of straight vodka or blowing off steam by yelling at someone (usually with their permission) until I felt a little better were the only ways to deal with rage.

On one occasion, I was upset at the office. I asked a few of our people to come into my office so I could swear at someone until I felt better. I screamed *to* them, not *at* them, about why the person who was causing me the problem was a jerk (not the word I used).

After about 10 minutes, the anger subsided. I thanked the people who had listened to the tirade. When I finally called the guy, I was calm and resolved the problem to everyone's satisfaction. Thanks again to anyone who let me yell at him or her to get it all out. It kept me from doing or saying something stupid.

After being on hormones a few months, the rage started to disappear. That is not to say that I don't get mad or upset any more, but it takes a lot more to set me off. The rage—the lousy feeling in my gut—is gone. Anger passes more quickly and I can more easily move on.

A new bonus that bubbled up when the rage went away was finding humor in situations which used to make me angry.

For example, rude people used to aggravate me. When people would cut me off on the road or when they were nasty to someone in public, the rage started in the pit of my stomach. I never did anything beyond occasionally saying something to the person, but it really bugged me. I'd give them "the look" and hold those feelings inside all day.

One day after I had been on hormones for a while, I stopped at the vet's office to get some medicine for Murphy, one of our little English Jack Russell dogs. One worker was seated behind the counter near the door. She was taking care of a lady, and another customer holding a baby stood behind her, apparently waiting in line. Around the corner behind the L-shaped counter was another uniformed worker. A person standing in front of her finished and started to leave as I walked up behind her.

This was the spot where I had previously gone to pickup medicine for the dogs, so I walked around the corner, stood in front of the worker and waited for her to look up and take care of me. She smiled and asked if she could help.

I said, "I am picking up the medicine for Murphy." figuring that they would remember Bailey and Murphy since they had been there several times, they were excitable (that is a challenge for any vet) and they were so cute.

As she started to say something, the second lady in the other line gazed at me with a piercing look of death (OK, maybe I'm a little melodramatic, but you could tell she was angry!) and said in a nasty voice, *"Excuuse* me"—a la an angry Steve Martin— "but I was here first."

I was surprised to hear her say that since I thought there were two lines for different purposes. I replied, "Oh, I'm sorry. I did not mean to cut in, I thought there were two lines."

She glared at me again and mumbled something. Another lady who worked in the office had been in the back and when she heard what was happening, she ran out to take care of the other woman who seemed so angry.

I paid for the medicine and, as I started to leave, decided to say something to the nasty lady. She had over-reacted and I had not tried to cut in front of her, but I still felt bad that she was so upset. I touched her on the arm (I never did that to a stranger when I was a guy, but it seemed appropriate and comfortable now) and said, "Ma'am, I'm sorry if I cut in front of you. I didn't realize there was only one line."

She glared angrily at me again and said, "Yeah, right."

The old me would have been annoyed and upset all day because frankly, the lady was acting like a jerk. The new me? I walked out the door and got a big grin on my face. It was hysterical to me that anyone would act like that. I thought it was funny to have seen it. She really was over the top.

My grin widened. I looked up at the beautiful morning sky and thought, "Dear Lord, thanks for not letting whatever happened to that lady to make her so crabby happen to me!" I felt so different than I would have in the past.

I like many of the new facets of me. I think my sense of humor has improved. At least I think more things are funny, and I laugh more often and longer than before.

I love *Calvin and Hobbes* comics. They have been out of the papers for many years, having run as long as the author thought they should go, but my kids bought me the complete, three-book set of every strip ever published. Now when I go on a *Calvin and Hobbes* streak and read a section of one of the books, I laugh so hard that I get tears in my eyes and occasionally have to gasp for air! It's fun, and once the laughing starts, it is hard to stop. Sometimes I get sore from laughing so long!

The last thing about hormones that really threw me is that I started to snort when I laugh and I do it almost every time I truly laugh. I used to always tease Jo because she snorts when she laughs. I never did it. I do it all the time now and often cover my mouth when it comes since it's embarrassing. I never heard of snorting being an effect of estrogen, but I have no other explanation. My editor suggests that since the goo of suppression is thinning, it's my natural laugh that the hormones have released!

Verification

When I finally acknowledged that I was transgender and needed to transition, I never regretted that I am like this or that I started the transition. I haven't regretted any of the steps made along the way.

I occasionally would get a feeling of disbelief—a thought that this could not be happening, that it was not real. I guess after so many years of hiding and suppressing, I could not believe that I was becoming a female. After a lifetime of terror worrying that someone would "find out," walking around the mall in a nice skirt feels so freeing and natural that I want to pinch myself to ensure it is real and I am not dreaming.

I didn't doubt that I did the right thing; it was more of a feeling of unreality that I had actually done it. I happily carried on when I would get this feeling. I was excited about the future. Many things happened to help me verify in my mind that this was real and I really had become a woman.

I was not confused or misled. I had not been coerced by other transgender people (some people believe we were recruited by other trans people or gays). No one talked me into anything, and I am not weird or sick.

Many experiences that I call "verifications" reinforce for me that I am on the right track. As it says in Isaiah 30:21: *"While from behind a voice will sound in your ears. This is the way, walk in it when you would turn from the right or the left."* God knew what has been happening. I think He or She is watching, and I had been keeping God informed about all my discoveries, decisions and changes. The Almighty would not let me get off track.

There has been much additional verification: I feel like I get better every day. Hormones take time. Hair grows slowly. All are too slow for me, but I am moving in the right direction. I should be better tomorrow than I am today. At least that is what I expect and how I feel.

At every milestone I felt a calm, a relief bordering on euphoria. When I started laser treatments for hair removal from my face and chest, I was anxious to get started, but also a little apprehensive since this was the first permanent change. I also expected it to hurt!

After my treatment, I was driving home. My face and chest were red and a little lumpy and sore. I was not hideous, but felt like they had zapped me. (They had!)

I started to feel exhilarated. I was so excited that I had started the long journey to remove all that disgusting (at least to me) hair. I thought, "How can I be so excited? I am red and sore, and nothing is going to happen for two to three weeks." It takes a few weeks for the treated hair to fall out after a laser treatment. I thought if I am this excited for something that hurts now and won't really show an effect for almost a month, I must be doing the right thing.

As my breasts started to develop—by the way, this does not happen quickly—I gave thanks every day for my development. I would pray, "Thanks for what I have, and if you can go a little bigger, that would be okay with me!"

Sometimes, I would get that feeling of unreality, like it could not be happening: I had breasts! I could not go back, and that was fine with me. I felt good that I didn't need fake breast forms any more and that my breasts were real.

If I could go from an A cup to a B, I would be satisfied. A is okay—no complaint, but I think for my body shape, B would be better. I did not feel any regret that I had been blessed with these changes.

I had a similar experience with my hair. As it grew longer, I liked it better. The curls were a giant plus. Even on a bad hair day I still am thankful that my hair looks nice and that I have a lot of hair. The curls vary with the weather. Some days it looks longer since the curls are looser, and some days it is shorter since the curls are curlier. There is a fine line between curly and frizzy.

I had similar thankful and verifying moments for many other things—wearing new clothes, having a purse to put your stuff in, being included in girl talk, being able to use the ladies room and not having to be macho.

With no offense intended toward the guys, many men's rooms are disgusting (especially when you don't want to be in that bathroom anyway), and no one in there is sociable unless they are drunk or bragging. The ladies rooms are better.

I've talked with several trans women who never liked sports or lost interest as they transitioned. As I mentioned earlier, I still like watching boxing and football, but I have lost interest in most other sports. I am starting to lose interest in football.

Something about boxing keeps my interest—probably because I have a hard time believing that boxers can do what they do. They endure 10 or 12 rounds of constant movement and punching and oh, by the way, someone is trying to hit you at the same time! They work through bruises, injuries, bleeding, dizziness and hometown refs who may not notice that the other guy is fouling you.

The macho stuff that goes with sports on TV turns me off. This is especially true now that I lost whatever macho feelings I had because of my shrinking testosterone levels. All that testosterone on the field—it's all lost on me. When you watch the replays or highlights, they show the celebration—guys jumping up and bumping each other (I never really understood that), the chest thumping (literally) and the trash talking and intimidation of the other team.

I understand competition and wanting to win, but you don't have to make your opponent look bad, do you? How about respecting your opponent? As the rehearsed celebration displays, dancing in the end zone, cut throat signals, in-your-face taunting and excessive celebrating increase, the team aspect decreases. Instead, it's "all about me." I just get tired of it.

Part of the attitude adjustment comes from my changes and some from age. I grew up watching the Browns play football in Cleveland. Jim Brown was an awesome player and did some things seemingly so far above what others could do that it was hard to believe. He didn't celebrate on the field. He didn't trash talk—he didn't need to talk at all. Many of the other players were afraid of him because he was so good. He was the best ever, or at least one of the very best, depending on who gives their opinion.

I heard Jim Brown being interviewed one time, and he said some interesting things (paraphrased from memory):
- "Why would I celebrate? I expected to score!"
- "It is disrespectful to the other team."
- "Celebrating and all that dancing make you look stupid." As a black player in the 1960s, he wanted to earn everyone's respect because he deserved respect and felt that others deserved respect.
- "Why would you celebrate when you score? It doesn't matter unless you win the game." I found this the most interesting.

Another benefit of cutting back on machismo and following sports is that it gives me more time to do other things! Like writing books, playing piano and my new pursuit – flower arranging!

Things People Don't Want to Know (But If You Do, Keep Reading)

I am a vocal person. I like to think through issues and deal with problems by talking about them. This can be boring or even upsetting to the person who listens to me while I am rambling, so I usually try to warn the other person that I am talking and thinking at the same time.

Oftentimes I'll ask their permission since much of the "conversation" is not really a dialogue, but to help me think through something. Jo is usually the recipient (participant?) of these vocalizations of thought and she tolerates them since she is a nice person who knows that this is how my mind works.

There are a few subjects where the listening can be more difficult or even painful for the listener. Listening to a description of a medical condition or procedure is sure to inflict suffering on the listener.

When that happens to me, I usually think, "I hope you are okay and thanks for sharing, but the details of your colonoscopy (or whatever the procedure was) are unnecessary and gross. The lesser the amount of time we spend on each gruesome detail, the better it is. No offense intended, and I really hope you are okay, but I really don't need to know how unpleasant barium tastes and how big the scope was!"

Sharing details of transgender treatments fall into this category. Some trans people may want to know what hormones do, or if electrolysis hurts, but everyone else can barely tolerate hearing about it. Electrology treatment is a good example for illustration.

I had been getting two-hour treatments every week with Barb Clayton in Indianapolis. She seems good, and several people recommended her. It's hard to compare her with anyone else since she was the first electrologist I'd seen, but she seems fast to me (not that electrology and fast belong in the same sentence).

She treats every hair with an electrical probe and then pulls it. With an estimated 10,000 hairs in your face, it feels like the treatments take forever. Laser got rid of a lot of the dark hairs, but a lot of facial hairs were left and I wanted to get them out as quickly as possible.

Barb's a nice, pleasant person. She encourages me to talk to make the time go faster. We chat on and off for two hours. It's hard to talk while she's doing your upper lip, but we can gab during the time she is working on the other areas.

When she's done with the two hour session, I get off the table, set the next appointment and pay her. She has a big mirror, and I look at my face with feelings of satisfaction in that we are making progress and another clearing has been opened up in the hair. It gets better each time.

This feeling is combined with despair, since there is still more to do. There are a lot of individual hairs to remove, and as I understand it, the hair grows in cycles. When a hair is permanently removed, there still may be a dormant hair right next to it that won't be visible for months. If you don't have (or can't develop) patience, you'll have a rough time with electrology. It's also expensive, especially since I went every week.

Barb and I would hit some artificial milestone—most of the dark hairs were gone; there was not much left on my lip; I could easily go a day or two without shaving and no one will notice; it only took 11 minutes to clean up my lip (as you might guess, this is the hardest spot to eliminate all the hair).

We'd laugh that we were making progress, and I'd be happy that there was less and less of that unwanted hair. Some weeks, I'd be more excited than others and would go home and ask Jo if she'd mind a couple of minutes of an electrology update.

I'd chatter about the new area that had been cleared up and express hope that I was getting closer to not needing to shave any more and not having all that hair. Then I'd thank her for listening. I felt better. She tolerated to be considerate. It works out.

A few other discussion topics falling into the same category include boob size changes, name change administrative details, permanent eye liner procedure description, comments made by other transgender people if I go to one of the meetings (unless they are touching or funny), and complaints about my nails breaking. I appreciate everyone who tolerates the rambling. That's especially true of Jo, who has listened patiently to all the boring updates.

While I am on the subject of electrology, I am glad that I found someone (Barb) who is technically good and also pleasant to be with. Mary Levell is another friend from the Indy area who is training to be a licensed electrologist, so soon I'll have two friends in the business. I rarely spend two straight hours within a foot of another person, so I would hope we get along. Also, I try to be amicable to any person holding a probe hooked up to an electrical current!

I am a process-oriented consultant by trade so I am usually interested in knowing how people work. When Barb would zap a hair two, three or even four times before she'd pull it out, I'd occasionally ask her what was different about that one. She'd reply that it was thicker than normal, or there was more than one hair in the follicle, or something like that. I asked if she liked working on those problem hairs since they were different, and she said she did.

I have "accused" her of making designs on my face via the pattern she used to remove the hair from an area on my face. I started to notice that she was working around a patch of hair under my chin, having cleared out on both sides of this patch. I asked her, "What are you doing under my chin—giving me an upside-down Mohawk?" She laughed and said that she'd never tell.

Names, Titles, Pronouns

People wonder how you address transgender people. What do you call them? Generally, an easy rule of thumb is to refer to and treat the person as the gender they present themselves to be. I expect to be called "she," "her" and "ma'am" (too old for miss!).

I don't think most people notice anyway, especially since I've been full-time female for a few years, but if they are not sure or think I may have formerly been a guy, they are almost always polite and respectful and act accordingly. Many people I have met only know me as JJ Marie, so they don't need to adjust at all.

The difficulty is with people who knew me before, sometimes long before the transition. Some have no trouble with the adjustment, but others have a hard time switching from Joe to JJ. They may see me, say "Hi Joe," and then catch themselves and apologize. Some get the name right, but forget when using pronouns.

It can be hard to get the gender pronouns correct, especially for our kids. When they introduce me to one of their friends, they'll say, "This is my dad, JJ." They still call me Dad, which is okay with me. The friend will either already know or figure out that I am transgender but they will usually call me he or him. After all, they know I am the dad.

I try not to let it bother me. As people get used to it, they get the names and pronouns right. As I said before, a few people aren't even trying. They call me Joe even though they know that is wrong. I let it go—for now.

We now have a new grandson – Vincenzo Cancilla Gufreda. He is very young, and doesn't talk so we can understand him yet. The adults usually refer to Jo and the Grandma from the other side of the family as Grandma and me as Nonna. It's Italian for Grandma, so it works for me. Of course, kids don't always do what you expect, so we'll see if the name sticks with Vinny. The nieces and nephews mostly call me JJ or Aunt JJ.

None of this name and gender-pronoun business is set in stone. I identify as female, but have a past as male. I am married to the same person as when I was male, so I am not sure if I am still a husband, spouse or what you'd call me. I'm still the father to the kids, even though the greeter at church (when I used to go to the regular church) wished me a Happy Mothers Day after Mass.

I look at it and think, "If name adjustments are the biggest problems I have, I'm in pretty good shape."

I appreciate it when people I've known for years remember and actually see me as JJ Marie rather than something that I used to be.

When I attended an Indy Girlz (M to F) and Indy Boyz (F to M) meeting in Indianapolis, they asked everyone to go around the table, give their name, how they identify their gender and then answer some icebreaker question. They also asked for family or friends/supporters to identify their relationships. The answers some people shared to the gender question were interesting:

- "Female" (person looked female)
- "Male" (person looked male)
- "Female" (person looked and dressed male)
- "Male" (person looked and dressed female)
- "Gender queer"
- "I am not sure"
- "I'm kind of in the middle"
- "I really don't care about what gender I am"
- "I guess I am androgynous"
- "I'm a male lesbian"

It's an interesting world!

Dreams

In my dreams (not hopes, but what I do while asleep), I have always matched what I looked like on the outside. I previously had looked like a male, and I was male in my dreams.

When I started to transition, it was like the button was pushed in my brain to what I really was. Suddenly I was female in my dreams. It literally happened overnight as soon as I stopped fighting it and accepted that I was female. I immediately changed to female in my dreams. It was fun!

The other interesting development with my dreams was when I would dream about some person, event or situation from the past. I have had dreams from previous times where I was a young girl in the dream. In my waking experience, of course, I never got to experience being a young girl, but I received some glimpses in my dreams. It has been a nice bonus that made up for some of the lost time from the past.

Two Directions on the Same Road

Early on, I attended a transgender meeting that included M to F transgender people as well as F to M. One of the F to M guys excitedly shared how his parents helped him pick out his new name, that he had gotten his first tie and how excited he was about the effects of testosterone—new hair was growing all over his body, he had to shave his face every day, hair was thinning on his head, his voice was changing, etc.

I recoiled at what he was saying. How could anyone be excited about all that hair? Wearing a tie was like torture. Shaving had been a daily reminder for me that I was in the wrong gender. Nothing he was saying made sense to me.

Suddenly I realized what I was thinking. How could I be so shocked with what he was saying? Even though I did not like the same things that he did, I knew that we are on the same road—just going in different directions. He is headed away from the female to the male end, and I am going the opposite direction towards female.

I smiled to myself and realized how difficult it can be to understand and empathize with another person. It was a good learning experience for me. This realization brings to mind a snippet of song:

There's a better me
I've been working on
I've got this belief now that I've been going on
That there's a place deep down where I come from
All the time, all the time

From singer/songwriter Natalia Zukerman in her recording, "Better Me" from the CD, *Brand New Frame* (used by permission)

Chapter 10

"Ick": The Definitive Answers to Questions on the Morality of Being Transgender, Gay, Bi or Lesbian

The Insider Report on Gays and Lesbians

Until I started my transition, I did not have much experience with gay and lesbian people. Most of the people I knew were married with children, so while I knew some gay people, I did not know them well.

When I started to attend transgender conferences and meetings, I knew that some of the people were gay, but it became confusing to figure out how to categorize each person, which seems so important in our society. It's a sort of double-edged sword; classifying people can be misleading but may also help understand what they are like.

The majority of people in the world are heterosexual, meaning that they are attracted to the opposite sex. There are fewer numbers of homosexuals and lesbians, who are attracted to their same sex. Bisexual people are attracted to both sexes.

There are differences between gays, lesbians, bisexuals and transgender people. For some, their sexuality—their sexual attraction—is different from the majority. For others, their gender identity does not match the way they looked when they were born. Lesbians and gays can try to hide their sexuality if they desire, while we transgenders have a harder time trying to hide our gender identity, especially if we are transsexuals and transition.

People may suspect that an unmarried guy who doesn't talk much about his social life may be gay, especially if they have "gaydar" and pick up the gay vibe (whatever that is). He can tell or not tell depending on the situation, people involved or circumstances.

A transgender might be undetectable to someone they just met, but it is hard to hide it when someone knew you as one gender and you show up another day as the other gender.

I met people like me who were transgender and stayed married to their original spouse. If the person was straight for their entire marriage, does changing their gender make them gay or lesbian? What about the spouse that stays with the person through the whole process and beyond? The spouse surely can't be gay because they did not change anything themselves. But my wife is now married to a woman, so …

You get the idea. It can be pretty confusing. I wonder sometimes what the Church and the Christian moralists would like me to do. If I am transgender and change my gender, do they think it is better for me to divorce, since they perceive me in a same sex marriage? But if I divorce, that breaks up a marriage of over 33 years. It causes a dilemma!

Kristen, a transgender friend of mine, is comfortable changing back and forth. She was born male. She enjoys being a girl, but works and does other things as a guy. I had never seen her as a guy, so she (or rather he!) came to my office one day so I could give her feedback on how I thought she "passed" as a guy. She thought she'd have a better chance to find a new position if she "stayed male." She had scheduled an interview for a new job. She did not want to look overly feminine, which in my view was burned into her being and demeanor.

Just so you know, even though she had long, highlighted hair, I thought that the only tell-tale attribute was that she was so used to sitting as a girl that she needed to "guy up" her demeanor a little. My assessment was she could pass as a guy if she's careful when she sits down!

As this story illustrates, some things that may initially seem to be black and white in perceiving other folks can in reality be a variety of shades of grey (or maybe pink and blue!).

It was funny having Kristen, who I only knew as a girl, ask me to check her out as a guy—which is what she was when she was born. She had to work at it to pass as a guy! It was a little weird, but I totally understood. I guess that someone who is not transgender would have a harder time understanding why she would want to do that. Welcome to my world!

Lesbians – Discovering How Much I Didn't Know

Several people have asked me if my changes made my wife a lesbian. I said that neither she nor I think she is a lesbian.

I hope she still is attracted to me, in whatever form I am. We are soul mates and dedicated to each other for the duration. I said that it is more likely that I might be a lesbian. Or maybe not! That struck me as funny since at the time I started my transition, I did not know many lesbians, did not know much about lesbians and did not know where they hung out.

The whole situation struck me as arbitrary and not important. What is of critical importance to others suddenly became irrelevant to me.

I attended one of the regional meetings of the National Gay & Lesbian Chamber of Commerce (NGLCC) and hung around after the meeting to talk with some of my friends. They were all lesbians.

We got onto the subject of the pros and cons of purses. Some of the girls liked wallets that they put in their pockets, and some liked to carry more stuff in a purse. One of the girls said that she could never be a "purse lesbian."

They all laughed, but I asked, "What is a purse lesbian, and what other categories are out there?"

They explained that many lesbians prefer either a purse or a wallet, but some use both depending on the situation.

I laughed and said that I must have missed the class in school where they explained these things!

A few years ago, I started taking a dance class at the Jesus MCC Church, now Life Journey Church on the other side of town. A person at one of the transgender meetings had announced that they were providing two hours of dance lessons every Monday and the cost was reasonable. I never was much into dancing, but since my transition to female I became much more interested in learning and I was becoming more social.

Leading Doesn't Have To Be Gender Specific

I was not sure what to expect. Ron, the instructor, was gay and would come with his boyfriend, Scott. There would be straight people, gays and lesbians in the class. What would it be like to see guys dancing with guys and girls with girls? When we started my first class, all Ron said was, "All the leads on this side and all the followers on that side."

Before my transition, I never considered being the lead or the follower to be negotiable or that it might change. I thought about it for a second, and thought, "If I am going to learn to dance, I want to learn the girl's part—the follower."

There were guys with guys, girls with girls and guys with girls. It did not seem to matter to anyone. They all just wanted to learn to dance.

I have to change to being the lead when Jo attends lessons. I told her that I like to follow and asked her if she wanted to learn to lead to dance with me. She said, "No way," and that was the end of that discussion.

I follow most of the time, and I like to react to the other person much more than being "in charge," but I am glad to switch over to dance with Jo. It is hard to learn both parts but I should be used to that!

It was interesting how quickly my attitude changed. When I was a guy, I never would have considered dancing with a guy. That would have been impossible. Now, I am comfortable and don't mind it at all. Most of the good leads are guys, so they can be the best to dance with. My good friend Barb and I go out dancing regularly. It is so much fun!

The people in the class are friendly. We all have fun, laugh at ourselves when we mess up, and enjoy the company. Ron and Scott are sweet people and delight in seeing others learn.

Getting the Scoop on GLBs

As I started my transition, I began to meet more gay people. I attended the NGLCC National Conference in June of 2008 in Minneapolis. I knew that I had the first transgender-owned company that the NGLCC certified as a minority business. Other represented businesses were owned by gays, lesbians and bisexuals. In addition to having a great opportunity to meet people from the NGLCC, other business owners and many potential clients, I would be able to make friends with a lot of gay people—a new experience for me.

From this conference and my experiences with many other gay and lesbian people, here is the summarized "inside" report:

A. Most gays, lesbians and bisexuals who I have met seem like genuinely nice people. They have been friendly to me. Most of the gay business people I meet are helpful to me and are most welcoming. They know that business is tough and that being in a minority can be difficult. I know that gay rights and gay marriage are two of the most divisive issues in our society. Now that I know more gays, I have a hard time understanding people being mad or mean to them because of their "lifestyle." A lot of the gay people I meet are interested in work, their families, their partners, eating dinner, paying bills, etc. Not really that exciting!

Also, many of the gay people I know will give me a hug

when they see me rather than shake hands. I got used to that quickly. It's hard to hate people who hug me when I see them!

B. *They are gay.* This may sound silly, but lots of people think that gays and lesbians somehow decided or chose to be that way. From my unscientific experience (you can read all the literature if you want) gay people are gay, meaning that they are attracted to their own sex rather than the opposite.

I think that people can be at different points on the scale below:

Attracted to own sex   Attracted to opposite sex

A   B   C   D

The people who are represented as A and B are generally considered gay, even though the amount of attraction or the way it manifests may be different from person to person. It is similar for the straight C and D people. A person in the middle is attracted to both sexes and is genuinely satisfied by an intimate relationship with either sex.

When I talk to some gay guys, it is clear to me that they just are not interested in girls. If the anti-gay (oftentimes they are Christian Moralists too) people are right that the gays are either confused or sinners, it seems hard for me to see what they should do or how they would change. Most wouldn't change even if they could.

Scott, my friend from dance class, described what I call the "Ick Factor." I asked if I could ask him some personal questions to test a theory and he said, "Sure."

I said that when I was in grade school (maybe third grade or so), a lot of the boys acted as if girls had "cooties" and when they got close to a girl, they said, "Ick" because they thought that girls were gross. They either were genuinely not interested in girls, or were being shy. They got over it within a few years, and eventually they wanted to be as close to the girls as possible.

I said to him, "It seems to me that you never changed from that 'Ick' feeling when you got older. You never have been interested in girls, right? That feeling never changed for you."

He agreed and told me that he never was interested in girls.

Based on my sample size of one, my observations and my gut feeling, I concluded that God makes some number of people gay, and that is the way it is. By the way, some gay people use the "Ick Factor" to describe something else, but that is another issue!

The "Quality Guru," W. Edwards Deming, taught and spoke about normal variation. You can measure variation to understand a process or population. It seems to me that there have always been LGBT people, so we must be part of the Normal Variation in humans.

The Australian/New Zealand Round Up (It Didn't Work for Hitler, Either!)

If we could somehow round up all the gay and lesbian people (by the way, I am using this as an example and not advocating we do this!!) and send them to a big island someplace, would we eliminate gays and lesbians from our society?

First, you would need a pretty big island, because there are lots of gay people. Maybe we could borrow New Zealand or Australia. Of course, we'd lose some talented people, so we'd be a lesser society for it. The Right Wingers would have less homophobia to discuss to try to scare us. Who would put on shows in the theatres? I *know* some of the theatre people are gay.

Second, I predict that eventually, more gays would eventually be born and we'd have to round them up again. And the great majority of their parents are heterosexual! It is similar to God creating left-handed people. It is the way it is. Why try to figure out if they are wrong or not?

We may try to understand why things happen the way they do, but ultimately, I think it is easier, much more Christ-like and more fun to accept people as they are and to *enjoy* the variety.

Between a Rock and a Hard Place

I have a hard time understanding the Church's, and some people's, beliefs about the morality of gays and lesbians. They expend a lot of effort telling gays what they can't do, but I don't see much effort spent telling them what *to* do.

Let's take a look at two gay guys in their late 20s. The Catholic Church says that you can't have sex before you are married. They also say that homosexuals are okay, but committing homosexual acts is not. I am guessing that they consider two guys having sex with each other a homosexual act. Two people of the same gender aren't allowed to get married in the Church. Let's break it down.

With a heterosexual couple, most of the time (not all, but most) the guy is more aggressive sexually. He may pressure the girl to try to get her to "give in." I've heard that younger guys think about sex many, many times a day. Females think about sex too, but not as much as the guys.

The guy may even ask the girl for sex, and tell her that he has been thinking about it all day. The girl may agree, but is more likely to focus more on the relationship and less about physical sex. He may be turned down or told that they have to wait. The guy may even get in trouble with the girl if he keeps talking about it.

In my example of two young guys who are gay, they may be thinking about sex all day like most guys. So they are both automatically interested when they connect if they are attracted to each other. The chance that both are interested in sex seems more likely than when compared to a heterosexual couple. Guys, on average, have a higher sex drive, so two guys would add up to more sex drive than a guy and girl.

Given this situation where both parties are attracted to each other, both are interested in sex and they are together -- according to the Church, they can't have sex unless they are married; they can't commit "gay acts;" and, unless they change their orientation (good luck with that) they can't ever have sex at all. That's if they go by what the Catholic Church tells them.

When, by definition, a person who is attracted to someone and interested in sex is never allowed to have sex, well, you see where the problems arise. It is an impossible situation for them. That's why many of them leave the Church.

Bisexuals

Bisexual people are also a small percentage of the population and not that visible. For me, if you are lesbian, gay, bisexual or transgender (LGBT) you have three things to deal with that most other people do not. You have to figure out that you are different and why you are different, and you have to figure out what to do about it: "come out," transition or deny or hide. If you are public, you have to share it with others and accept the consequences, both good and bad.

For bisexuals, it seems doubly hard to "figure it out," because they are attracted to both sexes and probably consider themselves straight and gay at different times throughout their lives. From my view, it's complicated for them!

My extensive insider's report to all the straight people, of which I used to be a member, is concluded. (I am not sure where I fit now!)

My perspective

One of the speakers at the NGLCC Conference in 2008 was Cynthia Wade, director of the Academy Award-winning documentary *Freeheld*. She showed the video to the group. It is an emotional story of a dying New Jersey police officer who is trying to leave her pension to her female partner. The film is enlightening and powerful, and some companies are using it as part of their diversity--training initiatives.

The officer and her partner experienced much discrimination and difficulty. It was interesting to see the reactions of the townspeople, the government leaders and her peers. I won't give away the entire story, but recommend you see it. Have tissues at the ready.

After the viewing of the film, one of the attendees asked Cynthia, who is married and has two children, her perspective on why straight people were so "mean."

Cynthia shrugged and responded that she did not know since even though she was straight, she did not behave that way.

I caught up with the gentleman after the session. I told him that I have been married for over 30 years and most of the people I know are straight, so I might have a good perspective on how to answer his question.

The answer I gave him can be summed up visually using this model:

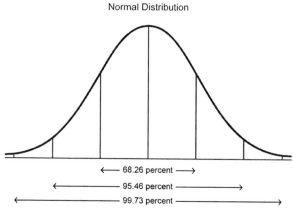

Normal Distribution

← 68.26 percent →
← 95.46 percent →
← 99.73 percent →

This is a normal curve describing a population—in this case, the variety of God's creation in human beings. Most of the people are around the average; there is more and more variety and less people different from the average as you go further out in the curve. There are less people on the ends and more in the middle.

The problem comes when someone does not know what is under the curve in the outer areas corresponding to the lower percentages, or when they have difficulty (or refuse) acknowledging that something is that far out on the curve.

For some, if they don't believe it, it cannot be real. Some people just can't accept that others are gay or transgender. To them, it may seem morally wrong. It is almost impossible (in my experience) to reason with these people and explain another perspective different from their own. They also may "not get it;" it just does not make sense to them. When that happens, they may react in a less-than-understanding or even a nasty way.

A non-transgender example might be helpful for illustration. My son Joey's fiancée is Katherin. She was born in the United States. Both of her parents were born in China and she has many relatives and friends in China. She speaks Chinese (both Mandarin and Cantonese) and is familiar with Chinese customs and lifestyle. Her roommate from college was a black girl named Coye.

Joey, Katherin and Coye went to China to see some of the country on a vacation. When they returned, they told me that Joey was an interesting person to many of the Chinese people he met because he was growing a beard and was naturally more hairy than the average guy. Many of the Chinese men were not very hairy, so Joey was an oddity and notable to them because he was so different. He always got second looks in the bathhouse where he went for back massages.

Coye was even more interesting to the people they encountered because she has a dark complexion and her hair is braided in rows. Some of the Chinese people asked to touch Coye's hair and skin, since they had never encountered anyone that looked quite like her. Her differences from them were extreme; they wanted to touch her to make it real for themselves.

Although in my example, the Chinese were curious and wanted to understand people different than them, many straight people don't understand and don't try. I think that variations in gender and sexuality are similar to this example for many people near the average. They don't understand or don't try to understand the other person, so that person or category of people never becomes real for them. It is as if the outlying people who are "different" do not exist because the "average" people don't have the experience or can't (or won't) process information about the seemingly oddball people.

When that is the case, people respond in some strange ways—from asking to touch the person, to ignoring that they exist, to active discrimination against them, or worse.

My answer seemed to make some sense to him. I realized that I am blessed with a perspective that few people have. I can see things from several perspectives—straight, gay, male, female. I can use my experience to try to see things from others' perspectives and have additional empathy for people.

I told a friend of mine that I could be a translator between people or groups who may not get along since I could see things from more than one side. She laughed when I said *trans*lator. Maybe we have come up with a new term and service that transgender people can offer to humanity! We'll talk more about this in the next chapter!

There is a book called, *Nine...Ten...And Out! The Two Different Worlds Of Emile Griffith,* by Ron Ross. Emile was a Hall of Fame fighter who had a twin burden. He tragically killed a man in the ring and lived a double life outside of it—he was a bisexual.

One quote attributed to the boxer was, *"I killed a man and most people understand and forgive me. However, I love a man, and to many people this is an unforgivable sin; this makes me an evil person. So even though I never went to jail, I've been in prison almost all my life."*

To the clean all things are clean, but to those who are defiled and unbelieving nothing is clean; in fact, both their minds and their consciences are tainted. They claim to know God, but by their deeds they deny him. They are vile and disobedient and unqualified for any good deed.
Titus 2 1:15, 16

Chapter 11

I am a Translator:
An Insider's Report on
Discrimination, Women, Straights and Gays

Prejudice and Discrimination

The '50s and '60s in Cleveland Ohio was a time of racial discrimination, racial violence, riots and ethnic conflicts. The city had many different neighborhoods, usually based on ethnic differences. We were Sicilian/Italian and lived in a mixed but mostly Slovenian neighborhood, but we were near the Italian neighborhood.

In the nearby neighborhood where Jo and I lived after we got married, there was an Italian church down the street from the Slovenian church. It was not uncommon to hear people speak their ethnic language rather than English, and it was easy to tell if they were not thrilled with you because you were the wrong nationality.

One lady who was not of Sicilian/Italian heritage was walking down the aisle at the grocery store. She walked up to me and bumped me with her cart a few times. I just looked at her and carried on. It was not a big problem for me since the ethnic prejudice and discrimination were not nearly as bad as the racial. I never experienced much of the racial discrimination firsthand, but it was all around us.

I did not have much familiarity with people who were black or other races until I went to Cleveland State University. I went to a white grade school and a white high school. At college, I tried to meet more people and make friends with people new and different to me. I had a black friend in one of my classes, but found that he did not want to hang around with me after class because he didn't want his friends to see that he had befriended a white person.

The two groups who were discriminated against the most were blacks and gays. I made a few black or gay friends over the years, but I had few points of common experience with them except for my gay friends from high school. I was against discrimination, but it did not affect me until the past few years. A consulting colleague is black. We have talked about her experiences and what it is like to be a black female. Besides being a great person and a good friend, she helped give me some perspective from her viewpoint.

I met some members of the Indianapolis Black Pride group at the local Indy Rainbow Chamber of Commerce meeting. I asked them if they had experienced much discrimination or had many problems after coming out as gay. It sounded like most of the discrimination they experienced was from being black, rather than gay or lesbian.

One guy, who had come out as gay in high school, said that he did not get much discrimination for being gay. But everyone still takes notice when he walks into a room of mostly white people. In his experience, the racial discrimination is at the forefront rather than discrimination against gays. Of course, you may or may not be able to tell he is gay, but it is easy to pick up that he is black!

It is interesting being transgender from the perspective of prejudice and discrimination. In my case, I rarely felt any prejudice or discrimination at all for over 50 years before I began to transition.

Then overnight, some (not a majority, but enough people to notice) started to treat me differently, ignore me or out-and-out discriminate against me. Prejudice and discrimination are difficult to get your arms around when you go your entire life with no discrimination and then instantly start to experience it.

It is as if we went back to the '60s in my hometown of Cleveland and you went to bed as a white person and woke up as a black. Immediately, people would treat you differently, you would be disliked or feared, your employment and housing opportunities would dramatically decrease, and your entire life would change. In addition to the shock to your being, the reaction of others might overwhelm you.

That is similar to the way I felt when I started to transition. I have not seen or talked with some of my old friends for a few years, and when they see me they get out of there as quickly as possible. It's not usually blatant, but more than a few people forgot my number and don't know how to look it up any more!

The Translator

I am in a unique position to empathize and try to understand other people. I can certainly see things from the white male perspective, since I tried to be a white male for over 50 years. I may not have looked at things like the "other" guys did, but I certainly thought I was seeing things from the male perspective. I have been married for over 30 years, so I understand the "married with kids" view of the world.

I had been a member of the Church, a volunteer, manager, entrepreneur, executive and member of what seemed to be the majority. Since I started my transition, I have started to get the perspective of people who are gay, lesbian, bi and transgender. I feel totally like a woman; as much as is possible for someone that wasn't born female, I have a female perspective. I don't know anyone who has changed their race, but I think that I can see things from a racial or ethnic minority better than most people because of my experiences. I have a decent idea of how religious minorities feel, since I am having serious difficulties with my church since I started with my changes.

When someone says, "If you want to understand someone, walk a mile in their moccasins," I can say that I have done that!

The new moccasins are a lot better for me, and you can never have too many!

Dealing with Repairmen and Salesmen

I wondered if my interactions with strangers would change when I went from male to female. In my consulting experience, I have met and worked with many female consultants, and I have been impressed with their knowledge, professionalism and skill.

There can be some problems, especially if the client is a guy with a larger-than-normal ego. Consulting can sometimes have the opposite effect on the client than you might expect. If we have a project and save clients millions of dollars, you'd think they would like this. Sometimes, however, they appreciate the savings, but their egos get bruised because some outsider found improvements that they may not have seen or could not do themselves. This can be aggravated if the person who made the improvements is female and the client is male.

Even though I feel and consider myself female, I lived many years, and have many experiences, as a male. My experience and my memories haven't changed since my gender change. How I view and interpret them might change, but the things I have learned have not changed.

I have worked as an engineer, even though that is not my training; I was in charge of tool-making and maintenance. I was never very inclined or good at making repairs, running machinery and doing home improvement work, but I got by.

Part of my job as husband and father was to fix stuff, so I did the best I could. I didn't really like to do it, (and like it even less now!) but I did my share of home improvement and repair projects. That comes with owning a house.

Since my transition, I've had a few interesting experiences related to repairs. One hot day, one of the tenants in our building told Joey (my son and Office Manager) that the air conditioning was out and it was sweltering in his office. Joey was leaving early to run an errand, so he asked me if I could stay until the repair guy came and fixed the air conditioning. I told him yes. He called the repair company and asked that someone come out as soon as possible. I told him that I'd stay until it was finished.

A repair technician quickly showed up, and I saw that he went back and forth between the tenant's office and the A/C unit outside the door in the rear of our building. After a little while, I went to see how things were going. I don't think the repairman knew that I owned the building or that we were paying for the repair.

I asked him how the repair was going.

He said that he was wrapping things up and he had fixed the problem.

I asked him what was wrong with the air conditioning.

He ignored me, started to walk away from me and walked into the tenant's (a man) office. He told our tenant that the A/C was fixed and that it would take about an hour for it to cool down again.

I asked him again, "What was wrong with it?"

He looked at me in a condescending way and said, "It was broken."

I thought this stuff happened, but it was still weird when it happened to me. I decided to keep going and see how things played out. Also, even if he didn't know it yet, I owned the building and wanted to know what went wrong. I don't want people in our building to be too hot in the summer.

I said, "I know it was broken because it got hot in here. What did you have to fix in order to get it to work again?"

He looked at me with disdain, and said, "The thermostat wire was broken."

That was an answer, but not really the amount of detail that I wanted. I wanted to know what happened to cause the A/C to stop working. I looked at him and asked, "Inside or outside?"

He looked surprised and said, "What?"

I repeated, "Inside or outside? The thermostat is inside and there is a wire connecting it to the outside unit. Which of those two were broken?"

He looked at me with a shocked look on his face, like he wondered how a girl would know such ineffable things as how the air conditioner works. He stammered, "The wire on the outside unit was broken."

I thanked him and walked back to my office. What a struggle!

On another occasion, I went to a local home repair supply store. We had a big flood in our basement, and to conserve money, I tried to fix the drywall myself; taking all the help I could get from friends and relatives. I had never done it before, and several people had told me that doing drywall yourself is difficult. The people who do it well had a lot of experience and skill. Still, I decided to take my best shot, since we had spent so much money on the cleanup and repairs already.

I went to the store and went to the drywall aisle. I asked an employee if he could give me an overview of how to do it, because I was going to try to do it myself and had never done drywall before. I also needed to know what to buy so I could get the job done without coming back to the store several times.

He explained it very simply, so it sounded like it would be a snap. From what some knowledgeable friends and my brother have said, it is not a snap at all.

I asked him several questions, and he continued with his simple instructions. I sensed (female intuition?) that he was leaving several parts out of the story; it couldn't be as simple as it sounded. He kept telling me that what he said was all I needed to know.

I bought the materials he suggested and got started. After two evenings, my brother called for an update. He has a lot of experience and has even taken classes on how to do different repairs. He reiterated that he can *do* drywall, but wasn't close to an expert.

After my discussion with my brother, I concluded that in order to make it simple for me (something a girl might understand) the gentleman at the store had left out a few important points:

- If the wall studs don't match the size of the drywall, you have to cut the drywall so it ends halfway on a stud. The new piece starts on the other half. That was an important fact that he left out!
- The corners are made of a metal corner bead nailed or screwed to the drywall and covered with drywall mud. It's close to impossible to do it if you don't have that.
- You need a paddle to put on a long rod hooked to your drill so you can thin the drywall mud and mix it up to a uniform consistency. Using it out of the bucket is difficult.
- Blending it in during the mudding process is extremely difficult. Mere mortals should proceed at their peril.

Now maybe I am sensitive. It seemed to me these two gentlemen were talking to me like I would never understand what they were telling me, and this never happened to me before I became female. I think I am just as smart now as I was before my transition started.

Maybe they were not good at explaining, or didn't know what they were talking about, but I think it is because I am female. I can certainly see why this would aggravate other women when it happens to them. Perhaps they think that brain matter decreases as breast size increases, but I don't think so!

Despite some problems, I am enjoying seeing life from the other side—and being a translator.

As a friend said, "If you think the world is flat, that affects how you travel!"

Chapter 12

A Business Trip to London:
Transition in Business

As I moved through 2007, I was convinced that transition was not one of my options—rather it was the only option. I could not go on as a guy. Every day that I was going back and forth—male at the office and female at home or someplace safe—was not working. Once my family and I had started working through all of our issues, the biggest remaining issue was what to do about my job.

I own a consulting company and have been in consulting as a profession for 25 years. Much of my professional experience has been in male-oriented work. I worked in several different factories as a supervisor and manager in production, materials, tooling and maintenance. My consulting experience has included automobile manufacturing, several parts plants, utilities, concrete manufacturing and foundries plus white collar, professional services and high tech. I've been in some nice companies and my share of nasty places.

Transitioning at Work – Considerations

As I started to sort out the issues involved in my transition, I thought about many potential problems:

- How do I "tell" the many people that I work with?
- Will I have more than one version or do it the same way for clients, consultants, associates and colleagues?
- How will I handle negative reactions if I get them?
- How will clients (especially in some of the rougher industries) react to me as a female rather than a male?
- Would I lose sales because I am transgender and female?

There were so many issues. Would all of this work out? Was I jeopardizing my career and income?

I had talked with and read about people who had transitioned at work. It sounded like some good companies helped their transitioning employees, gave training and assistance, covered the healthcare costs and really removed many of the work-related bottlenecks and problems. I also heard of people who had been harassed, pushed out of their jobs or fired for being transgender.

Learning about the others' experiences was helpful, but I needed to talk to people who were executives or owned the businesses. Their experiences would be closer to my situation. I talked to, read about and corresponded with a few executives who had transitioned at work, but I did not find anyone in my situation. I was the president, owner and public face of GEI.

I was about ready to stop hiding and start my transition, but I was uneasy since I had no frame of reference for how to do it in my position. After working with so many people during my career, I felt utterly alone.

I attended the Southern Comfort Conference in Atlanta in the fall of 2007. This is, as far as I know, the largest transgender conference. Several people who I had met previously were attending. I met lots of people, had a great time and enjoyed my first experience of living as a female for an entire week. I attended and learned from several education sessions related to transgender people at work, but still did not have what I needed to transition in my career.

Resources That Work

That all changed when I attended a presentation from the National Gay and Lesbian Chamber of Commerce (NGLCC) related to transgender business owners. When I got to the session, I found that the presenter was Aditi Dussault. She worked with the NGLCC.

She explained that the NGLCC was the chamber of commerce for LGBT (Lesbian, Gay, Bisexual, Transgender) businesses and that they were looking for transgender-owned companies to join the chamber. She also described their supplier-diversity program, which certified LGBT businesses as minority-owned and helped introduce them to companies looking for diverse suppliers.

She showed a slide listing some of the companies that supported the program. I was excited to see some large, well-known companies such as KPMG, Merck, Accenture, Continental Airlines, PepsiCo, Lilly, Cummins, and Ernst & Young (where I had previously worked before I formed GEI). Over the years at GEI, (www.geilean.com) our biggest engagements had come from large clients. AlliedSignal, Honeywell, Ford, Maytag, Nestle Foods, and Electrolux were some of the internationally-known clients that used our services.

I realized that I was now a minority, which was a new experience. The concern I had about the unknown was offset with the knowledge that the NGLCC could give me help and some opportunities could open to us because I was transgender. I didn't know how it would go, but I didn't feel alone any more.

I was bubbling with excitement after hearing Aditi's presentation. I thanked her and told her that I had not started to transition yet, but if they could help me through their programs, I was confident that I could transition at my business in a professional way. The diversity opportunities could provide new business for my company.

We agreed to stay in touch. I gave her my old business card (with the guy name), along with a card that I had printed with my female name and image on it. I told her that when I was ready to transition, I'd contact her so my company could become certified by the NGLCC as the first transgender-owned company to be a certified Lesbian Gay Bisexual Transgender Business Enterprise (LGBTBE).

I left the meeting feeling a sense of relief and looking ahead to a ton of work to make the professional transition happen. I was excited that the roadmap was taking shape.

As described earlier, on the drive home from Atlanta, the feeling of despair I felt knowing that I was going back to being a guy on Monday pushed me to make the final decision to transition—or at least get started on sorting out the detailed plan. I was exhilarated that the last seemingly impossible roadblock had been reduced to a large boulder, not Mount Rainier. I was ready to go. By the end of the year, I'd be ready to start the transition—personally and at work.

I started to go out more and more dressed female, but had never gone to the office or met clients as a woman. I worked hard at home, at work and in therapy developing a reasonable plan for transition. Every day that I waited was painful, but I wanted to do everything thoughtfully and carefully, giving myself the best chance for success in my business relationships.

Personal Support

I developed a plan that included as much detail as I could anticipate needing, wrote drafts of emails and letters so I could explain the changes to everyone, and worked to get as much in my life in coordination for my gender change. The last step was to tell a trusted friend who I had worked with for several years to get some advice and to start to get it off my chest.

The longtime friend, Charlie Colosky, had worked with me when I was at Ernst & Whinney (E&W). He was a smart engineer who joined us after working at Cummins Engine in Columbus, Indiana. I was impressed with his knowledge and consulting style, and I shared any consulting tips I had with Charlie since I had been in consulting a few more years. He was a good colleague and friend.

When Charlie left E&W, he became an independent consultant and worked with the Kaizen Institute of America.

When I left Ernst & Young (name changed after E & W's merger with Arthur Young), Charlie helped me with the change from consulting employee to consulting company owner and taught me how to develop my consulting practice and expand my consulting expertise.

After a few years of Charlie and I working together for a second time, I continued to build GEI and Charlie took a position with Apple in Cupertino, California.

Whenever Charlie and his wife, Shari, would come back to Indy, we'd try to get together and grab lunch or dinner. Just before I was ready to transition to full-time female, they were due for a visit. I thought this would give me a perfect opportunity for feedback from a trusted friend whom I had met in my professional life.

Charlie met me at a restaurant near my house and I told him the story. I talked quietly since I was still nervous about people finding out before I was ready to tell them.

He was helpful and supportive and gave me some good ideas and suggestions. He said transgender people were welcome at Apple and there was an internal employee group for transgender people and their supporters. I would later find out that several companies had support groups that included transgender people.

I had been nervous about telling my colleagues and friends from business about my changes, but as with most of my previous interactions with Charlie over the years, he gave me some perspective, a different viewpoint and a lot of friendship. I had developed the confidence and prepared to make the changes.

Since we didn't have much face-to-face client contact around the holidays that year, I decided that the first people I needed to tell were the tenants in our building. I wrote them this letter:

April 2008

To: Our Clients, Friends, and Associates,

Since we have known each other for some time, I wanted to write you and let you know about an important transition that is happening in my life.

For many years, I have been aware that I am transgender. This means that I mentally and emotionally identify myself as a woman even though I was born physically as a man. This is not something I have shared with others. I have been dealing with this issue for my entire life and am relieved that I finally have come to a clear understanding of this and can be my true self. As a result, I have decided to continue my life as a woman and need you to know that when you see me in the future it will be as a female. Instead of "Joe" I will continue my life as "JJ."

We have not shared this news widely, but are now telling people as appropriate. I do not plan to make any further formal announcements.

I have been in the consulting business for almost 25 years. My company, GEI, has been serving clients for almost 14 years and I plan to continue as before. I have the same experience, knowledge, skills and background, but I am more relaxed and less stressed because I am not suppressing this important part of me. I have found a lot of new and positive energy and am excited about the future!

I am taking this transition a day at a time, as this is a new experience for me as it is with all of those who are close to me. I understand that this change may take some time for you to "process" as well. Most of the people who are already aware of my transition have had a hard time getting used to the new name and using the female pronouns. That is completely understandable, given the circumstances!

I have gotten terrific support from my wife, family, friends and the business associates I have discussed this with. I look forward to continuing and improving our personal and business relationship. Feel free to call me if you have any questions, or just want to chat.

God bless,

JJ (formerly Joe) Gufreda

During the week between Christmas and New Years day, I started to go to work as JJ. The people in our building didn't bat an eye, chatted with me in the hallways like before, and called me JJ without hesitation. I thought, "Everyone has been so nice, it can't be this easy," but my first days going to work as JJ were a big non-event!

Business Transition Specifics

I developed an outline plan for the rest of my professional transition. Here's a summary of some of items in the plan:

- A. Start application for NGLCC supplier program.
- B. Pursue minority opportunities.
- C. Pursue certification as a woman-owned business.
- D. Write and finalize letter(s) to send to business associates.
- E. Make list of the initial people to inform, make lists of other people that need to know.
- F. Contact individual companies that have LGBT inclusive supplier policies.

There were detailed steps and lists to be developed. When I would "tell" someone, I added their name to the "They know" list and tried to be sure that I told everyone, but not to tell them more than once. I started with a pad and pencil, but eventually used a spreadsheet list so I could keep everything straight.

As we moved into the new year, I slowly started to tell people related to my business about my changes. In the first quarter of 2008, our business took a turn for the worst. The early stages of the worst economic downturn since the Great Depression had begun, and it is common for clients to stop or delay consulting projects as the economy slows down. The economy was not slowing down; it was quickly headed into the abyss.

Consulting can be a leading indicator for the economy— when companies slow down, they often cut outside resources before they cut employees. Even though we save clients money and make big improvements, some executives feel that it looks bad to keep consultants while they are eliminating their own people.

The good news is that occasionally, a company will recognize that slow periods are ideal for improvement and let us help them, but while logical, this is not nearly as common as you might think.

The good news is that consulting is also a leading indicator when the economy improves. As sales start to rise, many companies use consulting services to help them ramp up in a quick, reasonable and cost-effective way while improving quality, cost and customer service. We were prepared for the slowdown, which eventually developed into an international financial disaster.

While it was difficult, a slow period when I spent most of my time in the office (because we didn't have many clients) allowed me the time to transition, tell people, and shift from being a businessman to being a businesswoman. I didn't like the decrease in sales, but I appreciated the time to work through all the issues related to my gender change.

We increased our marketing and networking efforts and used the time to continue to tell all my business contacts about my changes. Everyone was interested in what was happening and since there wasn't much business to discuss, I used the opportunity to normalize my new feminine work persona.

Minority-Owned Business Certification

In early 2008, we completed our application for certification as a minority-owned business by the NGLCC. In February we received our certification, and GEI became the first transgender owned firm certified by the NGLCC.

We also joined the local LGBT Chamber of Commerce, The Indy Rainbow Chamber, and we were the first NGLCC-certified firm from Indiana. We have since joined the Chicago Area Gay and Lesbian Chamber of Commerce.

I started to contact the supplier-diversity and procurement people at several target companies and looked forward to the NGLCC national conference in June in Minneapolis. We were slow, so I was anxious to start what I was sure would be a slow process to get business as a minority and I was excited because this would be my first business trip as JJ. I would also get the chance to meet the NGLCC staff, network with other suppliers and start to build the relationships that (hopefully) would bring us some new business.

Supplier Diversity Initiatives

Many of the companies that were seeking diverse suppliers (certified minorities) were large Fortune 500 companies. These were excellent target clients for GEI. I wanted to learn about how the process worked. Each company was a little different, but generally supplier diversity initiatives work like this:

- The company develops or expands a supplier diversity initiative to help them gain access to the best suppliers, works with internal employee resource groups (ERG's) that want the company to encourage diversity inside and outside of the company, and takes advantage of the natural benefits of diversity. The initiative is often a result of some internal champions or the internal ERG working to expand opportunities.
- I found a hierarchy or pecking order amongst the minority groups. There is certainly cooperation, and many of the certification organizations work together for professionalism and consistency.

Aditi Dussault, the first person I spoke with at the NGLCC, is now the Project Manager, Disability Supplier Diversity Program, at the U.S. Business Leadership Network (USBLN). The national business organization currently represents their BLN affiliates and more than 5,000 employers using a "business to business" strategy to promote the business imperative of including people with disabilities in the workforce.

The experience Aditi gained at the NGLCC is likely helping her at the USBLN. Some diversity groups however, feel that they are competing with the other groups. The logic is something like this: companies first provided help to some racial minorities, then they expanded it to include more ethnic groups, then women, then veterans, then LGBT, and finally people with disabilities. Pretty soon, some worry, everyone will be considered a minority and will expect special treatment and access to more business. That might mean a smaller piece of the pie for them. From my experience, my company needs help to make up for the losses related to my gender change.

The more companies that participate, the more opportunities for everyone. In my opinion, minorities do need assistance, because there is more than enough discrimination to go around. As more and more people work with all kinds of companies, suppliers and people, the need for outside help will lessen.

- The diversity initiatives are organized in the management structure—usually through Procurement and/or Human Resources.
- Full-time and part-time resources are assigned to develop the relationships with the various certifying bodies, advocacy groups and with potential suppliers.
- Some companies institute general goals such as "give diverse supplier firms increased opportunities," or "encourage diversity," while others are more specific and measure corporate and departmental goals for diversity spending. Some of the more advanced companies measure the amount spent for each diverse category, so they encourage spreading the opportunities around to everyone.

Bringing Others On-Board With Bringing My Business On-Board—How Work Works

The first challenges that I encountered in trying to procure diversity business related to the way we sell GEI's consulting services. Our normal process to sell consulting projects does not fit in well with the way diversity spending occurs at many companies.

For example, if you are a diversity supplier who does graphic design, the buyer assigned to purchasing graphic design and marketing services would be made aware of your firm, and you would be asked to bid for upcoming work when opportunities arise. If you did construction work, you might be considered each time a construction project became known through a request for proposal (an RFP).

In GEI's 15 or so years as a consulting business, our engagements have rarely come through someone in Procurement. An executive that wants results—*fast*, usually hires us. In many cases, the executive calls or has someone call me, we agree on a rate and what needs to happen first, and we get started. The Purchasing and Accounting people may not even know that we were engaged until I call them and let them know.

I am a process improvement consultant, and I know that this scenario messes things up inside the client's company because the standard process is not followed. When I have the feeling that for the sake of speed and the critical nature of the project, the client has bypassed the normal process, I call Purchasing or Accounting to make sure everything is in order.

Also, I know if there is no purchase order approved in the system, we don't get paid! Believe me, starting a project without a P.O. or the normal paperwork happens more than you would think—at least when we are engaged.

One executive was fed up with the results he was getting and called me to tell me what he wanted us to do. He told me where the sites were, who was in charge at each location, and then said that he wanted consultants at each site on Monday.

We only had a few days to line up the consultants. Most of the site managers were not even told that we were coming (not the most comfortable way to start) and when I called Purchasing, they said that they had never heard of us and if there was no purchase order, we would not get paid.

I told the Purchasing person the name of the executive who had hired us, and asked if she knew who he was. She said that she did. I suggested that it might be better not to chastise him for not following the normal process (he was one of the top three people in the company), and that we would help her get the paperwork and approvals in order after the fact, since we already started the work.

She appreciated my candor and our helping her prevent problems and, after some paperwork and the executive's formal approval, we were in good shape. The consultants had already started getting some results and it was a week before we got all the administrivia completed.

We are happy to respond to RFPs or work on engagements where we have time to plan, but usually we get our projects when an executive is upset, frustrated and in "a big damn hurry." One manufacturing company client called me at home on a Sunday afternoon. He said, "Do you know about my plant in (such and such a place)?"

I said that I had heard about it, but didn't know much more than that.

He said that they were having lots of quality and delivery problems, he had already brought in several people from the division headquarters and corporate, and that they were not making any progress. He described it by saying that everyone was bailing water so the boat would not sink and if anyone stopped bailing to fix the hole, they would all go down. He said, "I want you to fix the hole in the boat!"

He surprised me when he said, "If you don't have two consultants in my plant by Friday, I am shutting the plant down!"

We had one consultant there on Tuesday and another on Thursday. By the end of the second week, we had six consultants helping to turn the situation around.

The project didn't last that long because he was right in his understanding of what was happening: While they bailed, we fixed the hole. The plant was running pretty well, and our consultants were finished within six weeks. The company had needed outside people who were aggressive and experienced. When they call, we respond.

In another situation, after we started work in a difficult problem area, one demanding client started emailing me requests for consulting resources in the morning. We would scramble to get the person lined up, and I would send him an experienced consultant by 7 a.m. the next day. We progressed from one person to 21 consultants within a month and a half, and we also engaged a partner firm to do customer research for the client.

Most of these opportunities came without much warning and without an RFP. We were hired directly by the executive. Having an advocate in supplier-diversity or procurement looking for opportunities inside the company is helpful, but I realized that we needed to have good relationships and build up trust before they would feel comfortable enough to plug us into situations and fill their needs.

Building on Our Successes

It takes time, but I keep working the process. The good news is that in each prospective client, we have at least one, and often several, advocates looking for projects for us to work together.

We like to partner with other firms and consultants and as a minority firm, we look for non-diverse firms that can benefit by teaming up with a certified minority firm. I knew it would be a slow process, but doors were opening.

I have been working for some diversity-related business for four years, but so far, we have not gotten any work from this channel. I am still trying, and we'll see if we can turn the relationships into business.

While we worked on developing the diversity-related market, we also pursued our regular consulting opportunities. In the spring of 2008, I talked with a client who I had worked with early in my consulting career—20 or 25 years ago. We had a great relationship when I worked with them, and had kept in touch over the years. They had a new initiative that they were starting, and my former client called me and asked if we would help them.

I was excited to meet her since I enjoyed working with them so much in the past, and because I looked forward to helping them improve. At this time, I had not told anyone at the client about my gender change and knew that I needed to tell her before we met in person.

We set a time to meet for lunch, and when I responded to confirm the meeting by email, I included a short note explaining my gender change and told her that I looked different. I had told many people, but this would be the first client to know and see me. I waited for her response.

She emailed me a few minutes later and wrote, "I look about the same! See you Tuesday."

Perhaps this would not be as difficult as I thought. I knew everyone might not have such a good attitude or sense of humor, but I had received so much good feedback by now, I wasn't worried any more.

When we met, we hugged, she said I looked great and we sat down to lunch and started talking business.

When we met with a larger group at their offices a few weeks later, I was pleased that I wasn't thinking about my gender, how I looked or what I was wearing. I was concerned with understanding the client's needs and sharing our approach and suggestions for improvement. I was relaxed—as much as possible—before an important client presentation, and was enjoying being myself and working with my client. It was different than in the past, but the same.

By the end of 2008, I had informed every business contact I could think of about my gender change and would share the news with anyone I missed as the opportunities arose. Our business started to improve a little, despite the economy.

I have had some folks not respond to my messages and emails. I've had a few people call, ask for something, and when I tell them why I sound different and why my name is different, they told me that they really didn't need anything after all and would call if things changed. It is surreal and disappointing when this happens, but I just try to find the opportunities in other places. It's tough to lose business and clients simply because of who I am.

All I can do is be myself, take advantage of the new relationships and opportunities, and not worry about what I don't know or the disappointments.

After my first year as a female CEO, we were doing fairly well, given the situation in the rest of the business world. The macro economy was a concern, but at least I was focused on business, not my gender.

By early 2010, we hit another slow point and then sales picked up the second half of the year. The economy seemed to be picking up, but most prospective clients were still reluctant to hire consultants. The Great Recession was a major factor in the malaise. I am not sure how much my gender is a contributor as well. Being transgender and a woman has certainly not helped so far. Time will tell.

To use my Left-Hander in London analogy, by now I was full-time left-handed. I was throwing and writing with ease, and could barely figure out how I ever had tried to be right-handed. I was comfortable in London!

Chapter 13

Business Reactions:

"I was going to…"

I initially told a few people in business about my gender change via phone or in person, but after a while I decided that the preferred method was by letter using email. I felt that a letter or summary email was the best way to explain the change and reiterate that our services and business relationships would not change.

The written story would give the person some time to digest the news before they responded or saw me. Knowing is not the same as seeing, so some "sink-in" time seems to be helpful for people. They could call or email right away or they can take their time. A few people did not respond at all, but I decided not to worry about this. I had to focus on the people who did respond.

One person I had told fairly early in the process was Joe Maxwell. I had known Joe for several years and worked with him when he was consulting. After he left consulting and went back into management, we did some consulting work for him at his new company. We had stayed in contact and were on each other's buddy lists for instant messaging.

When I was ready to change my picture to a female one on the instant message icon, I knew Joe would see the change and wonder what was going on. Following the "knowing before seeing" rule, I emailed him a letter explaining what was happening.

If you close your eyes and picture a New York business executive, Joe's face might come to mind. He has the East Coast accent and mannerisms and definitely has the New York attitude. If you get into a negotiation or disagreement with Joe, your best hope is to tie or break even. It is hard to win those battles.

I had sent the email in the early afternoon, but late in the day, I hadn't heard anything from Joe. I wasn't concerned because I know he is busy.

I left the office a little early to go to the grocery store on the way home from work. While I was in the frozen foods section, my cell phone rang. The voice on the other end said, "This is Joe Maxwell. I called to bust your balls, but I guess you already got rid of those."

I laughed and told him, "No, that hasn't happened yet, but I am getting close! We'll see when I have more money."

He continued, "I just have one thing to say to you." I wondered how he could top what he had already said. He said, "If you think I am going to be nice to you because you are a girl, forget it!"

I replied, "Joe, if you said anything different, I'd be disappointed."

We continued our conversation later when I was in a more opportune place.

The call started with the same good-natured joking that is always common when we get on the phone.

He then said, "You know, I've got about a million questions for you. Are you up to it?"

I said, "Let's see if I can give you some answers."

He hesitated and said, "Okay, but do you mind if I get a little personal?"

I told Joe that I didn't mind and I would try to answer his questions as honestly as possible. From there we spent about an hour discussing various topics from "Are you going to have an operation?" to "Do you pee standing up or sitting down?" He was direct in his questions as usual and we had a good conversation with the usual laughs.

He sounded indignant when he said, "It doesn't matter to me what type of clothing you wear, you are still the same person. I'm from New York."

I responded I didn't think he'd care, but I was sure he'd notice next time we got together and I didn't want to surprise him.

He said that he understood. "When you live around here, you get used to all different types of people. You work with people that look different every day—it just doesn't matter as much."

He paused a moment and said, "Oh, you're from Indiana. How's that going?"

I told him that it was okay and that it wasn't without some challenges, but I would get through those because I'm much happier now. I appreciated his call, his friendship, and was still chuckling after hanging up the phone!

Okay...Now Back To Work!

Most of the responses from people I worked with were brief and positive. Several people called me to ask questions, offer support or discuss the gender change. Many responded by email. Most of the responses followed this pattern:

- Support for me and my family
- Confirming desire to continue to work together
- Congratulations and best wishes for the change and in the future
- Let's get back to work

Most people offered two or three sentences of encouragement, and then returned to discussion about whatever business we needed to discuss. I was happy that I enjoyed so many good relationships and that I know a lot of nice people.

I sent most business associates letters similar to the one I shared in Chapter 12 but in some cases, I added some information about being a minority business to facilitate stimulation of people's thinking about business opportunities:

A few notes about my news - I am certified as the first transgender owned business in the supplier diversity program

of the NGLCC. This group certifies suppliers as Lesbian, Gay, Bisexual or Transgender owned business enterprises. If a company includes LGBT in their diversity program, we would be considered a minority supplier. This opens up many doors for our partners and us. I recently attended the NGLCC annual meeting and met with many major companies that are looking to try to work with me. Here are the links to the information about the program -
http://www.nglcc.org/programs/supplierdiversity/overview
http://www.nglcc.org/programs/supplierdiversity/participation

If you have any clients that have diversity supplier initiatives, or are considering this as a strategy, please let me know so we can team up. Most companies recognize several levels of supply including subbing arrangements.

Please note my new email address.

JJ (formerly Joe) Gufreda

I appreciated the way most people responded—a short personal note of support, and then back to business!

I was happy that as I moved through the year, almost everyone from my business dealings who needed to know, knew. Occasionally, when someone I hadn't communicated with for a while contacted me, I let him or her know about the changes.

I am sure that some people who don't call any more are uncomfortable with my gender change, but there have been so many good reactions too.

In the fall, Jeff Sipes, who had worked with me many times over the years, and his wife Anita invited Jo and I and another couple to a fund raiser at his church. I appreciated the invitation and was comfortable spending time with my friends. We bought several items for charity and had a lot of fun. Afterwards, I thought, "Things are pretty normal. Different, but I was comfortable in the space of the new normal."

My Experiences as a Female in Business

Here is a summary of the relationships I have had as a woman president and CEO:

- Most friends I have made through my professional work seem to appreciate the relationship we had and value my friendship, as I do with them. Good relationships helped ease the difficulty of transition.

- Most of the business people I know are focused on business first, and who you are and how you look second. While I have heard of discrimination that other transgender people have experienced, and suspected it a few times for me, if we continue to do a good job with our consulting practice and add value for the dollar spent by my clients, it seems like the other issues aren't really that important to people.

  Also, most of the business people I know don't want to risk their reputation, bad will or a lawsuit by discriminating against someone or treating someone unfairly. There may be a few nasty ones, but most seem to err on the side of inclusion. It seems to make sense and is good business.

- In spite of the mostly positive responses in business, there have been enough bad experiences that it has hurt our sales significantly. It is hard to quantify if people ignore you.

- Many business people value diversity and are happy to work with the best people they can find.

- I have been thankful that my company and I have a good reputation for being easy to work with and we try to be fair and ethical with everyone we encounter. That reputation, combined with our track record and great consultants, helped us during the transition.

- There is a long way to go to get back to the business levels we had in previous years.

- I really appreciate the many friends, colleagues and clients that have stuck with us.

Chapter 14

Pioneering

One of the problems/opportunities/joys of being transgender is that I have had many chances to educate people on what it means to be transgender, and what it is like for me to be different from other people.

Some people may be uncomfortable around transgenders, gays and lesbians, people of other faiths, people of different ages, different cultures, and people of different races because they may not know anyone similar to those people, or they may not understand the other person. Some people may just be mean-spirited and bigoted, but let's give them the benefit of the doubt and assume they are trying—just ignorant.

Several people have told me that they had never known anyone that was transgender before me. People can be nervous that you'll be "weird," whatever that means. Once they have talked to me in person, they usually loosen up and relax. I can *be* weird, but I don't think I *am* weird (you decide for yourself!).

I know there aren't too many transgender business owners. But there are some, and I am sure there are more than people realize.

As I said, I know of at least two other transgender people that live within a few miles of my house. This is in Greenwood, Indiana—not known as a hotbed of LGBT activity! There aren't too many, but we are here. It is a shame that so many have to hide.

Pioneering Spirit Disappears for Some

One problem with helping people get familiar with transgender people is that many transgenders live a pattern something like this:

- They are silent or hiding as they figure out what is happening with them and then they decide to be out in public, and transition or not, as they are so inclined.
- They are out in the LGBT community and connect with other trans people and often lesbians, gays and bisexuals. They attend meetings, join groups, meet people, attend conferences, etc.
- If they are going to transition, they change their gender and live as their true gender.
- After they are comfortable in their new gender, they disappear into regular society as their new gender. They stop or at least reduce their identification as transgender and simply identify as female or male. When they disappear into general society they usually are not available or interested in helping other transgender people.

Some transgender people may pass perfectly and may take steps to hide or erase evidence that they weren't always what they appear to be. This can be critical if they don't want to risk their job because their employer does not know their background and may not react well if they were to find out. Sometimes, trans women find love and romance with a partner who does not know her background.

This scenario is not good or bad, but it makes pioneering efforts more difficult because people that could advocate may disappear from sight.

Practical Matters

There are issues related to transgender people that aren't relevant to the rest of the population. To be certified as a transgender minority, you have to show you are transgender. Evidence is available: You can show documentation showing you received therapy to help sort out your gender issues; there can be evidence of different treatments—electrology, laser, a myriad of facial treatments, genital reassignment surgery; a doctor's letter regarding hormone therapy and other medical treatments.

The standards vary between organizations and definitions of different categories of people are not consistent. The NGLCC is one of the best at looking at any and all relevant factors and realizing that each person's situation may be different.

I tried to get GEI-certified as a woman-owned business. The state of Indiana requires a birth certificate that says "F" for their certification. I told the person in the appropriate office that the ability for an M to F transgender person to change the gender on their birth certificate varies by state.

In some states (as far as I know, including the state where I was born) they will not change the gender marker for any reason. In other states, it may be as simple as stating that you have changed gender and they will change the documents for you.

Many states require genital reassignment surgery before they will change your documents. Even this can vary. I won't go into detail about what kinds of surgery people have had done, but it should suffice to say that some get everything changed, and some get some parts changed. The issue is that defining someone's gender can be difficult and is not consistent.

It was suggested to me that I could talk to my representatives about changing the law in Indiana. It's possible that eventually the law will be changed, but I am not holding my breath.

I know some good people with Indiana Equality Action, the group that lobbies for LGBT rights in the political arena, and eventually joined their Board of Directors. National organizations also deal with these issues, but it is difficult to change these things. In many states, including my own, we are still fighting for basic rights. Since I was the first person who had called inquiring about this issue, I don't think they will be changing the law for JJ Marie.

I also checked with a national certification body to try to be listed as a woman-owned minority business, but after writing a long business case arguing my position and waiting several months, they aren't going to change their rules. They require an "F" on the birth certificate and as far as I know, I can't change mine.

It seems odd to me that they weren't interested or responsive because I am transgender. I expected them to be more sensitive to gender discrimination.

I also have a real concern that if I change my driver's license and other documents to read "F" I might jeopardize my marriage. There are a number of people that want to "protect marriage" by legally defining it as only between a man and a woman. How another type of marriage endangers heterosexual marriages is beyond me, but I don't want Christian Moralists, conservative politicians and the Religious Right trying to invalidate my marriage of over 33 years.

There aren't enough transgender people to have a loud voice for change. The good news is that other minority groups, especially the gay and lesbian groups, help us and support our causes. Eventually these things will change.

Personal, if Reluctant, Pioneering

For me, I am trying to help where I can. If I can lead the way on issues related to my business, it will be easier for others. It is tough accepting discrimination, especially since it is a fairly new phenomenon for me. Still, you have to choose your fights, and some problems won't be solved quickly.

GEI was the first LGBT certified firm in Indiana. There are more in Indiana now, and the number is growing. I work on issues related to transgender-owned firms. I recently became a

Board Member and then President of the local Indy Rainbow Chamber of Commerce.

If I can help these inclusive and supportive groups and make it easier for others, that is a good thing, right? There are many advocates and allied supporters for LGBT people, and there should be. ENDA (Employment Non Discrimination Act) has been in the works for years, and groups trying to help with its passage abound. They keep trying. We have made some progress working with individual counties and cities in Indiana.

When I first heard of the effort, I tried to explain it to Jo. I told her that it was to try to stop people from being fired for their sexual orientation or gender identity.

She was shocked and asked, "You mean it is legal for companies to fire someone for that?"

I replied that unfortunately, it was in many places and it has been difficult to change that. Indiana is known as an "at will" state, which means an employer can pretty much fire anyone for any (or no) reason.

I didn't have the desire to be an advocate, spokesperson or pioneer. I have to stay focused on my family and my company. However, things need to be done, and if I can help, I do. We're all in this together. Any progress one makes can help everyone.

I guess if I write a book called *Left-Hander in London: A Field Guide to Transgenders, Lesbians, Gays and Bisexuals - In the Family, On the Job and In the Pew,* and I'm on the board of Indiana Equality, and I'm making presentations about my book, and helping INTRAA, and I'm president of Indy Rainbow Chamber of Commerce, then maybe I *am* a pioneer.

Muddying the Midwestern Waters – Warning: Politicians' Heads May Explode

I can also put a messy spin on issues that some people thought were black and white. I went to the Indiana Statehouse to talk to my representatives about the "Marriage Protection Amendment." We call it the "Marriage Discrimination Amendment."

I told them that I have been married to the same person for over 33 years, and we have stuck together through thick and thin, raising three children, and going through a gender change. If they pass this amendment, one of the provisions being kicked around is that it nullifies same-sex marriages that happened out of state. That would mean that our lifetime commitment of marriage could be void (we were married in Ohio when I was a guy).

I said that I didn't think supporting family values should mess up my family.

One representative said that he believed that a marriage is between a man and a woman.

I said, "Okay if you believe that, but is it right to try to end a 30 year marriage in support of family values?"

I don't think that they knew how to respond. Two of my duly elected officials said, "I have to go," and turned and walked away.

One of the equality advocates suggested that there are a few of our state representatives whose heads would explode if they met me!

I told him that I certainly didn't want that, but if I did meet them, we should get a few pictures of it!

Slow, But Some Progress

There is a long way to go, but from the positive viewpoint:

- A majority of business people seem not to care about your gender, sexuality, race, or anything else. If you are good and do good work, they will work with you.
- Discrimination is bad for business. Who wants to have a reputation as a bigoted, non-inclusive business or state?

- There are organized groups and people available for support. For me, the existence of the NGLCC was enough to feel confident enough to start my transition.
- There are many talented and impressive LGBT people in all walks of life. If you want the best people, look for the best people—wherever you can find them.

Nearing the Tipping Point

One way to look at the inclusion of LGBT people in all facets of life is to compare it with the trend towards "business casual."

Years ago, early in my career, the norm for many businesses was for people to wear traditional attire—suits and ties for men and suits or classically-styled clothes for women. Some companies started to go casual on Fridays, and then during the week. Soon the entire company was casual all the time. When a few influential companies made business casual mandatory for their people, they pushed the movement over the tipping point.

In some industries, it was understood that business casual was the acceptable way to dress. Some accepted only when forced. At one client, many of the men wore suits and kept their jackets on all day, but did not wear a tie. Others were happy with the change. At GEI, we usually are in a similar style or a little dressier than the average when we meet a client.

I believe that we are approaching a similar tipping point for acceptance and support of LGBT people in companies. Several of the Fortune 500 companies already have some sort of LGBT supportive initiative for their employees and suppliers. The Human Rights Campaign (HRC) has for nine years published their Corporate Equality Index of the major U.S. businesses that are supportive of their LGBT employees. The numbers of supportive corporations increase each year.

When those companies become the majority and the support crosses that tipping point, being unsupportive of LGBT people will become unpopular and a negative mark on the company. They may do it for the right reasons, or to not look bad, but for whatever reason, most companies will need to be on the bandwagon.

We just need to hang on, keep pushing and let it happen. And to the people still hiding or experiencing discrimination—I hope the day comes soon enough so you can enjoy it.

Chapter 15

Moving Down the (Sometimes Bumpy) Road

A Different Point of View

The first day I consider myself to be out in society as a female was December 25, 2007. Our kids bought tickets for the musical *Wicked* in Chicago for Jo and me and booked a night in a hotel for us as a Christmas gift. We looked forward to a short weekend vacation after Christmas, but I also was excited because this would be one of my first opportunities to go to a nice show as JJ. I packed a pretty dress and heels and we headed to Chicago.

In addition to a very pleasant weekend with Jo, I appreciated being in public as myself. I enjoyed the trip, spending time together, going out to eat, walking (even though it was freezing) to the show. *Wicked* was terrific.

I had not heard much about the show – only that it was good. The actors were talented, the singing great and the show was very well done. I was surprised about how the story unfolded.

Wicked is the story of the Wizard of Oz, but from the perspective of the Wicked Witch. It was very interesting to see how different the story and perceptions could be when approached from another direction. I won't give many details – you should see it, but as an example, consider how tough it would be to grow up if you had green skin like the "Wicked Witch." That could be a source of the other kids making fun of her at school!

The play sure gave me a different take on the story! As we walked back to the hotel, I thought about the many things that might be different if viewed from alternate perspectives.

The experience and the story from the musical would be a good introduction to how my life would be as I developed into a woman. I see things differently than I did before my transition. Many people that I know and society in general see me much differently than before. Some see me differently because I am a woman, others because I used to be a guy.

Increasing Comfort Zones

I mentioned previously that I was on a new road and my family and friends were on the same road, but probably traveling at a different (slower) speed. As time goes by, our speeds are coming together and soon, I hope, we can be traveling at the same rate. We have progressed to the "new normal" where I am female and my gender is not an issue.

This situation is highly relative depending on who is involved. My family and friends have made great strides with me. Some are very comfortable, but others still struggle. I have friends that treat me like I was always female, and others that still use male pronouns when they talk with me. It grates on my psyche, but I try to go with the flow – if it's an accident.

The majority of people I am acquainted with either know me as female or realize that I am a transgender woman. I have progressed to where I expect respect whether the person accepts me or not. As someone spends time with the new me, they usually get more comfortable if they weren't already.

I moved from terror that someone would discover that I *was* a guy, to concern that they might realize I had *been* a guy, to rarely thinking about it at all. *I live my life as a woman.*

Construction Zones in My Future?

I had previously hoped that I could get facial feminization surgery to make a few features more feminine, but after years of being a full-time female, I can survive without it. I am accepted as a woman, so looking prettier would be nice, but is not necessary.

I have not had the genital reassignment surgery (GRS). Surgery is expensive and business is tough (to say the least).

I need to be on a better financial footing to spend that kind of money on anything. Also, the surgery is *surgery*. Any procedure has risks, and I would need to take time off work for a hospital stay and recovery. It's a big decision and until the financial situation is better for the family, I can't proceed with the final physical changes.

I know other transgender people who prioritized surgery much higher than I do. Some felt ready for surgery as soon as they realized (admitted) that they were transgender. Others lost everything (financially) in order to get the money for surgical changes. Some transgenders have told me that they consider their birthday to be the day of their genital-reassignment surgery.

It is not as important to me, especially since I have promised myself and my family that I won't consider it until we are in better financial shape. If consulting revenues improve, I find a new career, or I make a few million dollars selling books, maybe.

Curiosity

One interesting facet of being transgender is that people might ask questions that can be rude, inappropriate or offensive more often than they might with non-transgender people. I try to not take offense and consider that people are curious about aspects of gender, especially if they are not familiar with transgender people.

If someone has a question, I tell him or her, "You can ask me anything, but I may not answer every question you have."

For example, it would be rare for a stranger that knows little about a woman to ask her, "Do you have a penis or a vagina?" It is rude to ask in that way to a transgender person as well. A better way to say it might be: "Have you had reassignment surgery?" I can understand why someone would be curious to know.

Que Sera, Sera

Practically, I hope I can get GRS as soon as feasible and if I am lucky enough to have a successful procedure, based on previous experience, I expect that I would be more satisfied than I had anticipated. Each treatment or step along the way so far was better than I expected, and I don't anticipate this major step being any different.

I consider myself a female. Yes, I am transgender, but that is not my identity. I had to focus so much time and energy on my gender change that being transgender consumed me. After some time, things have settled down. I just live my life as the person that I am.

Legal Considerations

There are some other practical and legal concerns. I live in Indiana. Every year conservative "family-oriented" groups push for introduction of legislation for a constitutional amendment outlawing same-sex marriage. If this becomes part of the state constitution and includes a provision annulling out-of-state same-sex marriages for persons living in Indiana, it could potentially invalidate my marriage.

After, all, depending on the law in each state, most of the time a person who has had permanent genital altering surgery is considered the new gender. It is a grey area.

After surgery, if I am "legally" (whatever that means) a woman, could they stop recognizing my marriage of over 33 years since it is now between two women? After all, religious zealots, Christian Moralists and many churches may consider it a same-sex marriage.

I shouldn't have to fight for the basic right to stay married to a person who also wants to *stay married* to me. It is increasingly frustrating because many of the groups that push for these laws say they are doing it to "protect families." How does hurting my family protect other families? I have become more active as an advocate for equal rights. I said that I did not want to do this, but it seems necessary. Fighting for basic rights in America seems stupid, to me at least, but it is what it is. I must consider these realities when I make the final decision for surgery.

The Church, Christian Moralists and I Don't Seem to Be on the Same Road

I wrote with much frustration in Chapters Seven and Eight about the problems I have encountered with Christian Moralists and the Catholic Church. The more I learn about the Church's pronouncements and observe Christian Moralists, the more resigned I have become to the reality that these situations won't change any time soon.

I try to check myself because I don't want to jump to conclusions. I caught myself judging or at least expecting people to be prejudiced if they were what a friend called "Pious and Overly Devout" (PODs). It still seems odd that most of the people who have given me trouble have been the most vocal about being religious Christians. The Catholic Church leadership stubbornly and fervently holds on to the old patriarchal ways. I still struggle when people try to hurt me or anyone else in the name of God or religion. I am careful to protect myself, and try to not be judgmental. It's a great effort some times.

It seems that much of it comes down to the church being self serving rather than serving others. If the church doesn't want me around, is that what God wants, or is it that they don't want another potential problem at the same time they are being exposed for covering up child abuse and being hypocritical? If they attack gay marriage is that because it really is a sin, or because there are a lot of gay priests and they don't want people to know? I don't have anything against gay priests, but suspect that the church leaders don't want us to know about them.

When people have said that they don't agree with my "choices" two thoughts come to mind. First, what business is it of another person what my choices may be? Second, for many transgender as well as other LGB people, the choice is become your true self or eventually commit suicide. If they don't like my choices, would they have preferred that I commit suicide?

I wonder how people can judge others and go so far as to hurt them in the process. If God appeared to you and asked you to help judge someone, would you really vote hell rather than heaven? I certainly would not want to be responsible for sending someone to hell, regardless of whether I think they are sinning or how many bad things they have done in their lives. I met a gay man that was "consigned to the devil" by his church. I wonder who gave them this power, but also why they would do something like that if they had the chance. I was the kind of coach that didn't want to cut anyone. I don't want to think that someone would end up in hell because of me!

Buy me a sandwich

I tried to approach this logically: Many people honestly believe that others (never themselves) are going to hell for some sin or transgression. They may want to point out that not only will the other person be spending eternity suffering in hell, but they will be *aware* of the eternal suffering.

I have two reactions to this. First, I have to give them some credit that they are smart enough to figure this out. It took me fifty years to figure out that I was transgender and needed to transition to female. I must not be that sharp. These people apparently not only know how they are doing, but they can also figure out if someone else is sinning. They must be a lot smarter than me.

Secondly, if I am going to hell (and they are sure I am going), I ask how long they think I will be suffering. Eternity is a long time, as I understand it. A hundred trillion years would only be a drop in the eternity bucket, but let's use that as an example. If I am going to be consciously burning and suffering for a hundred trillion years for what I did during my lifetime (I think they think it's mostly for being transgender) then *why be mean to me now?* How many years do I have left on the earth? Fifty at the most. Why not treat me nice now since I have a hundred trillion years to suffer afterwards? Do something nice for me like *buy me a sandwich.* That's the least you can do!

Big Deal, I'm a Chick Now

I look into the future and consider what life holds for me. Much of the "novelty" of transitioning to female is gone. I enjoy being a woman; I like being myself. I finally feel like I am in synch with the universe. I feel that I am still improving as a woman to become all that I can be, but I am not dissatisfied with where I am now.

Even though I had so many years that I tried to live as a male, my male memories are fading. I have a difficult time remembering how I felt when I was a guy. I remember people and events, but how I was as a male is hard to recall and visualize. My occasional sense of disbelief that I had transitioned to female is being replaced with difficulty remembering that I had ever been a guy. That seems so long ago, even though it has only been a few years.

I am female, but also transgender. I don't want to disappear into society and hide my past. The past *did* happen. I don't want to hide from the past any more than I would like to go back to hiding and suppressing my real identity. I live in the present, but embrace my past.

Wardrobe Additions

One fantasy/wish that many closeted transgender girls

have is going shopping and getting clothes with a genetic girl. Recently, a girlfriend of mine told me that she had gone through her closet and was getting rid of things she no longer wears. She asked me if I wanted to look through the boxes.

I appreciated that she thought of me, and was excited about the prospect of some new clothes, especially since we have similar taste and like the same styles. I was excited to add to my wardrobe. Lots of girls like to get more clothes as I do, but I also like to get new clothes because most of my wardrobe is relatively new. I don't have that favorite skirt from ten years ago like some women. I didn't have any skirts ten years ago! I appreciated the new clothes and her thoughtfulness. The novelty of it was not there.

They're Against Us?

I am always interested to learn why people are in fear of or discriminate against LGBT people. I think I am pretty normal.

I went to the NGLCC national dinner in Washington in late 2009. The night before the dinner, they had a reception at the Rayburn House Office Building. The cab dropped me off; I found the room, grabbed a glass of wine and started chatting with a friend.

She asked, "Did you see the protestors when you came in?"

I answered, "What protestors? I didn't see anyone."

She responded that there were Tea Party protestors at the main entrance. Apparently the cab driver had dropped me off in the back.

I asked, "What are they protesting?"

She looked at me, paused for a few seconds, and said, "Us."

I asked, "Why would anyone be protesting us?"

She told me that LGBT meetings occasionally draw "conservative" protestors.

It did not make much sense to me that anyone would be protesting this meeting. It was just a reception for a bunch of business people and a few elected officials and staff. Sure, many were gay or lesbian, but so what?

I exclaimed, "I want to go out and talk with them. I want to get an understanding of why they would be protesting us and what they want. I am going out there to see who they are."

She told me that it probably wasn't a good idea to do that and finally talked me out of it. I didn't want to pick a fight, just to try to understand why someone would picket us—why they would picket *me*!

Too Normal for Comfort With Stardom

Nick Turner is a young man who recently graduated from Ball State University in Indiana. He met me at an Indiana Equality lobby day session at the Indiana State Capitol at the suggestion of a mutual friend. He was a photojournalism student and wanted me to be the subject of his senior capstone project.

I like to help students when I get the opportunity, but asked him, "Why would you want to do a story on *me*?"

He told me that it would be interesting to talk with my family and me and take some photos for his project.

I told him that I'd be glad to help, but thought that I might be a boring subject. He was professional and met Jo and I several times for taped interviews and photo sessions.

It feels weird to have a photographer take pictures of me while I am walking the dog or playing the piano. I told Jo and Nick that I didn't see how celebrities ever get used to it.

If you're interested, here is how to access the video: http://nicholasturnerphoto.com/stories/the-walls-we-build

Reluctant Civil Rights Activist

I feel the need to help others as they cope with dealing with friends and loved ones that are LGBT and help LGBT people become all they can be. We have a long road ahead for LGBT people to have the same civil rights as everyone else—in the US as well as around the world. We can move in a positive direction by contributing to society and being "out there."

I hope that each generation of LGBT people will be helped by the experiences of the people that came before. It should not be as difficult a life simply being yourself as it has been for many of the people I know.

Parallels in the Boxing World

I tape all the boxing programs on TV that I can find. It is common for a boxing show to begin with a story about a boxer's background, especially if he had a difficult childhood, grew up poor and homeless, turned his life around, etc. I saw a program about two brothers that have become world-class professional fighters. They grew up in poverty, slept in the bus station, ate food they found, and through boxing, became successful in boxing and in life. It is a great story and helps people identify with the struggles of the athletes.

I would like to see a time where the majority in our society empathizes with LGBT people in a similar way. Why shouldn't they? Each LGBT person feels different from others. They have to figure out why they feel different, then decide what to do about it, and then risk everything when they transition or "come out." Does our society show concern for their struggle and journey like we do for an athlete who pulls him or herself out of poverty? Hopefully hearing my story and learning about other LGBT people – your child, your relative, your friend, your work associate, your spouse…will help all of us understand each other better.

Meet JJ: Weird, but Not Weird

In many cases, I am the first transgender person people have met. I hope it is easier for both parties when they meet the next transgender person. Our progress is linked to LGBs as well; if one group gains, we all benefit. I may be weird, but not because of my gender. I think it is my sense of humor.

Humor's a Great Shield

I am thankful that I have a good sense of humor, which has improved as I moved through my transition. It's helpful to have fun and greet life's situations with a smile if you can. A good sense of humor is necessary to counteract any negative and bigoted people that I encounter at one time or another.

Deliberate Consciousness In My Relationships

One of the blessings of being transgender is that the decision to transition or, to come out in the case of lesbians, gays and bisexuals, causes a conscious pause in each relationship we have. It is easy to live your life in the world with friends, acquaintances and loved ones and rarely stop to consider how you really feel about each person.

When I considered telling someone with whom I have had a relationship—for a month, a year, or my lifetime— that I am transgender, I was forced to consider my relationship with that person, whether I wanted to tell him or her, and how to tell them so our relationship would continue and thrive.

In turn, he or she must consider how to interact with me and what they will do at that decision point where they decide whether to continue on the road with me. Sadly, some have decided that they don't want me in their lives. Fortunately, almost everyone in my inner circles and many of my other friends, colleagues, clients and acquaintances are happy to journey with me.

A Road Well Traveled – and With Companions!

Becoming my true self has been an interesting journey. I have experienced profound disappointment because of lost friendships, rejection and discrimination. I have observed and experienced the pain inflicted on so many LGBT people.

I feel so much better about myself and I'm thankful that I finally not only figured out that I was "left-handed" but I could live a better life because of my trip to London – living, working and worshipping as a Londoner and a translator. I occasionally look back at all the hiding, suppressing, and neurotic behavior I have had. No more hiding in the closet (literally), no more dressing and walking around at night when no one is around, no more sneaking into the ladies department to pretend I was buying a present, but in fact was longing to buy those clothes for myself.

I also have met many great people and learned so much. If a result of this book is that it only makes it easier or better for just one LGBT person, one high school kid that figured out that he is gay, one woman that has been hiding her attraction to other women for her entire life, or one transgender person longing to change to their true gender, then that is pretty good! Further, if by reading this book and considering how they want to treat others, a shocked mother or father, surprised sibling, confused work colleague or struggling long-time friend has a better time understanding their friend or loved one, and can actually *enjoy* the person more now that they are more honest and whole, then we are making real progress!

I am not alone being left-handed. Despite the occasional rain, London is a great place to be!

Pray for Peace.

Summary

Left-Hander in London:
A Field Guide to Transgenders, Lesbians, Gays and Bisexuals
In the Family, On the Job and In the Pew
By JJ Marie Gufreda

You Can Just Be Yourself

Left-Hander in London is intended to help lesbian, gay, bisexual and transgender (LGBT) people that want to "come out" or, in the case of some transgender people, transition. It discusses relationships and describes how a person can be successful in the journey, despite the inevitable difficulties. Many gay, lesbian, bi and transgender stories are focused on the losses incurred, discrimination faced and a myriad of problems unsolved. While I have undergone my share of difficulties, I want to share that a person can become their true self and not lose everything and everyone. In fact, the journey can be rewarding and fun, especially if you have a positive attitude and a good sense of humor.

It took me many years to discover and understand my true self. I have enjoyed a successful business career, which includes manufacturing industry management and engineering positions, consulting and college teaching positions. A published author, I have contributed to three business books and written several magazine articles. My wife and I have been married for over 33 years, and we have three grown children. I always knew that my gender identity did not match that of everyone else I knew.

After hiding and suppressing my real identity, I worked very hard to come up with the best transition plan for my family, those close to me and myself. I know of many LGBT people that are hiding or are outcasts. I was determined that this would not happen to me and that I would keep my relationships with the people most important to me. This journey taught me valuable lessons about myself and my relationships with others. These lessons can benefit other people, if they apply some of what I have learned to their lives and relationships.

Help for Your Circles – A Guide for Family and Friends

According to some estimates, between 5% and 10% of the US population is LGBT, meaning there may be as many as 30 million people personally interested in *Left-Hander in London*. The book is also intended to help friends, colleagues and families of LGBT people. Many people are shocked to hear that someone close to them is sharing their true gender identity or sexual orientation (or both); they ask, "What can I read to help me process this news about (their relative or friend)? How do I react to this?" *Left-Hander in London* discusses how I told people and shares many of the loving, questioning and funny reactions I received. I also discuss those who did not respond positively—or at all.

Pioneering Translator

Since I am transgender, I can identify with and empathize with gays, straights, lesbians, married people, minorities, parents, men, and women. I have been a member of many of society's majority groups as well as several minority groups. Know the old saying about having to walk a mile in someone's shoes before you can understand them? I have definitely done this in a way that most people have not. My unique perspective helps me "translate" between the different groups, build bridges and aid in better understanding and communication.

I am a transgender business owner. During my transition, I had a hard time finding businesspeople like me to give me advice or help me learn. I found that to be successful, I needed to be a pioneer. In many cases, I was the first transgender person that a business associate ever met. My company was the first transgender-owned business certified as a minority business by the National Gay & Lesbian Chamber of Commerce (NGLCC), and we are trying to make other LGBT people's journey easier for them. *Left-Hander in London* gives transgender businesspeople some of the insights that I wanted during my transition. If I can clear the way for others while I am helping my own business, we have accomplished good things for everyone.

Religion, Spirituality, People and God – Part of the Journey

Left-Hander in London includes a discussion of spirituality and my experiences with the Catholic Church. Many in organized religion shun and reject LGBT people rather than showing the love to be expected from a religious group. It is probably more correct to say they attack the gays and are afraid of transgender people because they really don't understand us. When I am with a group of transgender people, it is common (unbelievable to me, but common) to hear someone say, "My parents won't talk to me any more and have rejected me from the family. You have to understand: they are very religious." The rest of the group groans with an understanding sigh and shows their sympathy. Shouldn't the reaction be the exact opposite? Shouldn't a religious family embrace their own flesh and blood and help them with their struggles? My thoughts on my experience and the Church should make some thought provoking reading for people of any and all faiths and beliefs.

Chapter Synopses

Introduction

Included is basic information about me—I have a family, business and a sense of humor. I am spiritual and religious and had been active in the Church. I discuss what I hope the reader will gain from reading *Left-Hander in London* and why it is targeted to LGBT people and their friends, business associates and family.

Chapter 1: Left-Hander

My journey of discovery is similar to the experience that many left-handed people undergo. Depending on when and where they grew up, they may have had to hide or suppress their natural condition because it was inconvenient or even perceived as evil. I was surprised to find out that there were other transgender people like me.

Chapter 2: My Personal Odyssey—Uncovering the Real Me

I spent many years struggling with my gender identity, attempting to discern why I felt different or "weird" as a male. The sheer ordinariness of my external life and the anxiety caused by trying to maintain my "man mask" led me to realize something *had* to change. In my naiveté, I thought becoming my true self was impossible, and for years I lived accordingly – if fairly miserably.

Chapter 3: In London

When I figured out that I was transgender and that other people were too, I had to decide what to do. It wasn't as simple as wishing you would become a girl when you wake up in the morning, and it happens. But I learned that it is possible to change into a female. It is as "simple" as getting therapy (I have used 5 therapists so far), laser and electrolysis treatments, coloring your hair, taking hormones, telling everyone you know that you are changing genders, getting a new wardrobe, changing your name and, if you have the money, getting facial and genital reassignment surgery. It is a long and difficult process, but *it is possible.* I previously never considered that any of this was feasible until I met other transgender people and researched to get more information. I use an analogy of traveling to London to illustrate the journey: If you've never been there, you might doubt that it's real. But once you see and experience it, you realize that it has been there all along.

Chapter 4: Transition and Circles—Setting Priorities and Boarding the Plane for London

One of the most important parts of my transition was figuring how to tell people what was happening. I wanted to do it in a way that would maximize my chances of a successful outcome while showing empathy and concern for everyone I knew. I put together a plan based on circles. The most important people were in the inside circle, and as you moved to circles further out, the people were less important. More accurately, if their reactions were not supportive, it would not be as bad a loss as if someone in my inner circles objected to my change and ended our relationship. I was determined not to end my marriage or lose my family. I also set up some rules about how to tell people. One was "telling before seeing" which would reduce the shock to my friends and family. I did not want to show up in a dress and say, "Guess what?"

Chapter 5: More in the Outer Circles

I share how I told my family and our friends. I learned much about myself and about how people perceived me. I told a friend about my gender change early in the sharing process, and after I finished my prepared "speech," she said, "Where is the punchline?" She thought I was kidding. I had to convince her that I was serious and re-tell the entire story now that she believed me. I also found that many people were nervous about "seeing" me for the first time. If they had no relevant experience or frame of reference, it might take some time for them to get comfortable with JJ.

Chapter 6: Reactions—"How Ya Doin'?"

I received a lot of good responses from friends and family. How people reacted and what they said meant so much to me. I hope that others can learn from my experience so they can respond in a caring and loving way, regardless of what they learn about a loved one or friend. I noticed that my supportive friends and family reacted with empathy, friendship and love in addition to a myriad of questions and other responses to the news that I am transgender.

Chapter 7: In or Out—The Creeping Darkness of Christian Moralism

I noticed a profound difference in some people's reactions to me. Most showed me love, empathy and concern and then told me how they felt about my transition. The outpouring of human love and concern for my family and me touched me. I refer to many in the other group as Christian Moralists. They reacted first with judgment and then with an argument about how I was sinning—and cited chapter and verse (literally) confirming their position in the Rule Book, i.e., the Bible. (Actually, the Bible never mentions anything about transgender people.) When one person took the time to look up all the Biblical passages that he thought would condemn me and wrote me a letter whose only nod to compassion was, "Dear Joe, (my male name) Glad to hear your family is doing well… you are living in sin," I did not feel any friendship or love at all. The letter only displayed judgment and justification for his position. This judgmental attitude is very dangerous for our society, because much of the negative behavior is justified in the name of religion. This chapter will likely invoke controversy, but I hope that through my experiences, others may learn to better tolerate people that may be different from them.

Chapter 8: Bad News and Good News—The Church, Morality and Spirituality

Jesus said there is one sin that can't be forgiven. He meant "sins against the Holy Spirit," but many people in our society are sure he was talking about homosexuality, abortion, gay marriage or voting for a pro-choice candidate. The Catholic Church—at least my pastor and the Vicar Judicial—rejected me and refused to answer any of my questions. Since then, I have become aware of many illogical (at least to me) and hurtful actions by the Church against divorced people, LGBT people, victims abused by priests and others. I reflect on a secret document that gives the Catholic Church's position on transgender people. The author seems to have never met, talked to or made an effort to understand a transgender person; the sole purpose of this hurtful, self-serving article was to protect the Church.

The hierarchy and a group of zealots (considered good Catholics) are becoming more conservative, while anyone different is shunned, bruised and rejected. I encounter more and more of these bruised people as I move along my journey. They are searching for the Divine, but are shunned rather than aided by the Church.

Chapter 9: Junk that JJ Learned

This chapter covers exciting changes I experienced, people I met, and random things I learned.

- Hormones: JJ Unleashed
- Adapting My Voice to Match My Gender
- Crying Takes on a Whole New Importance
- The New Me Can Rise to the Top
- Temper Recedes and Humor Bubbles Up
- Verifications – Proving To Myself London's the Place for Me
- Things People Would Rather Not Hear – Electrology, Boobs and the Like
- Names, Titles, Pronouns – Please Respect Me
- Dreams – Self Expression in My Sleep
- Two Directions on the Same Road – F to M and M to F and Anyone in the Middle

I started to attend meetings with other transgender people, and I met a number of Female to Male (F to M) transgender people. I had never met an F to M before and was curious to learn more about them. One of the guys excitedly told how he had gotten his first tie, how his parents helped him select a name, and how he was so pumped up because his testosterone treatments caused hair to grow everywhere and that the hair on his head was starting to fall out. I thought to myself, "What are you thinking? Are you crazy? Why would you want all that body hair? Wearing a tie is like torture!" And then I quickly thought, "How can I even think that? I am on the same road as him, but we are going in opposite directions." I realized how difficult it could be to understand another person, even if you're trying to empathize and be a friend. That is why it is hard for some people to understand me. A less serious example of what I learned after 50 years as a male: When I began taking hormones, I started to snort when I laugh.

Chapter 10 "Ick" The Definitive Answers to Questions on the Morality of Being Transgender, Gay, Bi or Lesbian

Our society expends a tremendous amount of energy criticizing, judging and condemning LGBT people—especially gays and lesbians. Based on history, there have always been LGBT people. The ones that I know seem pretty nice! They also did not "choose" to be gay or were not "won over" in a recruiting push (as some people believe). If God creates a certain number of gay people (estimated to be 5 to 10% of the population), maybe it would be better if we accepted them rather than trying to change their natural state and condemning them! The Catholic Church teaches that you should not have premarital sex and that people of the same sex can't get married. Extending that logic, gays and lesbians are never "allowed" to have sex. That seems pretty difficult and harsh! Perhaps we can put more energy in loving and helping LGBT people and less in judging and condemning them.

Chapter 11: I am a Translator: Another Insiders' Report—Discrimination, Women, Straights and Gays

I reflect on my unique position and experience with many of both the majority and the minority groups. I have been male and female, and associated with gay and straight groups. I *have* walked in another person's shoes. It's more difficult to do in heels, but if they fit well, I can do it—no problem!

Chapter 12: A Business Trip to London—Transition in Business

I found a number of LGBT people that came out or transitioned on the job. Some had very high executive positions; some did not. Some told their employer and were helped and supported. Others were demoted or fired. Many companies have formal policies that support the inclusion of LGBT people. Transgender people that own their businesses are harder to find. As a transgender business owner, I can't just tell my boss and the HR department—I have to tell associates, partners, current clients, former clients, consultants and other business contacts. I had to announce my gender change many times. This chapter also describes how the National Gay & Lesbian Chamber of Commerce (NGLCC) was very helpful and supportive and how I am running my business as a businesswoman.

Chapter 13: Business Reactions—"I was going to…"

In this chapter I describe reactions from business associates. The responses have been overwhelmingly supportive. Many have also been hysterically funny. The typical reaction from a business associate is something like this: "Wow, thanks for sharing the news. That must have been hard on you and your family and I am glad for you that you are becoming your true self. When are you going to send me that proposal?" Very friendly and encouraging - then back to business!

Chapter 14: Pioneering

In many cases I encountered situations where I was one of the early pioneers, or where I was the first in breaking new ground. Many of the people I encounter have never met or known a transgender person; so I can help them learn more about diversity and help them understand what it is like to change gender. Our business was the first transgender owned business certified as a minority owned business and I am happy to try to change things for the better. It helps me as well as making the journey for people that come after me easier and smoother.

Chapter 15: Moving Down The Road

Early in my transition, I described that I was on the road and that my family and friends were on the same road with me, but traveling at a slower speed. As time has gone on, I have slowed down. Transitioning affects many aspects of my life and held much of my focus during those nervous, critical early steps. I am comfortable being female and no longer focus on being transgender. I learned from my experiences and enjoy being JJ. I am not alone being left-handed. Despite the occasional rain, London is a great place to be!

Index of Useful Sections:

Questions Section

Questions to Ponder:

This is, of course, not a comprehensive list of everything under the sun you may be wondering about LGBT matters, but at least it should give you some food for thought in your search for a mental footing -- particularly concerning someone who is transgender making the transition from one gender to another. As I've frequently told people, you can ask anything you like, I just may not answer everything you want to know. In that spirit I am providing my answers on those questions I've been asked. The second list of questions is more to stimulate your own thought processes.

In order for this to be a good guide, you need to be able to take something from the book that you can use in your life, your world. As I related in chapter 6 about my friend Dan, if I had had the chance to reflect on this matter beforehand, I would have reacted much differently. If you can think about these things in advance, you won't be as surprised and will react better. Here are many of the questions you may have either for someone who is coming out or transitioning, *or* for yourself *concerning* your attitudes, internal or external reactions to such news.

****

Things Folks Have Asked JJ:

Q: What is the difference between being transgender and gay? Are transgender people gay?

A: Transgender is more about gender identification. Gay is related to sexual attraction – attraction to the same gender rather than the opposite gender.

Q: What did your kids say? How do they feel about Dad being a woman?

A: Their responses varied from being glad that I was not so stressed anymore, to sadness at the loss of their father. It has been a difficult journey, but they have been great.

Q: How do people react to you?

A: Some of my old friends and contacts won't talk to me. Many treat me like any other woman (this has its pros and cons!) People I encounter in public and people I meet treat me as a woman. I don't tell people I am transgender unless it is relevant.

Q: Is your wife a lesbian? Are you a lesbian?

A: No. Probably not. I am still married to a woman. I dance with guys. What does that make me? It is confusing, so I don't care.

Q: Do you think LGBT people will ever be "accepted" by churches and organized religions?

A: Not in this lifetime, but if we can move it in the right direction, I am glad to help. Remember that (if you believe in God) God made all of the people, so I think He or She loves us all. I sometimes wonder if Jesus himself appeared and asked some PODs (outwardly religious) people to back off from criticizing LGBT people because he didn't like it, I think some might dismiss him as wrong and keep doing it! Misguided beliefs based on religion are almost impossible to change.

Q: Does God think you (or any gay or lesbian) are sinning? Are you risking damnation?

A: He/She hasn't said anything to me and I have no guilt for being who I am. If God damns me to hell, I'd at least like to ask what the heck he/she was thinking when I was made this way!

Q; Is being LGBT a choice?
A: Is having blue eyes or being right- or left-handed a choice? I am not smart enough to choose to be this way. For me and many others, the choice is suicide or become true to yourself.

Q: Is it possible to be gay or transgender and not "act" on it?
A: If you can do it, you are stronger than me. I held it for a long time. I can't do it any more. It makes me physically sick. And by the way, for those people that say that they choose to be straight and not gay: If you wake up in the morning and have to make a conscious choice to not be gay — you are probably gay! Most heterosexual people I know don't make decisions about sexual attraction.

Q: Do you think your upbringing contributed to being transgender?
A: Possibly. There are many theories. I think you are susceptible because of your makeup. My friend Chloe has a scientific explanation of why she is trans. I don't. If they figure it out, fine. I don't care if I know or not. If a scientist could explain (and they probably can) why someone is left-handed, does it really matter?

Q: Why do you think being left-handed is similar to being LGBT? I am left-handed. Are you saying that I am transgender?
A: Yes, you are transgender! No, seriously, I just think it is similar because left-handers have been persecuted for being how they were born as are some LGBT people. By the way, I am right-handed.

****

Things You May Want To Ask
(Of Yourself or Another Regarding Someone Who Is LGBT)

Editor's Note: There are no answers provided to these open-ended questions. They are for stimulation of thought concerning these matters. Hopefully you will find things within this book that will help you formulate answers of your own.

Q: How do I treat people that I perceive as gay or transgender? How would I like to treat them?

Q: How do I know that people are gay or transgender?

Q: Do I know any same sex couples? How is my relationship with them? How would I react if I found that a friend, family member or colleague is in a same sex relationship?

Q: Do I judge the morality of LGBT people? Why? Is that my right or responsibility?

Q: Do I think being LGBT is a choice? If I believe it is or isn't, how does that affect my relationship with LGBT people?

Q: How do my religious beliefs affect my relationships with LGBT people? What is the basis of my beliefs?

Q: What are my views on the Nature vs. Nurture debate? Does it matter why a person is transgender, gay, or left-handed?

Q: Are you left-handed? Are you in a minority? Are you disabled? Have you felt different from others?

Q: How do you compare the journey of an LGBT person against your personal journey? How about comparing with the journey of a poor or disadvantaged person?

Q: Do you know anyone that has struggled or is struggling with his or her sexual attraction or gender identity? Have you helped, supported or thwarted them?

Q: How do the "What If" Twins (see Chapters 2 and 3) affect your day-to-day life and relationships? How much fear do you invent yourself?

Q: Have you used JJ's concept of circles (Chapter 4) or something like it to help set priorities?

Q: Have you had an experience with a friend, family member, loved one or colleague telling you the truth about their sexuality or gender identity? How have you reacted? If you had it to do over again, would you do the same? Was your response supportive and helpful? Negative or judgmental? Disinterested?

Q. If you are lesbian, gay, bisexual or transgender (or some combination), how have you treated others? Are you helpful and empathetic when people are surprised to learn about your true nature? Are you judgmental of people that you think may be not very open or understanding?

Q: How do you compare your relationship before you found that someone was LGBT with after?

Q: Have you used religion to judge other people? Have you used the Bible or another holy book to determine if another person is doing the right thing? How do you respond to people that have different religious beliefs or act in ways not consistent with your beliefs? What was your reaction to JJ's Morality Rule (Chapter 7)?

Q: Do you agree or disagree with JJ's description of Christian Moralists (Chapter 7)? Do you perceive this as a problem? Are you a Christian Moralist, or a "Moralist" of another faith or tradition?

Q: My company policy is supportive of LGBT employees and vendors. I am personally uncomfortable with them. If I say what I truly believe, I might lose my job. How do I reconcile this problem?

Q: How do JJ Gufreda's Rules of Ethical behavior (Chapter 7) match your beliefs and the practices and policies of your company?

Q: JJ contrasts two types of responses to her "news" of being transgender – supportive and loving and non-supportive and judgmental. Which style matches your behavior and how would you like to be in the future?

Q: What is your reaction to JJ's simplistic explanation of Gay, Lesbian and Bi people? Could it be that simple?

Q: What are your feelings about legislators and courts related to gay rights or anti-gay initiatives?

Q: If we rounded up all the gays and lesbians, what would change? What would some of the effects be? If there were no gays and lesbians in society, would that eliminate them forever?

Q: What is the gay agenda? Is there one?

Q: JJ claims to have experience as a translator – being able to see things from more than one side or view. Do you see things more as shades of grey or more as black and white? Is trying to be a "translator" a positive or negative thing?

Q: If female, have you felt that men sometime talk down to you? If male, have you done this?

Q: Describe the policies and actual practices in your organization or company: Are you accepting/encouraging/ supporting of minorities or more uniform and closed. Are all minority groups treated similarly, or are some treated well and others not so well?

Q: Do you track progress for supporting minorities? Do you use and partner with minority suppliers? Is your effort sincere, or more for show or for good PR?

Q: What are your views and standards around same sex couples, gender markers (M or F) when the person's gender may not be clear or is in flux, name changes, etc?

Q: Would you like to move beyond tolerance and acceptance to *enjoying* diversity?

****

Resources and Unabashed Hucksterism

I am not endorsing any particular product, service or group with this section, I am simply sharing those programs or people that have helped me along the way with issues such as generalized anxiety, panic attacks and the like. There may be resources here that you may find helpful as well. Take my recommendations or don't—as you choose.

In no particular order:

- www.healing-anxiety.com
David Johnson of New Zealand's Freedom From Fear Recovery Program is a terrific program to combat the incapacitating effects of anxiety. David has become a wonderful friend as well as a resource, and helped me identify and banish those pesky, debilitating "What-If" Twins. The paralyzing effects of allowing what-if-this and what-if-that to keep one in the anxiety state *can* be overcome!

- http://www.claireweekes.com.au/
Prior to my finding David Johnson's program, the books of Dr. Claire Weekes helped me tremendously with managing my anxiety. I would recommend them as helpful tools.

- http://www.dignityusa.org/
This group helps those hurt by both the treatment by and estrangement from the Church. Their counsel, encouragement, celebrations of Mass and safe haven have been invaluable in enabling me to retain the good parts of my faith with less bitterness and resentment.

- http://www.exceptionalvoice.com/voicefeminization. html
Kathe Perez has helped with the feminization of my voice.

It is one of the last pieces of my male identity to go, and I have been able to make tremendous progress in sounding more like a female through use of her techniques.

- http://www.nglcc.org/

National Gay and Lesbian Chamber of Commerce. The national LGBT Chamber of Commerce, promoting business just as any other CoC in the country does.

- *http://www.nglcc.org/programs/supplierdiversity/ overview*
- *http://www.nglcc.org/programs/supplierdiversity/ participation*

The NGLCC provides invaluable support to LGBT minority-owned businesses, and I am very proud for my firm to have been certified as the first transgender-owned business registered with their organization.

- www.geilean.com

Okay, just look at this section's title. I'm good at what I do, I have the most professional staff and consultants around, and I think GEI's status as an acknowledged supplier and our track record grants me the bragging rights to place this website on my list. My consulting firm has been operating successfully since 1995. You will find no better firm to help your business!

- http://www.hrc.org/index.htm

Human Rights Campaign – The largest national LGBT civil rights organization working towards equal rights for everyone.

- www.pflag.org/

Parents, Family and Friends of Lesbians And Gays is a national organization with over 350 local affiliates. They promote the health and well-being of LGBT people, their families and friends.

- http://www.gayindynow.com/

Indy Rainbow Chamber of Commerce. This is the local
  LGBT Chamber in the Indianapolis area. JJ is the
  current President.

- http://www.indianaequalityaction.org/
  http://www.indianaequality/org/

Two of the key organizations working to end discrimination
  based on sexual orientation and gender identity in
  Indiana. JJ is a Board Member of IEA.

- http://www.intraa.org/

INTRAA –the Indiana Transgender Rights Advocacy
  Alliance works for freedom of gender expression and
  the right to gender self-determination in Indiana.

- http://www.gendersanity.com/

The Center for Gender Sanity works on aspects of
  transition in the workplace.

- http://www.be-all.org/

The Be-All Seminar is one of the premier Transgender
  events held in the Spring of each year.

- http://ixe-in.org/

IXE Iota Chi Sigma is a gender support group in
  Indianapolis. They hold monthly meetings.

- http://glchamber.org/

The Chicago Area Gay and Lesbian Chamber of Commerce
  promotes economic opportunities for the LGBT
  community and advocates for member businesses. GEI
  is a member of the Chicago Chamber.

- http://lifejourneychurch.cc/

Life Journey Church, formerly Jesus Metropolitan
  Community Church, is a supportive and accepting
  church in Indianapolis.

- http://omaram.hypermart.net/thelesbiantherapist/
Michele O'Mara, therapist extraordinaire. She is in the
     Indianapolis area and also works with people via the
     internet.

- nrbrand@iupui.edu
Norman R. Brandenstein, is a Licensed Mental Health
     Counselor who has been serving the central Indiana
     community for over ten years, providing services for
     adult individuals and couples. He has also focused on
     supportive counseling for the local LGBTQ population
     regarding healing and transitions of sexuality and
     gender.

- http://sites.google.com/site/tennesseevals/home
Tennessee Vals – The Vals is a social and support group
     located in Nashville, Tennessee for transgender people.
     The Vals were my home away from home when I first
     started going out as JJ.

- http://www.sccatl.org/
The Southern Comfort Conference is a major transgender
     conference in Atlanta.

- http://www.riseconsulting.org/index.html
Glossary provided by T. Aaron Hans. of Rise Consulting
     with support from Melisa S. L. Casumbal, Ken Carl,
     Alicia Schmidt, and NYAC. These terms reference
     and draw on the ground-breaking work of many trans
     scholars and activists, who Aaron and company wish
     to thank and acknowledge: Kate Bornstein, James
     Davis-Rosenthal, Dallas Denny, the former American
     Educational Gender Information Services, James Green,
     Shadow Morton, Leslie Feinberg, Nancy Nangeroni,
     Kiki Whitlock, Riki Anne Wilchins, Female to Male
     International, and Gary Bowen.

- http://www.transworkplace.blogspot.com/

Dr. Jillian T. Weiss is a Professor of Law and Society at Ramapo College. Her research area is transgender and transsexual workplace law and policy. She consults with organizations to ensure successful workplace gender transitions.

Gender Terms Glossary

Today's Terminology: A Moving Target

The following glossary of terms and definitions helps provide a common language for discussing gender identity and transgender issues. The glossary incorporates vocabulary from various sources. The list developers intend this dictionary to continue to evolve to reflect new understanding and changing gender identifiers and norms. When I transitioned from Joe to JJ, I became a member of the "gender community" and the "LGBT community." It has been interesting meeting different people and becoming familiar with some of the classifications because in many cases, I was not familiar with the terminology and had never met anyone quite like some of the people I have met.

Initially, when I met someone that was so different from what I had experienced that they didn't quite make sense or were difficult to understand, my tendency was to think, "this (situation) must be wrong" or "I don't get it." Fortunately, based on the experiences I described in LHIL, rather than jump to conclusions, I reconsidered and really tried to understand the other person as best I could. Just because they were different from me did not make either of us better or worse, good or bad. It was like trying to figure out a double or triple negative - after I thougt it through, it started to make some sense. If I eventually came to a conclusion something like this then I think I did well: "I somewhat understand what they are saying, even though it is difficult for me because I am different from them, but they seem to be what they are describing and if they are happy, I am happy for them."

I believe that God created the universe and all of us. There are others that don't believe in God, but regardless of what we believe, we seem to be here and there are a lot of us - almost 7 billion! Whether God put us here, or we got here through some other process, I have a hard time believing that we shouldn't expect a lot of diversity. When you read through the list, you'll see that there is indeed, a great variety.

This list was adapted from the glossary created by T. Aaron Hans, with support from Melisa S. L. Casumbal, Ken Carl, Alicia Schmidt, and NYAC.

Gender Terms:
Words We Speak, Words We Tweak

ADDITIONAL PRONOUNS: Pronouns such as "ze," "hir," and "per," which do not denote rigid masculinity or femininity. Coined by trans activists and scholars, such gender-bending pronouns emerged (and may continue to emerge) in opposition to, and in recognition of, the insufficiency of gender-specific pronouns (i.e., him, her, his, hers, she, and he) to refer to trans and gender-variant people. Some people may also use they, their or them. (See also ZE, HIR, PER.)

ANDROGYNY (ALSO ANDROGYNOUS): A person who expresses and/or presents merged culturally/socially defined feminine and masculine characteristics, or mainly neutral characteristics. May or may not express dual gender identity.

ASEXUAL:
An individual who is not sexually attracted to others. Within the asexual community there are a variety of ways this plays out in individual lives and relationships; people who identify as asexual my have different levels of emotional, spiritual, or physical attraction to others.

ASSIGNED GENDER: The declaration by doctors of what one's gender is based upon what one's genitalia appear to be.

One is then expected to grow up and exist within a certain set of gender roles "appropriate" to one's assigned gender. (See also GENDER [SEX] ASSIGNMENT).

BI-GENDER: A person who identifies as both or some combination of the two culturally prevalent genders. A bi-gender individual may shift their gender identity and/or expression from one gender to another, or a combination of genders, in ways that make sense to them – such shifting may occur on an hourly, daily, monthly, or yearly basis.

BINARY GENDER SYSTEM: A culturally/socially defined code of acceptable behaviors which teach that there are men and women, who are masculine and feminine, and that there is nothing outside of this system. Most popular discussion on gender assumes a binary gender system. Discussion of trans issues and identities, however, challenges a binary gender system and forces us to think of gender within a multi-gender system.

BINDING: The practice of wrapping or taping in order to compress the chest or "breast tissue" so that one can pass as a man. This is done with extremely tight bras, elastic bandages, binders and other methods.

BIPHOBIA: The irrational fear of people perceived as bisexual. Biphobia also includes refuting the existence of bisexuality by promoting the belief that every individual is either homosexual or heterosexual.

BISEXUAL (BI): An individual who is emotionally, spiritually, physically, and/or sexually attracted to those of either gender (clinical term). Within bisexual communities, many find themselves attracted to multiple gender expressions and gender identities, and actively oppose a binary gender system.

BOTTOM SURGERY: Surgery "below the waist," to create either a vagina (for a male-to-female, or MTF), or a penis and testicles (for a female-to-male, or FTM). Factors people consider in deciding whether or not to have bottom surgery include: degree of desire or need, expense, physical health, age, and access to medical care and information. There are risks and complications associated with these surgical procedures, which should be discussed with medical professionals. Such risks and complications are also a factor in individuals' decision-making regarding these surgeries.

BOYDYKE (AGGRESSIVE): A female-bodied person who intentionally or non-intentionally expresses and/or presents culturally/stereotypically masculine, particularly boyish, characteristics. (See also DYKE.) Also, one who enjoys being perceived as a young male (See PASSING).

BUTCH: This term can be used to identify any person who expresses and/or presents culturally/stereotypically masculine characteristics. A person, who self-identifies, mainly with the stereotypically masculine end of a gender characteristic spectrum. Within lesbian, bisexual women's, and trans communities, a female-bodied person who self-identifies as butch and understands the intricacies of, and exhibits, a masculine spirit. ("Butch" is not, however, a term used by lesbian, bisexual women's and trans communities exclusively.)

BUTCH QUEEN: A masculine gay man.

CAMP (Also CAMPY): A culturally specific play on gender, sexuality, and heterosexual norms that occurs within the LGBT community.

CISGENDER: A term used to identify a person whose gender identity is congruent with their assigned gender and the gender role expectations that society expects of them. This term is used instead of "gender normative" and "bio-male/bio-female;" and can be used as a prefix, i.e. cis-male or cis-female.

COMING OUT: The process of becoming aware of, understanding, and accepting the sexual orientation, gender identity, and/or gender expression of oneself, one's family member(s), one's partner(s), or one's friend(s). Also, the ongoing process of decision-making about the level of openness a person feels in disclosing such information about oneself or one's family member(s), partner(s), or friend(s) to others. (See also IN THE CLOSET.)

CROSS-DRESSING (ALSO TRANSVESTITE, TRANSVESTITISM): A person who, on occasion, wears the clothing considered typical for another gender, but who does not desire to change their gender. Reasons for cross-dressing can range from a need to express a feminine or masculine side to attainment of erotic/sexual/fetish gratification. Cross-dressers can be of any sexual orientation; the majority of cross-dressers tend to identify as heterosexual/straight.

CROSS-LIVING: Cross-dressing full-time (also referred to as 24/7), and living as the gender that one believes oneself to be.

DRAB: Acronym for "Dressed as a Boy."

DRAG (ALSO DRAG KING, DRAG QUEEN, FEMALE/ MALE IMPERSONATOR): Wearing the clothing of another gender, often involving the presentation of exaggerated, stereotypical gender characteristics. Individuals may identify as Drag Kings (female in drag) or Drag Queens (male in drag). Drag often refers to dressing for functional purposes such as entertainment/performance or social gatherings. Drag has held a significant place in LGBT history and community. Can also be an acronym for "Dressed as a Girl."

DSM IV: The Diagnostic and Statistical Manual of the American Psychological Association, Fourth Edition. This is the handbook used by mental health professionals. The Fourth Edition is the edition in which the diagnosis "gender dysphoria" first appeared.

DYKE (ALSO FEMME DYKE, BUTCH DYKE, BI DYKE): A person who identifies as a woman, and who is emotionally, spiritually, physically, and/or sexually attracted primarily to women. This term is reclaimed or appropriated in a positive way by many types of people for the purpose of self-identification, and can be political. "Dyke" has been historically used in a pejorative way, to ridicule and label lesbians who were/are perceived to express or present stereotypically masculine characteristics.

EFFEMINATE: A term used to identify a person (usually male) who expresses, and/or presents, culturally/stereotypically feminine characteristics. Often used in a pejorative way, due to sexism.

F2M, FTM, FEMALE TO MALE (TRANS MASCULINE): A term used to identify a person who was assigned a female gender at birth or is female-bodied, and who identifies as male, lives as a man, or identifies as masculine. Some use this as an identifier to let others know where on the spectrum they come from and the direction they might be headed. Others in the community use the signifier MTM, male-to-male, to affirm their belief that their assigned gender was inaccurate.

284

FAG (FAGGOT): A person who identifies as a man, and who is emotionally, spiritually, physically, and/or sexually attracted primarily to men. This term is reclaimed or appropriated in a positive way by many types of people for the purpose of self-identification, and can be political. "Fag" has been historically used in a pejorative way, to ridicule and label gay men who were/are perceived to express or present stereotypically feminine characteristics. This term is becoming more gender neutral; therefore, one does not have to be a "man" to identify as a fag (i.e., a person who identifies as a "faggy" dyke).

FEMALE: A medical label used to signify a "human sex," the biological designation based on genitalia (a vagina and clitoris). Can also be a socio-political term, used by an individual to label their gender identity.

FEMALE-BODIED: A term used to recognize a person who was assigned a female gender at birth, or who had/has a female body with some variation of genitalia, chromosomes and phenotype as those of a female. Trans or gender variant people who are female-bodied may or may not choose hormonal, surgical and/or other body modification to create a "more male" body. Someone who is female-bodied can never, however, have a male body in the same way as someone born male, with some variation of genitalia, chromosomes and phenotype as those of a male.

FEMININE: An often ambiguous term that refers to self-expression, performance, actions, behaviors, dress, grooming, adornment and speech popularly associated with someone who is female-bodied within a binary gender system. People of all genders can self-identify as feminine or as having feminine characteristics.

<u>FEMME:</u> This term can be used to identify any person who expresses and/or presents culturally/stereotypically feminine characteristics. A person, who self-identifies, mainly with the stereotypically feminine end of a gender characteristic spectrum. Within lesbian, bisexual women's, and trans communities, a person who self-identifies as femme and understands the intricacies of, and exhibits, a feminine spirit. ("Femme" is not, however, a term used by lesbian, bisexual women's, and trans communities exclusively.)

<u>FEMME QUEEN:</u> A feminine gay man, who may or may not cross-dress, do drag, or be trans-identified.

<u>FULL-TIME:</u> Living 24/7; living all the time as the gender with which one self-identifies.

<u>GAY:</u> A person (who usually identifies as a man) who is emotionally, spiritually, physically, and/or sexually attracted primarily to members of the same gender. Someone who accepts their same-gender attraction and identifies as gay.

<u>GENDER:</u> Both an innate sense of oneself and a social construct based on a group of emotional and psychological characteristics that classify an individual as feminine, masculine, androgynous, or other. Gender can be understood to have several components, including GENDER IDENTITY, ASSIGNED GENDER, and GENDER ROLE.

<u>GENDER (SEX) ASSIGNMENT:</u> The process by which doctors determine what one's gender is, based upon what one's genitalia appear to be. One is then expected to grow up and exist within a certain set of gender roles "appropriate" to one's assigned gender. (See also ASSIGNED GENDER.)

GENDER-BENDER (ALSO GENDER-BLENDER): A person who merges characteristics of any gender in subtle ways or intentionally flaunts blurred stereotypical gender norms for the purpose of shocking others, without concern for passing.

GENDER DYSPHORIA: An intense, continuous discomfort resulting from an individual's belief in the inappropriateness of their assigned gender at birth and resulting gender role expectations. Also, a clinical psychological diagnosis, which many in transgender communities are offended by, but is often required in order to receive medical services such as hormones and surgery.

GENDER EXPRESSION: Any way in which an individual chooses to present or explain their gender. The self-expression, performance, actions, behavior, dress, grooming, adornment, and speech of individuals according to culturally proscribed norms associated with gender within a binary gender system (i.e., female and male, feminine and masculine). Also refers to self-expression, performance, actions, behavior, dress, grooming, adornment, and speech of individuals in ways which do not conform to gender within a binary gender system, and do not follow culturally proscribed notions of man/male and woman/ female or masculine and feminine.

GENDER IDENTITY: The inner sense of being man/male, woman/female, both, neither, butch, femme, two-spirit, multi-gender, bi-gender or another configuration of gender. Gender identity usually matches with one's physical anatomy, but sometimes does not. Gender identity includes one's sense of self, the image that one presents to the world, and how one is perceived by the world.

GENDER OPPRESSION (CISGENDERISM): The verbal, physical, and emotional violence and legal discrimination against people who do not conform to socially acceptable gender roles.

GENDERQUEER: A term used by some people who may or may not fit on the spectrum of trans, or be labeled as trans, but who identify their gender and sexual orientation to be outside of the binary gender system, or culturally proscribed gender roles.

GENDER AFFIRMATION SURGERY, GENITAL REASSIGNMENT SURGERY (Formerly: GENDER/SEX REASSIGNMENT SURGERY-SRS): Permanent surgical refashioning of genitalia to resemble the genitalia of the desired gender. Sought to attain congruence between one's body and one's gender identity.

GENDER ROLE: The social expectation of how an individual should act, think and feel, based upon one's assigned gender. The social expectation that an individual must be defined as man or woman. Gender role includes behavior characterized as feminine or masculine according to culturally prevalent or stereotypic standards.

GENETIC: A term often used to refer to the gender assigned at birth. Also used to refer to the discussion of the chromosomal makeup of an individual.

GETTING READ (ALSO CLOCK, TO BE CLOCKED): Being detected as a person who is "cross-dressed," or is not living in their "assigned gender."

HETEROSEXUAL: An individual who is emotionally, spiritually, physically, and/or sexually attracted primarily to those of the opposite gender (clinical term).

HIR: (pronounced "here") Used in place of "him/her," a pronoun coined by trans activists to refer to individuals who identify as existing/presenting outside of a binary gender system and its rigid delineations of "male" and "female."

HOMOPHOBIA: The irrational fear of love, affection, and erotic behavior between people of the same gender. Expressed as negative feelings, attitudes, actions, and institutional discrimination against those perceived as non-heterosexuals. Often directed at those perceived as expressing or presenting stereotypically non-heterosexual characteristics and/or blurred gender roles, regardless of individuals' actual sexual orientation or gender identity. (See also TRANSPHOBIA)

HOMOSEXUAL: An individual who is emotionally, spiritually, physically, and/or sexually attracted primarily to those of the same gender (clinical term). A term often viewed as negative, overly clinical, or disempowering by many members of LGBT communities.

HORMONE THERAPY (ALSO HORMONE REPLACEMENT THERAPY, HRT): Administration of hormones to affect the development of secondary sex characteristics of the opposite gender than that one was assigned; this is a process, possibly lifelong, of taking hormones to change the internal body chemistry. Female-to-males (FTMs) use androgens such as testosterone, and male-to-females (MTFs) use estrogen and progesterone. Hormone therapy is safest when administered by a medical professional, and after discussion of potential health risks. Some effects of prolonged hormone use are irreversible.

IDENTITY: How one views, labels, or chooses to identify oneself.

IN THE CLOSET: Not disclosing (See COMING OUT), or being secretive about, the sexual orientation and/or gender identity of oneself or one's family member(s), child or children, sibling(s), or friend(s).

INTERNALIZED HOMOPHOBIA (ALSO INTERNALIZED TRANSPHOBIA): The belief that same-gender sexual orientation and/or transgressive, non-conforming gender identity are inferior to heterosexual orientation and/or traditional masculine or feminine gender identity. The internalization of negative messages, feelings about oneself and one's group, and beliefs about how one should be treated, which often results in self-hate and difficulty with self-acceptance. Also, an irrational fear of deviating from stereotypical gender roles.

INTERSEX (ALSO HERMAPHRODITE): A person born with anatomy or physiology which differs from cultural ideals of male and female. Intersexuals may be born with "ambiguous genitalia," and/or experience hormone production levels that vary from those of culturally "ideal" female and male. Intersexuals may be born with "full or partial" internal genitalia, and/or "full or partial" external genitalia. Intersexual genitals may "look nearly" female, with a very large clitoris, or they may look "nearly male," with a very small penis. They may be truly "right in the middle," with a phallus that can be considered either a large clitoris or a small penis; with a structure that might be a split, empty scrotum, or outer labia; with a small vagina that opens into the urethra rather than into the perineum.
Intersexuals are typically assigned a single gender at birth, and often undergo surgery on their genitals in infancy to force a more culturally acceptable gendered appearance — one which "matches" their assigned gender. Many intersex people who undergo such surgery in infancy later report feeling a sense of loss of an essential aspect of themselves.

Examples of the medical diagnoses used for intersexuals include: adrenal hyperplasia (CAH); ambiguous genitals; androgen insensitivity, full or partial (AIS/PAIS); clitoromegaly; early genital surgery; hypospadias; Klinefelter's; micropenis; and testicular feminization.

LESBIAN: A person who identifies as a woman, who is emotionally, spiritually, physically, and/or sexually attracted primarily to members of the same gender. Someone who accepts her same gender attraction and identifies as a lesbian.

M2F, MTF, MALE TO FEMALE (TRANS FEMININE): A term used to identify a person assigned a male gender at birth or is male-bodied, and who identifies as a female, lives as a woman, or identifies as feminine. Some use this as an identifier to let others know where on the spectrum they come from and the direction they might be headed. Others in the community use the signifier FTF, female-to-female, to affirm their belief that their assigned gender was inaccurate.

MALE: A medical label used to signify a "human sex," the biological designation based on genitalia (a penis and testicles). Can also be a socio-political term, used by an individual to label their gender identity.

MALE-BODIED: A term used to recognize a person who was assigned a male gender at birth, or who had/has a male body with some variation of genitalia, chromosomes and phenotype as those of a male. Trans or gender variant people who are male-bodied may or may not choose hormonal, surgical, and/or other body modification to create a "more female" body. Someone who is male-bodied can never, however, have a female body in the same way as someone born female, with some variation of genitalia, chromosomes and phenotype as those of a female.

MAN: A term referring to someone who identifies as such, who may often exhibit masculine or male characteristics (see MASCULINE and MALE). Popularly understood within a binary gender system to refer to someone who is male-bodied.

MASCULINE: An often ambiguous term that refers to self-expression, performance, actions, behaviors, dress, grooming, adornment, and speech popularly associated with someone who is male-bodied within a binary gender system. People of all genders can self-identify as masculine or as having masculine characteristics.

MULTI-GENDER: A term used to describe a person who identifies with all genders at some level, and may display gender in a variety of ways.

NO-GENDER (ALSO NON-GENDER): A term used to describe a person who identifies as neither of the two genders existing within a binary gender system. A no-gender person may "live outside of" gender, and play with various types of gender or anti-gender expression.

NON-OP (Abbreviated for NON-OPERATIVE): A term used to describe transgender, transsexual or gender variant individuals who have not attained and may not desire to attain gender reassignment surgery. Such individuals may or may not take hormones. For many individuals, self-identification and self-expression alone (through cross-living or other methods of gender expression) achieve harmony or congruence between one's body and one's gender identity. Such individuals may feel no need for surgical reconstruction.

OPPRESSION: A system of exploitation, and imbalance of power and control, in which one social group benefits over another. Oppressed groups are often made to feel invisible, devalued, disempowered, unimportant, and "abnormal," and are systematically denied legal rights and economic, political, and cultural access and privilege given to and maintained by groups with greater power within an oppressive system.

PACKING: The act of creating a visual, physical, and tangible form of a penis in one's pants. This can be done using a variety of techniques and materials, including socks, gel-filled condoms, prosthetic penises and dildos.

PANSEXUAL (ALSO OMNISEXUAL): A person who is emotionally, spiritually, physically, and/or sexually attracted to those of any gender or physical makeup.

PASSING: The ability to present oneself as any gender other than that assigned at birth, and be accepted as such.

PER: (pronounced "purr") Abbreviated form of the word "person." Like HIR, used in place of "him" or "her." A pronoun coined by trans activists to refer to individuals who identify as existing/presenting outside of a binary gender system and its rigid delineations of "male" and "female."

POST-OP (Abbreviated for POST-OPERATIVE): A term used to describe transgender, transsexual, or gender variant individuals who have attained gender reassignment surgery, and/or other surgeries to change secondary sex characteristics.

PRE-OP (Abbreviated for PRE-OPERATIVE): A term used to describe transgender, transsexual, or gender variant individuals who have not attained gender reassignment surgery, but who desire to and are seeking that as an option. Such individuals may or may not currently be cross-living full time; may or may not undergo hormone therapy; and may or may not be seeking surgery to change secondary sex characteristics, but who may look at this as an option for the future.

PRESENTATION: The totality of one's appearance, including attire, voice, behavior, body language, etc.

PRIMARY SEX CHARACTERISTICS: Identifiers such as genitalia, body fat distribution, and hair growth patterns that are commonly used to assign or label someone's gender as male or female within a binary gender system.

QUEER: Historically and currently used as a slur targeting those perceived to transgress "norms" of sexual orientation and/or gender expression. In the 1980's and 1990's, "queer" was increasingly reclaimed and popularized by some LGBT communities as a positive term of self-identification. More recently, this term has been used to identify trans, bisexual, lesbian, intersex, gay, and heterosexual individuals who are progressive sexual and gender outlaws in some way or another.

REAL LIFE TEST (Also LIFE TEST): A period of time required of individuals seeking gender reassignment surgery during which they must live full-time expressing and presenting the gender in which they identify. Many doctors require a Real Life Test of two or more years before advancing to surgery.

SAME GENDER LOVING: In the spirit of self-naming, and of ethnic/ sexual pride, the term "same-gender-loving" (SGL) was introduced to fortify the lives and illuminate the voices of black and African-American homosexual and bisexual people of color; to provide a powerful identity not marginalized by "racism" in the gay community or "homophobic" attitudes in society.

SECONDARY SEX CHARACTERISTICS: Physical characteristics that emerge with the onset of puberty, including but not limited to: facial and body hair growth, muscle development, voice changes, breast development, and the ability to reproduce.

SELF-DEFINED GENDER: A gender identity that one chooses for oneself without regard for limitations imposed by social norms or a binary gender system. May or may not be fixed, may evolve and change. Often determined as a result of an individual's questioning and exploring gender issues, examination of gender roles, and through a process of self-discovery.

SEX: 1. A term used historically and within the medical field to identify genetic/biological/hormonal/physical characteristics, including genitalia, which are used to classify an individual as female, male, or intersex. 2. (Also SEXUALITY, SEXUAL BEHAVIOR) Activity engaged in by oneself, with another or others to express attractions and/or arousal.

SEXUAL ORIENTATION: A continuum of affectional, erotic, fantasy, or sexual arousal toward an individual of the same gender, the opposite gender, or other genders. Terms used to identify sexual orientation include: gay, lesbian, bisexual, pansexual, transsensual, straight, heterosexual, homosexual, same gender loving, two-sprit, dyke, fag, queer, women who have sex with women, men who have sex with men, and asexual. People experience sexuality in three ways: sexual orientation, or how one experiences attractions; behavior, or how one acts based upon such attractions; and self-identification, or how one chooses to define or identify oneself.

SHAPE SHIFTER (ALSO METAMORPH): A term used by some people (who choose not to identify as transsexuals) to express their belief they are not changing their gender, but changing their body to reflect their inner feelings and gender identity.

STANDARDS OF CARE: A set of minimum guidelines formulated by the World Professional Association for Transgender Health (WPATH), formerly the Harry Benjamin International Gender Dysphoria Association, Inc. (HBIGDA), for care of transsexual, transgender and gender nonconforming individuals. Provides requirements for consumers and service providers, version 7 was released in 2011.

STRAIGHT (ALSO HETEROSEXUAL, HET): A term used to describe a person who is emotionally, spiritually, physically, and/or sexually attracted primarily to members of the opposite gender. A person who accepts their opposite gender attraction and who identifies as straight or het.

THIRD GENDER: A term used to describe people who feel they are other than male or female, or a combination of both.

TOP SURGERY: Surgery "above the waist," usually breast augmentation for MTFs and breast reduction for FTMs. Factors people consider in deciding whether or not to have top surgery include: degree of desire or need, expense, physical health, age, and access to medical care and information. There are risks and complications associated with these surgical procedures, which should be discussed with medical professionals. Such risks and complications are also a factor in individuals' decision-making regarding these surgeries.

TRANSGENDER (ALSO TRANS): A term used to describe those who transgress social gender norms; often used as an umbrella term to mean those who defy rigid, binary gender constructions, and who express or present a breaking and/or blurring of culturally prevalent/stereotypical gender roles. The term trans includes but is not limited to transsexuals, intersex individuals, bi-genders, no-genders, androgynes, cross-dressers, gender-benders, feminine men, masculine women, shape shifters, transvestites, and sometimes Two-Spirit people. Transfolk, transperson, transpeople and trannies are other more casual terms used to refer to people who identify as trans or gender variant.

TRANSGENDER COMMUNITY (ALSO TRANS/GENDER COMMUNITY): A loose association of individuals and organizations who transgress gender norms in a variety of ways and perform advocacy and education on trans issues and trans liberation. Celebrating a recently born self-awareness, this community is growing fast across all lines. The central ethic of this community is unconditional acceptance of individual exercise of freedoms around gender, sexual identity and orientation.

TRANSGENDERIST: An individual who chooses to cross-live full time, but who chooses not to have SRS/GRS. Such individuals may or may not take hormones. For many individuals, self-identification and self-expression alone (through cross-living or other methods of gender expression) achieve harmony or congruence between one's body and one's gender identity. Such individuals may thus feel no need for surgical reconstruction.

TRANSITION: The period during which a transgender person (usually transsexual) begins to live a new life as their true gender. Can include the period of full-time living (see REAL LIFE TEST) required before gender reassignment surgery. After transitioning and surgery some transexuals who are living full-time identify only as a man or as a woman.

TRANSPHOBIA (ALSO GENDERPHOBIA): The irrational fear of those who are perceived to break or blur stereotypical gender roles. Expressed as negative feelings, attitudes, actions, and institutional discrimination. Often directed at those perceived as expressing or presenting their gender in a transgressive way, defying stereotypical gender norms, or who are perceived to exhibit non-heterosexual characteristics — regardless of individuals' actual gender identity or sexual orientation. (See also HOMOPHOBIA.)

TRANSSENSUAL: An individual who is emotionally, spiritually, physically, and/or sexually attracted to those of any trans-identified genders or a specific trans-identified gender.

TRANSSEXUAL: An individual who experiences intense, persistent, long-term discomfort with their body and self-image due to the belief that their assigned gender is inappropriate. This individual may then takes steps to adapt or change their body, gender role and gender expression in order to achieve congruence with their gender identity, (what they believe their true gender to be). Such steps may include cross-living, hormone use, surgery, and/or other body modification. Taking such steps may or may not lead to a feeling of harmony or congruence between a person's body and gender identity. After transitioning and surgery some transexuals who are living full-time identify only as a man or a woman. (See also F2M/FTM/FEMALE-TO-MALE, M2F/MTF/MALE-TO-FEMALE, PRE-OPERATIVE, POST-OPERATIVE, NON-OPERATIVE)

<u>TUCK:</u> The technique of hiding male genitals.

<u>TWO-SPIRIT:</u> A term used by some indigenous/First Nation/ Native American people to describe the experience of being, in Euro-American-centric terms, lesbian, gay, bisexual, or transgender.

<u>WOMAN:</u> A term referring to someone who identifies as such, who may often exhibit feminine or female characteristics (see FEMININE and FEMALE). Popularly understood within a binary gender system to refer to someone who is female-bodied.

<u>ZE:</u> (pronounced "sea") Used in place of "she/he," a pronoun coined by trans activists to refer to individuals who identify as existing/presenting outside of a binary gender system and its rigid delineations of "male" and "female." (See also ADDITIONAL PRONOUNS.)

This dictionary is a work in progress, so feedback and more words are always appreciated – adapted for Left-Hander in London, created by t. aaron hans © 1996, 2001, 2003, 2011.
All Rights Reserved. vs. 8.11

To contact, please email at tahans@riseconsulting.org
or call at 831.869.9392

CPSIA information can be obtained at www.ICGtesting.com
Printed in the USA
LVOW090230181111

255539LV00002B/1/P